Elementary School Literacy:
Critical Issues

Elementary School Literacy:
Critical Issues

Edited by
Mariam Jean Dreher
Wayne H. Slater
The University of Maryland

Christopher-Gordon Publishers, Inc.

Table of Contents

Chapter 5: The Elementary Vocabulary Curriculum: What Should It Be?

*Chapter 11: Reading as Cognition and the Mediation
   of Experience*

*John T. Guthrie and Michael Pressley, University of Maryland at
College Park* 241

Preface

In March 1991, teachers and researchers travelled through an ice storm to attend the *Maryland Conference on Literacy in the 90s* which we had organized at the University of Maryland at College Park. These professionals braved the storm because their commitment to the improvement of literacy in the elementary school compelled them to do so. They were particularly attracted by the opportunity to hear the ideas of a number of distinguished researchers who have consistently generated important scholarship for both theory and practice related to elementary school literacy.

The chapters in this volume grew out of that conference. Our purpose in editing *Elementary School Literacy: Critical Issues* was to provide a thorough grounding on important topics in elementary school literacy for two overlapping audiences: experienced teachers and graduate students early in their programs. Experienced classroom teachers and reading/language arts specialists will find this volume valuable for providing current, research-based information related to their practical concerns and to school-based research. Beginning graduate students–who often do not know exactly what topic they would like to investigate–will find a solid introduction to important issues helpful in identifying an area for focused inquiry.

Although there are many books for researchers and advanced doctoral students, this volume assumes an interest in research yet does not assume an advanced research background. Drawing upon perspectives derived from cognitive psychology and instructional research, the chapters in this book strike a balance between scholarly reviews aimed at experts and practitioner articles. In addition, it is long enough to allow thorough and scholarly coverage of the topics and yet is accessible to beginning researchers and experienced teachers. In additon, the extensive reference lists will give readers a start in developing in-depth literature reviews on instructional and research topics in the field.

This volume opens with an introductory chapter which provides a context for considering research related to the improvement of elementary school literacy. The eight core chapters deal with a number of critical issues in elementary school literacy: grouping and reading instruction, emergent literacy, learning to read and write in at-risk children, developing vocabulary, learning in the social studies, reading and the learning disabled, literacy in an age of integrated media, and authentic assessment in reading and writing. This book closes with two reaction chapters. The first focuses on the instructional implications of the ideas presented in this volume; the second extends the research implications. All of the chapters challenge readers to address unanswered questions.

Many people have helped bring this book into reality. First, we thank the contributors to this volume; it was a pleasure working with all of them. Second, we are grateful for the financial support from the University of Maryland which allowed us to host the conference that gave impetus to the chapters in this volume. The College of Education (Jean R. Hebeler, Acting Dean) provided the original seed money through its competitive grants program. This support allowed us to obtain matching funds from the Graduate School and the Department of Curriculum and Instruction. We are grateful to Jacob K. Goldhaber, Dean of Graduate Studies and Research, and Ann C. Howe, Chair of the Department of Curriculum and Instruction for their support. Third, we owe a debt to those who helped us with various aspects of manuscript preparation. Grace Lechert assisted by typing portions of the manuscript. Deborah Menke and Sharon Teuben-Rowe helped with proofreading. Rebecca Sammons helped to index this text and wrote the first draft of the summaries of the individual chapters used in Chapter 1. Finally, Sue Canavan, Christopher-Gordon Publishers, helped us put all the pieces together.

M.J.D.
W.H.S.
March, 1992

1

Elementary School Literacy: Critical Issues

Mariam Jean Dreher and Wayne H. Slater

Introduction

Those involved in literacy education in today's elementary schools are faced with a wide range of proposals for instructional improvement by almost everyone from educational critics (Flesch, 1983; Kozol, 1986, 1991; Ravitch, 1987) to prestigious policy groups (Carnegie Foundation for the Advancement of Teaching, 1988; National Commission on Excellence in Education, 1984; Rand Corporation, 1984).

One recurring criticism is that current literacy education is directed toward the development of a low level of literacy instead of what is termed *high literacy*. According to Chall (1990), Resnick and Resnick (1977, 1985), and Venezky (1990, 1991) low literacy as well as high literacy are identifiable educational traditions. Mass education evolved from low literacy which concerned itself with the minimum levels of reading required for religious ceremonies (Resnick & Resnick, 1977, 1985). In contrast, high literacy has been reserved for the upper class in Europe and the United States. Its purpose has been the development of breadth and depth in linguistic and comprehension abilities, literary and fine arts standards, and civic knowledge necessary for the leaders of society.

In this chapter, we contend that instruction and curricula could probably benefit from improvement in the direction of high literacy. But we will not address the strengths and limitations of the high literacy tradition as it has developed over time. Scholars from different disciplines offer compelling arguments and different ideas about what is central to a high literacy curriculum and what is peripheral (e.g., Bailey & Forsheim, 1983; Bloom, 1987; Bruner, 1960; Greene, 1988; Hirsch, 1987; Ong, 1982; Ravitch & Finn, 1987; Scribner, 1988). Instead, we focus on elementary schools where teachers are attempting to achieve the best instruction possible.

In this chapter, our purpose is to accomplish two objectives. First, we present a framework from which to consider suggestions for instructional improvement. Specifically, we discuss a prototypical teacher whose goal is to help students become independent learners and we consider issues related to such teachers achieving high literacy for their students. Second, we overview the remaining chapters in this volume.

Achieving High Literacy

In this section, we consider some of the thinking of Bereiter and Scardamalia (1987a), Berliner (1986), and Shulman (1986). We begin by discussing three prototypes of elementary school reading/ language arts teachers. After discussing the three prototypes, we turn to a discussion of the cognitive prerequisites for high literacy. Then we discuss the cognitive abilities students need to achieve high literacy. Finally, we consider whether or not the third prototype of teaching, the model which probably has the best chance for helping students achieve high literacy, is attainable.

Three Prototypes of Elementary School Reading/ Language Arts Teachers

Bereiter and Scardamalia (1987a) have constructed three prototypes of elementary school teachers that serve as discussion points for understanding and providing instruction for higher literacy in reading/ language arts.

Teacher One

Teacher One makes reading assignments with minimal reflection as to the purpose for reading and then asks students to respond to oral or workbook questions about the readings. Teacher One then rehearses the reading assignment with the class by asking more questions and telling students what the passage says in order to help those who did not comprehend it. Writing assignments are essentially made in the same manner. In other words, Teacher One reflects little on the purpose for the writing assignment. When the students turn in their papers, Teacher One evaluates them by considering language and content and then provides comments on how students can improve them. Students are rarely asked to make revisions suggested by the teacher or by the students' peers.

According to Bereiter and Scardamalia (1987a), the Teacher One prototype represents the current situation in many classrooms and is based on long-established customs that have become accepted to the extent that teachers do not consciously understand why they are using them.

Teacher Two

Teacher Two targets students' background knowledge. Reading assignments are sequenced in such a way as to build on students' prior knowledge in a gradual and logical manner. Before students read a selection, Teacher Two provides prereading instruction, activities, and materials designed to link the content of the selection to what students already know. This might be accomplished by discussing the reading selection topic with the class, by providing a preview, or by asking students to make predictions. Concepts and terms unknown to the students are taught by the teacher. In addition, students are directed to important information in the text, warned about difficulties at specific points in the content, and provided with questions to answer. When students have finished reading, Teacher Two conducts discussions with questions designed to help students construct inferences from the text and to establish links between what they have read and their background knowledge. As far as writing is concerned, Teacher Two often asks students to write on topics about which they possess extensive prior knowledge. If the teacher decides to assign a topic, students will devote several days to prewriting activities in which they gather information for the topic by researching, reading, brainstorming, interviewing, mapping, outlining, and numerous other exercises in order to compile the necessary and sufficient information for their papers. However, students usually select their own topics while Teacher Two meets with them individually helping them to focus and narrow their topics in such a way that students write in areas that intrigue and interest them. In addition, Teacher Two helps them establish plans and goals for their papers. Additional conferences between teacher and student are scheduled after students have completed their rough drafts in order to help students generate a better second draft.

The Teacher Two prototype is based on what Bereiter and Scardamalia (1987a) call a knowledge-based approach. It is grounded in a series of studies which demonstrate the important role of background knowledge in the comprehension of texts (Rumelhart, 1980; Voss, 1984). The important notions that support this approach are 1) that the critical factor in performance in reading and writing is the amount of relevant world knowledge that the student can access and 2) that the cognitive skills needed for performance are either already available or will develop as they are needed by the student.

Teacher Three
Teacher Three's approach can be characterized as including all of the strategies that Teacher Two employs in the classroom in addition to attempting to teach students to use those strategies independently. To be sure, students cannot immediately use these strategies independently so Teacher Three's instruction is similar to Teacher Two's. However, Teacher Three's ultimate objective is to make students independent learners. Eventually, Teacher Three should not have to prepare prereading activities to engage students' background knowledge, to direct questions to them constructed to link new information to prior knowledge, and to provide other such experiences. Instead, Teacher Three's goal is to have students engage in these strategies independently and on their own initiative. Teacher Three expects students to eventually identify what is new information and what is old information. In planning instruction, Teacher Three gradually stops asking students questions and instead models the process of asking questions about the text or asking questions of oneself about the material being studied. Teacher Three then coaches students in the use of the modeled activities. In

writing, Teacher Three provides scaffolding by using modeling, prompts, and cooperative learning to assist students in conducting their own discussions. Through these discussions students not only engage their own knowledge but also evaluate and reassess it in relation to what they are attempting to write.

Usually Teacher Two attempts to reduce the problems and difficulties students encounter in reading and writing. In contrast, Teacher Three will occasionally make reading and writing assignments that pose specific difficulties for students in order to create instructional opportunities for teaching problem solving strategies. When problems and challenges arise in lessons, they are considered intriguing opportunities for analysis and investigation. With this focus, students become students of learning processes in reading and writing.

According to Bereiter and Scardamalia (1987a), the Teacher Three prototype is based on research which focuses on the development of learning and thinking skills (Brown, Bransford, Ferrara, & Campione, 1983; Paris, Wasik, & Turner, 1991; Weinstein & Mayer, 1986). At a more general level, the Teacher Two and Teacher Three prototypes are grounded in Piaget's notions of learning as a constructive process and in Vygotsky's notion of the social transmission of competence (Piaget, 1952; Vygotsky, 1978).

Keeping in mind that Teachers One, Two, and Three are simply prototypes of how instruction may have developed from what was perceived as tradition, best practice, and research, most educators and researchers would probably agree that Teacher Two and Teacher Three represent important improvements when compared to Teacher One. The Teacher Three prototype is beginning to develop in important ways because of significant instructional studies designed to enhance higher literacy abilities (Bereiter & Scardamalia, 1987a; Brophy & Good, 1986; Brown, Bransford, Ferrara, & Campione, 1983; Palincsar & Brown, 1984; Paris, Wasik, & Turner, 1991; Scardamalia, Bereiter, & Steinbach, 1984). The goals related to Teacher Three are not new. Without question, many teachers nurture the development of independent learning in students, reward it when they observe it in their classrooms, and attempt to provide opportunities for it in their instruction. But as long as teachers adhere to Teacher One or Teacher Two prototypes, their attempts to develop independent learning in students are external to the curriculum. In contrast, the goal of independent learning is embedded in the curriculum for the students of Teacher Three.

The unique characteristic of the Teacher Three prototype is that it reconceptualizes instruction so that the curriculum is essentially about the deliberate transfer of those strategies that belong to the teacher in the Teacher One and Teacher Two repertoires (Bereiter & Scardamalia, 1987a; Weinstein & Mayer, 1986). Singer and Donlan (1989) presented the same concept when they pointed out that a good teacher helps students progress "from a teacher-centered to a student-centered classroom and from dependent to independent learners" (p. 375). As Singer and Donlan explained, good teachers combine individual strategies in an instructional framework that extends across an entire year; these teachers phase themselves out and phase in the students. The phase in/phase out process is accomplished through instruction that moves students from teacher modeling to group work to individual work to internalization of concepts and strategies.

Whether or not the Teacher Three prototype is superior to the other two prototypes in developing higher-level literacy remains a research issue. As prototypes, the three cover a fairly comprehensive spectrum of teacher behaviors. We do not know what the findings might be if we compared a teacher with Teacher One attributes who was dedicated to nurturing independence in students, with a teacher with Teacher Three attributes who lacked dedication and commitment. Similarly, research results are probably going to be influenced by such variables as the extent to which the curriculum is open or arbitrary, the degree of bottom up or top down administration, and whether or not the extent of involvement by teachers and students is required or voluntary. However, even in the best schools, Teachers One and Two will not be able develop a high level of literacy for the majority of their students. We believe that the Teacher Three prototype has the potential to make high literacy an accessible goal even for those students who are not raised in high literacy environments. To advance this position, we will now turn to a discussion of the cognitive prerequisites for high literacy.

Cognitive Prerequisites for High Literacy

Although most educators probably do not agree, the current curriculum suggests that high literacy is a remote goal for most students (Bereiter & Scardamalia, 1987a; Resnick & Resnick, 1985). Generally, those elements of the existing curriculum that are related to the high literacy tradition are usually reserved for students labeled gifted and talented. Many seem to think that a high literacy curriculum requires special screening procedures that permit access to only gifted children.

This counterproductive selection process is probably understandable as long as there appears to be no principled way to separate essential high literacy curricular content from nonessential curricular content. If this difficulty cannot be resolved, then the only logical approach to high literacy is to replicate the classical curricula created for the best public and private schools. When this is the option, significant numbers of children will have problems adjusting to the curriculum. While the explicit specification of this curriculum is not within the scope of this chapter, we do think that one strategic approach exists for establishing an intellectual foundation for high literacy. That approach considers expert-novice perspectives derived from cognitive psychology (Anderson, 1990; Bereiter & Scardamalia, 1987a; Berliner, 1986; Shulman, 1986). This approach not only considers what types of performance or background knowledge separates experts from novices but also examines what experts know and what novices do not do or do differently or do less frequently. As a result, researchers can map a fairly direct link between expert-novice differences and a variety of instructional goals. It is important to understand that expert-novice comparisons are relative. The comparisons can include certified experts and beginners, but in other contexts, such as in reading and writing research, the comparisons may be made between groups such as less proficient and more proficient students or elementary school students and high school students. No matter which comparison groups are used, specific higher order strategies and skills consistently distinguish more competent readers and writers from less competent readers and writers. The strategies and skills can be categorize into four types: 1) problem-solving or fix up strategies, 2) self-regulatory procedures, 3) executive structures, and 4) intentional learning procedures. We shall discuss each in turn.

Problem-solving and Fix up Strategies

One of the more consistent research findings is that experts working in their areas of expertise, do significantly less problem solving than might be expected (Anderson, 1990; Lesgold, 1984). Apparently, they possess a repertoire of problem types linked to well-established solutions.

As a result, tasks that would require problem solving by the nonexpert are carried out as a fairly straightforward application of pre-existing knowledge by the expert. To be sure, experts encounter novel problems, and they typically have strategies for addressing them. This appears to be true with expert readers and writers. For example, Bereiter and Bird (1985) asked proficient adults to think aloud while they read various texts. Then they analyzed the protocols to identify strategies these readers used when they encountered comprehension problems. These proficient adult readers used four strategies: summarizing the text in simpler terms; going back to the location of needed information; establishing cognitive monitors (e.g., generating questions which link knowledge in the text to important related knowledge in other sources); and identifying comprehension difficulties as problems to be solved. By using a combination of direct instruction and think-aloud modeling, Bereiter and Bird then provided instruction in the use of these strategies to seventh- and eighth-graders. The results showed a significant increase in the students' use of three of the four strategies. And apparently as a consequence of their increased use of the strategies used by proficient adults, these students made significant and substantial gains in reading comprehension when compared with other groups.

Self-regulatory Procedures

A typical list of self-regulatory procedures includes monitoring, checking, planning, testing, revising, and evaluating (Brown & Campione, 1981). These procedures do not solve problems. Instead the procedures are used to avoid problems or to identify problems should they develop. In the past, most of these procedures have been categorized as study skills. Research indicates that experts differ from novices by their significantly greater use of self-regulatory procedures in reading (Paris, Wasik, & Turner, 1991) and writing (Bereiter & Scardamalia, 1987b). Moreover, research has shown significant performance effects for in- struction on self-regulatory procedures in reading (Palincsar & Brown, 1984), writing (Scardamalia, Bereiter, & Steinbach, 1984), and study skills (Dansereau, 1985).

Executive Structures

Executive structures select goals to be achieved, monitor progress toward achieving those goals, identify obstacles, and solve problems in particular areas such as writing and reading (Bereiter & Scardamalia, 1987b). For example, the skilled writer differs from the average writer by more than a repertoire of fix-up and self-regulatory procedures. For the skilled writer, many more parameters of writing behavior, such as powerful rhetorical strategies, are under strategic control. In other words, the skilled writer can access and manipulate more complex executive control structure for writing than the average writer (Bereiter & Scardamalia, 1987b). This is not the same as possessing conceptual knowledge about the process. For example, studying a text about effective writing will not provide the novice writer control over the necessary parameters for skilled writing. However, it may lead the novice to an understanding of what those parameters are. The skilled writer's more complex control structure achieves more than proficiency. It enables the writer to develop complex goals (e.g., the goal of developing an idea through the use of an extended metaphor) that the novice writer probably cannot accomplish.

Expert-novice research focused on writers and readers has supported differences in executive control structures (Anderson, 1990; Bereiter & Scardamalia, 1987b). Research on composition suggests that the novice's control structure is a fairly simple procedure for retrieving information from memory that addresses topic and form requirements. Bereiter and Scardamalia (1987b) have described this as a knowledge telling model. In this model, the writer has little strategic control over the process of generating content. As a result, goals serve a minor role in composing. In contrast, experts seem to use a knowledge transforming model, in which content and rhetorical problems are solved interactively in the direction of objectives to be achieved in the paper. Similarly in reading, research supports differences between expert and novice models. For the expert reader, reading is a strategically-guided knowledge-constructing process. In contrast, the novice's reading allows minimal goal-directed knowledge-constructing comprehension (Paris, Wasik, & Turner, 1991; Scardamalia & Bereiter, 1984).

We do not know the extent to which instruction can enhance the development of more complex executive control structures. The most promising approaches seem to focus on providing some form of scaffolding or external structure that support learning while the student is in the process of constructing more elaborate internal configurations (Bruner, 1983).

Intentional Learning Procedures

In most school situations, students are solving problems, answering questions, discussing issues, reading stories, and .writing compositions. Often learning is a result that is intended by the teacher. But it may be unintentional as far as students are concerned (Bereiter & Scardamalia, 1987a). Intentional learning may be defined as " . . . the setting and deliberate pursuit of cognitive goals–goals to learn, to solve, to understand, to define, and so on" (Bereiter & Scardamalia, 1987b, p. 361). For example, in the protocols of proficient writers, there is evidence that as they are writing an assignment, they are also devoting effort into learning to write. That is, they are deriving knowledge from the experience of their writing assignment that will help them in future writing assignments. More generally, there is also support for the notion that some students, in addition to meeting the basic requirements of writing and reading assignments, are also investigating higher-level goals such as learning something for their personal enlightenment and generally enhancing their understanding and knowledge by working on units and assignments (Bereiter & Scardamalia, 1987b).

Most students seem to differ in their attitudes toward intentional learning. Researchers are only beginning to investigate what is required to support high levels of intentional learning. A series of studies support the notion that intentional learning can be encouraged in students from first grade to post-university (Bereiter & Scardamalia, 1985). Nevertheless, major instructional reforms which move from Teacher One and Teacher Two prototypes to the Teacher Three prototype, will probably be required to create a climate in which intentional learning can be supported.

Cognitive Abilities Required for High Literacy

If the focus of the school curriculum is low literacy, students will probably have little need for problem-solving and fix up strategies because the content is not demanding. As a result, there are few assignments or units that provide challenges in reading and writing. If the Teacher Two model prevails in a school, teachers will attempt to address problems before they develop by using prereading and prewriting strategies. But a curriculum which is more challenging and reflects more high literacy expectations through the use of more difficult material or more demanding goals will pose potentially important problems for students. If schooling is to be improved in important ways, students must deal with these problems in such a way that will enhance their problem-solving strategies and develop their knowledge base (Anderson, Hiebert, Scott, & Wilkinson, 1985; Bereiter & Scardamalia, 1987a; DeFord, Lyons, & Pinnell, 1991).

Self-regulatory procedures become critical when students are required to rely on their own resources in learning. At one level, a high literacy curriculum might not appear to require more self-directed learning than a low literacy curriculum. At the same time, it is reasonable to argue that in a high literacy curriculum students would need to learn more from texts and from other students' reading of texts rather than from the direct instruction of teachers or from exercises. If this is the situation, students will require a firm command of planning, checking, monitoring, testing, and revising strategies. Of particular importance are students' strategies for monitoring their own proficiency in comprehending texts (Bereiter & Scardamalia, 1987a; Paris, Wasik, & Turner, 1991). If students cannot identify their own comprehension difficulties, they will have no way to use the problem-solving strategies discussed earlier.

Elaborate executive structures for both reading and writing are probably better viewed as the possible result of a high literacy curriculum rather than the requirements of such a curriculum. However, unless we provide students with explicit experiences with executive control structures, there is a possibility that students will use coping strategies that circumvent educational objectives. This will result in hindering the development of the more efficient and expertlike control structures (Bereiter & Scardamalia, 1987a; Paris, Wasik, & Turner, 1991).

Taken together, these cognitive requirements (i.e., problem solving strategies, self-regulatory procedures, and executive control structures) are subsumed under the more comprehensive requirement that students following a high literacy curriculum be able to function as intentional learners. In effect, the students must be able to generate and carry out their own learning agendas that are not simply the minimal responses to the day-to-day expectations of the curriculum. Without intentional learning, it is difficult to imagine how literacy levels can ever rise above the current level. Thus, the Teacher Three prototype appears to be indispensible. It is the only prototype in which intentional learning is an explicit goal rather than an amorphous expectation.

Achieving the Teacher Three Prototype

The objective of developing independent learners is not a new one. In many ways, it is a critical factor in the description of ideal teachers (Good & Brophy, 1991; Singer & Donlan, 1989; Wittrock, 1986). Those teachers whose teaching styles actually map onto Teacher One or Teacher Two prototypes often espouse the objectives of the Teacher Three prototype. Regardless of their stated objectives, the Teacher One and Two prototypes lack the ways and means to support the kind of independent learning strategies required for high literacy. At this point, the critical question is whether the Teacher Three prototype can be adopted by practitioners and whether it will achieve the goals described.

As far as the research on this issue is concerned, the findings offer only partial support but provide important directions for further inquiry (Brophy & Good, 1986; Palincsar & Brown, 1984; Pearson & Fielding, 1991; Roehler & Duffy, 1991; Slater & Graves, 1989). When we consider the high level of children's enthusiasm and excitement in most elementary school classrooms as they are introduced to new learning or experiences, it is not surprising that teachers conclude that students are already engaging in intentional learning and that this intentional learning only needs to be nurtured. However, the examination of children's thought processes while they are learning suggests that intentional learning rarely occurs (Bereiter & Scardamalia, 1987a, 1987b; Paris, Wasik, & Turner, 1991; Resnick & Neches, 1984).

In considering the Teacher Two prototype, the difference between children's natural abilities and their acquisition of knowledge could be attributed to the schools' getting in the way of their natural drive to learn. However, if we consider the Teacher Three prototype, this difference may simply suggest some specific instructional deficits. For instance, we might compare becoming an intentional learner to becoming a carpenter or a musician. These fields require a special interest and a particular aptitude. While most individuals who enter these fields may be assumed to have these attributes, they do not achieve proficiency automatically. Through instruction and apprenticeships, they are required to learn how to do carpentry or how to perform music. The important difference here is that we have some pretty solid notions about how to teach carpentry and music. In order for the Teacher Three prototype to be successful, we must find ways to teach intentional learning.

Again, the idea of promoting intentional learning is not a new one. But a recent line of inquiry–learning strategies research–suggests a route for developing intentional learning. It is this line of inquiry that is providing a basis for the development of the Teacher Three prototype. Let us consider the four cognitive components of high literacy discussed earlier: 1) problem-solving or fix up strategies, 2) self-regulatory procedures, 3) executive structures, and 4) intentional learning procedures. Learning strategy research supports the idea that the first two can be taught. Problem-solving strategies and self-regulatory procedures for improving reading comprehension have been taught successfully using various combinations of direct instruction and explicit modeling of the thinking processes involved in comprehension (Bereiter & Scardamalia, 1987a; Paris, Wasik, & Turner, 1991; Roehler & Duffy, 1991). These teaching strategies that begin with a gradual release of responsibility model of instruction in which the teacher models and then gradually delegates more of the control for learning to students have been shown to be effective for reading comprehension (Pearson & Fielding, 1991; Slater & Graves, 1989) and in prewriting planning for composition assignments (Bereiter & Scardamalia, 1987b). Comprehensive changes in executive structures as a result of instruction remain to be demonstrated.

Considering that a major amount of research conducted learning strategies is fairly recent, the results do offer preliminary encouragement for attaining the Teacher Three prototype for teaching high literacy. However, a major question remains: Is the Teacher Three prototype sufficient to promote high literacy? That is, would a cluster of methods determined to be effective in promoting high literacy in reading and writing be adequate to enhance high literacy in students who lack the family and environmental support for it? In the vast majority of cases, the answer is probably no.

Given the nature of high literacy and the type of intentional learning it probably requires, more than cognitive abilities is required. One of those factors is motivation, the dedication and tenacity to devote additional time and effort to learning far beyond that required for achieving success in typical classroom assignments. In other words, it is not simply motivation to do well in class, but it is a type of motivation to achieve beyond the typical level of performance expected in classrooms. This type of motivation becomes a problem when learning objectives are unclear, and this will probably be the case in any program designed to achieve high literacy.

The challenge then focuses on helping those students who lack the background knowledge necessary to understand what high literacy is. In contrast, students who possess this background knowledge because they grew up in highly literate environments have a tremendous advantage. They usually understand what they need to achieve and what rewards may be in store for them should they attain their goals. For those students who lack this background, educators and schools need to establish the necessary environment within the school. At the same time, it is important to understand that an enhanced school environment supporting high literacy cannot be created instantly. A school environment which supports high literacy for all students must evolve over time through the systematic work of teachers, students, administrators, and researchers.

One of the best terms that we have found to describe this ideal school environment for achieving high literacy is briefly discussed by Shulman (1986) and Berliner (1986) and alluded to by Bereiter and Scardamalia (1987a). That term is the guild. In this educational guild, teachers, students, administrators, and researchers are involved and committed members. The focus of this community is the constant and continuous growth and development of literacy. Teachers, administrators, and researchers need to function as good and conscientious students of reading and writing. In addition, teachers, administrators, and researchers need to be committed to achieving higher levels of literacy than they have currently achieved. That is, their quest for even higher levels of literacy never ends. At the same time, we need teachers who are well grounded in the content knowledge of reading and writing, curricular knowledge, and pedagogical content knowledge to teach the higher-order cognitive skills that will empower all students to flourish in an educational environment in which intentional learning is pervasive. And to complete our description of this educational guild, we need teachers who possess the ability to involve students in supporting each other's learning and to engender in those students the same level of professionalism that exists among the teachers, administrators, and researchers in this environment.

To be sure, this elaborated version of the Teacher Three prototype will be a challenge to attain and the financial costs will probably be formidable. At the same time, it is important to note that it does not require a knowledge base or abilities that greatly exceed those that most teachers already possess. The current research does not suggest that the task will be simple, but it does suggest that the task is feasible.

Contributions in this Volume[1]

We began this chapter by noting the many and varied proposals for instructional improvement which today's educators encounter. We have implied that these proposals should be judged in relation to their value for helping students move toward high literacy–a level of literacy that is most likely to be developed for the most students as the instructional norm moves toward the Teacher Three prototype.

Similarly, as readers consider the·remaining chapters in this book, they should think not only of the ideas for instructional improvement, but also how these ideas can fit into the Teacher Three repertoire. We believe that higher-order literacy for the majority of students can only be achieved by teachers whose goal is to create independent learners.

To accomplish a move toward the Teacher Three prototype, we argue that well-informed, empowered teachers are needed. Teachers need to believe in their critical role as decision makers (see Dreher & Singer, 1989), but they must also be well informed. To this end, this volume provides a thorough grounding on critical issues in elementary school literacy. Although these chapters do not comprise all issues in elementary school literacy, they do cover a wide range. These chapters can serve as a springboard for in-depth study of lines of inquiry all aimed at the improvement of instruction.

Chapter 2

Although she acknowledges that many decisions are made for them by the school administration, Rebecca Barr points out that teachers, nevertheless, make crucial decisions about grouping and instructional materials that affect their students' learning. She notes that these key decisions, made early in a school year, tend to be highly stable: they affect students' learning for the entire year. Barr presents findings to explicate the complex interactions between students' learning and how teachers group students, how they use materials, and how they schedule instructional time. She concludes by considering recent instructional ideas that may lead to improved learning by changing the way teachers use instructional time.

Chapter 3
Jana Mason, Carol Peterman, David Dunning, and Janice Stewart describe three models that represent differing perspectives on how children learn to read. Developmental models of reading describe stages through which children progress in their ability to read words–each stage characterized by key changes in children's understanding about reading. Cognitive processing models describe readers' mental activities as they attempt to comprehend text. Social cognition models of reading explain how language, culture, and interactions with parents, teachers, and other children impact on children's construction of concepts about reading. Mason, Dunning, Stewart, and Peterman conclude that all three models contribute to an understanding of the reading process and that all are important to consider in obtaining the most complete understanding of how to teach children to read.

Chapter 4
Connie Juel discusses the development of reading and writing in a group of at-risk children as they progressed from first through fourth grade. She found that early attainment of word recognition skills in the primary grades is critical for later success in both reading and writing. Her chapter explains the factors, such as phonemic awareness and cipher knowledge, that influenced these results and discusses why the students who were poor readers at the end of first grade were still poor readers at the end of fourth grade.

Chapter 5
After presenting an historical overview of vocabulary research and summarizing current knowledge about vocabulary size and vocabulary instruction, Michael Graves presents a comprehensive plan for vocabulary development in the elementary school. His plan consists of two parts: a curriculum of individual words and a curriculum of strategies for learning words. For each, he describes appropriate learning tasks and presents guidelines for incorporating these tasks into the vocabulary curriculum.

Chapter 6

As they examine elementary school social studies instruction, Isabel Beck and Margaret McKeown note that many students have difficulty making the transition from narrative to expository text. Prime factors in this difficulty appear to be that expository textbooks lack structural coherence and that they assume levels of prior knowledge which students do not have. Both revising textbooks to improve structural coherence and building background knowledge prior to reading will lead to better comprehension of the content. However, improved background knowledge alone does not compensate for problems in the text presentation. Beck and McKeown argue that particular emphasis should be placed on exposing students to richer, more varied materials. They offer two key recommendations for teachers who want to increase social studies learning: 1) go for depth by choosing a few critical, related topics and covering them extensively, and, 2) make connections between ideas.

Chapter 7

Joanna Williams focuses on reading comprehension instruction and learning-disabled students. She describes research on the difficulties learning-disabled students have in finding the main idea in expository texts and the effects of instruction on their performance. She then reports on learning-disabled students' ability to identify the themes in narrative material, noting similar problems to the ones they exhibited with main idea in expository texts. As she draws implications for improving the instruction of learning-disabled students, Williams stresses that techniques helpful to learning-disabled readers are also appropriate and helpful for poor readers who are not labeled learning-disabled.

Chapter 8

Diana Miller, John Bransford, Nancy Vye, Susan Goldman, Charles Kinzer, and Salvatore Soraci, Jr. explore how combining print and video technology with oral and written language can be used to facilitate learning. They describe potential benefits that an integrated media system might have for education, including the capacity both to provide background knowledge, and their potential for helping students construct mental models of what they read. To illustrate their points, Miller et al. describe two integrated media projects, one with older elementary school projects and the other with young non-readers. They argue that new integrated media technologies make it possible to provide learning environments that are superior to what either text or video alone can offer.

Chapter 9
Robert Calfee examines the concept of alternative assessment by focusing on teachers' assessment of their students' use of reading and writing in elementary school classrooms. First, Calfee details an example of a teacher's ongoing assessment of her students. He uses this description to concretize the characteristics of authentic assessment. Then he presents a conceptual framework from which to view classroom-based assessment. Calfee raises a number of issues which need to be addressed if alternative forms of assessment are to survive as accepted educational practice.

Chapter 10
Linda Gambrell reacts to the chapters in this book from the point of view of instructional implications. As she offers her insights into the classroom applications of the ideas presented in this volume, she notes a number of recurring themes including the need to teach for depth, the crucial role of teacher decision making, and the concern for at-risk students.

Chapter 11
John Guthrie and Michael Pressley react to Chapters 2 through 9, arguing that these chapters can be categorized into those that address the cognitive bases of reading and those that relate reading to particular types of experience. In reacting to the ideas in this volume, Guthrie and Pressley return to the notion we have presented in Chapter 1 that there is a need for development of higher-order literacy. They argue that higher-order literacy is most likely to be developed when literacy goals are immersed in substantive content. They then present five hypotheses about improving students' literacy based on their viewpoint. For example, they posit that students will better comprehend a text if they see it as a means for learning a new idea than if they view it as an object to be recalled. Guthrie and Pressley challenge readers to investigate these hypotheses for their classroom validity.

End Note
1. Rebecca Sammons drafted the first version of the summaries of Chapters 2 through 9.

References
Anderson, J. R. (1990). *Cognitive psychology and its implications* (3rd ed.). New York: W. H. Freeman and Company.

Anderson, R. C., Hiebert, E. H., Scott, J. A., & Wilkinson, I. A. G. (1985). *Becoming a nation of readers: The report of the Commission on Reading.* Washington, D. C.: National Institute of Education, U. S. Department of Education.

Bailey, R. W., & Forsheim, R. M. (Eds.). (1983). *Literacy for life: The demand for reading and writing.* New York: Modern Language Association.

Bereiter, C., & Bird, M. (1985). Use of thinking aloud in identification and teaching of reading comprehension strategies. *Cognition and Instruction, 2,* 131-156.

Bereiter, C., & Scardamalia, M. (1987a). An attainable version of high literacy: Approaches to teaching higher-order skills in reading and writing. *Curriculum Inquiry, 17*(1), 9-30.

Bereiter, C., & Scardamalia, M. (1987b). *The psychology of written composition.* Hillsdale, NJ: Lawrence Erlbaum.

Bereiter, C., & Scardamalia, M. (1985). *Intentional learning in school contexts.* Unpublished report, Intentional Learning Project, Centre for Applied Cognitive Science. Toronto: Ontario Institute for Studies in Education.

Berliner, D. C. (1986, August/September). In pursuit of the expert pedagogue. *Educational Researcher, 15,* 5-13.

Bloom, A. (1987). *The closing of the American mind: How higher education has failed democracy and impoverished the souls of today's students.* New York: Simon and Schuster.

Brophy, J., & Good, T. L. (1986). Teacher behavior and student achievement. In M. C. Wittrock (Ed.), *Handbook of research on teaching* (3rd ed.) (pp. 328-375). New York: Macmillan Publishing Company.

Brown, A. L., Bransford, J. D., Ferrara, R. A., & Campione, J. C. (1983). Learning, remembering, and understanding. In J. Flavell & E. M. Markman (Eds.), *Handbook of child psychology* (4th ed.) (pp. 77-166). New York: Wiley.

Brown, A. L., & Campione, J. C. (1981). Inducing flexible thinking: A problem of access. In M. Friedman, J. P. Das, & N. O'Connor (Eds.), *Intelligence and learning* (pp. 515-529). New York: Plenum.

Bruner, J. S. (1983). *Child's talk: Learning to use language.* New York: Norton.

Bruner, J. S. (1960). *The process of education.* Cambridge, MA: Harvard University Press.

Carnegie Foundation for the Advancement of Teaching. (1988). *Report card on school reform: The teachers speak.* Princeton, NJ: The author.

Chall, J. S. (1990). Policy implications of literacy definitions. In R. L. Venezky, D. A. Wagner, & B. S. Ciliberti (Eds.), *Toward defining literacy* (pp. 54-62). Newark, DE: International Reading Association.

Dansereau, D. F. (1985). Learning strategy research. In J. W. Segal, S. F. Chipman, & R. Glaser (Eds.), *Thinking and learning skills: Vol. 1: Relating instruction to research* (pp. 209-239). Hillsdale, NJ: Lawrence Erlbaum.

DeFord, D. E., Lyons, C. A., & Pinnell, G. S. (Eds.). (1991). *Bridges to literacy: Learning from reading recovery.* Portsmouth, NH: Heinemann Publishers.

Dreher, M. J., & Singer, H. (1989). The teacher's role in students' success. *The Reading Teacher, 42,* 612-617.

Flesch, R. (1983). *Why Johnny still can't read: A new look at the scandal of our schools.* New York: Harper Collins.

Good, T. L., & Brophy, J. E. (1991). *Looking in classrooms* (5th ed.). New York: Harper Collins, Publishers.

Greene, M. (1988). *The dialectic of freedom.* New York: Teachers College Press.

Hirsch, E. D. (1987). *Cultural literacy: What every American needs to know.* Boston, MA: Houghton Mifflin.

Kozol, J. (1986). *Illiterate America.* New York: New American Library.

Kozol, J. (1991). *These young lives: Still separate, still unequal: Children in America's schools.* New York: Crown Publishers.

Lesgold, A. M. (1984). Acquiring expertise. In J. R. Anderson & S. M. Kosslyn (Eds.), *Tutorials in learning and memory* (pp. 31-60). San Francisco, CA: Freeman Publishers.

National Commission on Excellence in Education. (1984). *A nation at risk: The full account.* Portland, OR: U. S. A. Research, Inc.

Ong, W. J. (1982). *Orality and literacy: The technologizing of the word.* London, UK: Methuen.

Palincsar, A. S., & Brown, A. L. (1984). Reciprocal teaching of comprehension-fostering and monitoring activities. *Cognition and Instruction, 1,* 117-175.

Paris, S. G., Wasik, B. A., & Turner, J. C. (1991). The development of strategic readers. In R. Barr, M. L. Kamil, P. Mosenthal, & P. D. Pearson (Eds.), *Handbook of reading research: Volume II* (pp. 609-640). New York: Longman.

Pearson, P. D., & Fielding, L. (1991). Comprehension instruction. In R. Barr, M. L. Kamil, P. Mosenthal, & P. D. Pearson (Eds.), *Handbook of reading research: Volume II* (pp. 815-860). New York: Longman.

Piaget, J. (1952). *The origins of intelligence in children.* New York: International Universities Press.

Rand Corporation. (1984). *Beyond the commission reports: The coming crisis in teaching.* Santa Monica, CA: The author.

Ravitch, D. (1987). *The schools we deserve: Reflections on the educational crisis of our time.* New York: Basic Books.

Ravitch, D., & Finn, C. E. (1987). *What do our 17-year-olds know? A report on the first national assessment of history and literature.* New York: Harper & Row, Publishers.

Resnick, L. B., & Neches, R. (1984). Factors affecting individual differences in learning ability. In R. J. Sternberg (Ed.), *Advances in the psychology of human intelligence: Volume II* (pp. 275-323). Hillsdale, NJ: Lawrence Erlbaum.

Resnick, D. P., & Resnick, L. B. (1977). The nature of literacy: An historical exploration. *Harvard Educational Review, 47*(3), 370-385.

Resnick, D. P., & Resnick, L. B. (1985). Standards, curriculum, and performance: A historical and comparative perspective. *Educational Researcher, 14,* 5-20.

Roehler, L. R., & Duffy, G. G. (1991). Teachers' instructional actions.

In R. Barr, M. L. Kamil, P. Mosenthal, & P. D. Pearson (Eds.), *Handbook of reading research: Volume II* (pp. 861-883). New York: Longman.

Rumelhart, D. E. (1980). Schemata: The building blocks of cognition. In R. J. Spiro, B. C. Bruce, & W. F. Brewer (Eds.), *Theoretical issues in reading comprehenion* (pp. 33-58). Hillsdale, NJ: Lawrence Erlbaum.

Scardamalia, M., Bereiter, C., & Steinbach, R. (1984). Teachability of reflective processes in written composition. *Cognitive Science, 8,* 173-190.

Scribner, S. (1988). Literacy in three metaphors. In E. Kintgen, B. M. Kroll, & M. Rose (Eds.), *Perspectives on literacy* (pp. 71-81). Carbondale, IL: Southern Illinois University Press.

Shulman, L. S. (1986, February). Those who understand: Knowledge growth in teaching. *Educational Researcher, 15,* 4-14.

Singer, H., & Donlan, D. (1989). *Reading and learning from text* (2nd ed.) Hillsdale, NJ: Erlbaum.

Slater, W. H., & Graves, M. F. (1989). Research on expository text: Implications for teachers. In K. D. Muth (Ed.), *Children's comprehension of text: Research into practice* (pp. 140-166). Newark, DE: International Reading Association.

Venezky, R. L. (1990). Definitions of literacy. In R. L. Venezky, D. A Wagner, & B. S. Ciliberti (Eds.), *Toward defining literacy* (pp. 2-16). Newark, DE: International Reading Association.

Venezky, R. L. (1991). The development of literacy in the industrialized nations of the west. In R. Barr, M. L. Kamil, P. Mosenthal, & P. D. Pearson (Eds.), *Handbook of reading research: Volume II* (pp. 46-67). New York: Longman.

Voss, J. F. (1984). On learning and learning from text. In H. Mandl, N. L. Stein, & T. Trabasso (Eds.), *Learning and comprehension of text* (pp. 193-212). Hillsdale, NJ: Lawrence Erlbaum.

Vygotsky, L. S. (1978). *Mind in society: The development of higher psychological processes* (M. Cole, V. John-Steiner, S. Scribner, & E. Souberman, Trans.). Cambridge, MA: Harvard University Press, 1978.

Weinstein, C. E., & Mayer, R. E. (1986). The teaching of learning strategies. In M. C. Wittrock (Ed.), *Handbook of research on teach-*

ing (3rd ed.) (pp. 315-327). New York: Macmillan Publishing Company.

Wittrock, M. C. (Ed.). (1986). *Handbook of research on teaching* (3rd ed.). New York: Macmillan Publishing Company.

2

Teachers, Materials and Group Composition in Literacy Instruction

Rebecca Barr

As educators, we can view teaching and learning from a number of different perspectives. We can, for example, focus on the details of what individual students say and do during a reading or writing activity. Or we can consider the interaction of group members as they participate in literacy events. Through a somewhat more broadly focused lens, we can view the texture of activities participated in by teachers and students across the school day or year. Even more broadly, we can examine the interconnections between what students and teachers do and what occurs in schools and school systems more generally.

In this chapter we view teaching and learning from this more general vantage point as it occurs in school systems. This way of thinking about classroom instruction derives from a sociological perspective that concerns itself with organizational processes and the social processes of groups. In this chapter, I view instruction as influenced by the key structural decisions made by teachers and school administrators. Sociological perspectives that stress social organization complement the psychological perspectives more common to the field of reading in understanding instructional processes.

In developing this sociological perspective, I draw heavily on my own instructional research over the past two decades. The book, *How Schools Work,* (Barr & Dreeben, 1983), was based on a detailed study of 15 classes in the late 1960s. In this chapter, I present evidence from our second major instructional study conducted in the 1980s involving 13 first-grade classes and 11 fourth-grade classes. We observed instruction intensively and extensively; in the first grade classes, for example, we observed a full day of instruction 12 times over the school year. We analyzed curricular materials, interviewed teachers at the beginning of the school year and after each observation, and assessed the learning of children at several points during the school year. I draw on this evidence to illustrate concepts developed later in the chapter.

The chapter is organized in the following way. First, I describe the perspective from which I view classroom instruction. In subsequent sections, I explore the complex set of relations between how teachers group students for instruction, the nature of curricular materials and how teachers use them, time scheduling, and learning. In the final section, I consider changes now occurring in literacy instruction and discuss the applicability of a sociological perspective in understanding these changes.

Sociological Perspective

Classrooms are part of large complex organizations, and the work of teachers is shaped both by classroom and school-wide conditions. In many respects, teachers "play the hand they have been dealt." At the same time, they also make key decisions that influence the opportunities their students have to learn. Decisions about grouping, materials, and time, usually made at the beginning of each year, shape instruction and learning over the remainder of the school year. These key decisions are important precisely becasue they influence how much time students have for reading and writing, the materails they read, the instruction they receive, and their learning. We view the work of educators as characterized by a division of labor among levels of school organization, each with its own productive activities. Each has a different role to play in the organization and implementation of schooling (see Table 2.1).

Table 2.1 A sociological perspective on organizational decisions that influence instruction.

	TEACHER EXPERTISE	CURRICULAR MATERIALS	TIME SCHEDULING	STUDENT COMPOSITION
DISTRICT LEVEL	Recruitment Salaries Staff Development	Curricular policy Curricular selection Budgeting	Daily time Yearly schedule Vacations	School boundaries Busing Grouping policy
SCHOOL LEVEL	Teacher class assignments Staff development Instructional support	Curricular use policy Monitoring Assessment	Schedule of special subjects Lunch, Duties	Class assignments Cross-class groupings
CLASSROOM LEVEL	Teacher goals Teacher expertise	Teacher materials Selective use of materials	Scheduling of in-class time Group time allotments Time use	Grouping pattern Group membership
GROUP LEVEL	Teacher develops an appropriate literacy program			Instructional group
INDIVIDUAL LEVEL	Student participates in instructional activities			Student learning Student feeling

At the district level, for example, administrators are responsible for such activities as procuring and maintaining buildings, securing personnel, obtaining the resources that teachers need for instruction, and the like. Decisions made at this level have direct consequence for the work of teachers. For example, setting school boundaries and district busing policies establishes the social and intellectual composition of the student population that attends each school in the district. Similarly, policies concerning the length of the school year and the school day and the scheduling of vacation time have direct implication for when and how long children attend schools. District wide committees typically select instructional materals for reading and language arts.

Significant decisions are also made at the school level. These concern assigning students to teachers (a process that also establishes the composition of classes), developing the school time schedule, distributing instructional materials, and assessing learning. Each of these decisions has marked consequences for the work of teachers in classrooms. For example, teachers can tell early in the school year whether they have a class that will work well together, or whether it is going to be an extremely challenging year because of the number of children requiring special support. It is interesting to be with teachers, particularly first grade teachers, when they first learn that gym and library are scheduled in the morning. This means that they will have relatively little time two or three mornings a week to undertake reading instruction when the children are most alert and teachable.

At the classroom level, teachers work within the set of conditions that have been established by district and school decisions: the composition of their class, their weekly time schedule, and the available instructional materials. At the same time, teachers also make many significant decisions to establish the character of their instructional program given the resources at their disposal. For example, an important first decision pertains to whether they will instruct the class as a whole, in groups, or as individuals. Whether teachers decide to group students for instruction or to instruct the class as a whole influences the design of instruction. If teachers group children for instruction on the basis of ability, to some extent they solve the problem of matching the difficulty of materials with the prior knowledge of children. That is, when they limit the range of a particular group of children in prior knowledge, it is easier to find reading materials that are of appropriate difficulty for all group members. But the ability grouping solution makes teachers less available to work directly with pupils who are not in the immediate subgroup they are teaching. It also means that students will work on seatwork tasks for long periods of time while the teacher works with other reading groups. Alternatively, the solution of total class instruction may solve the problem of teacher availability, but because it typically involves using a single set of materials, the work is usually inappropriate for a number of students–too hard for some, too easy for others.

When teachers design instruction for their students, whether as a whole class, in groups, or as individuals, they must decide how to use the available in-class time. Especially when they have their students for most of each school day, they must decide how much time to spend on reading and writing, and how much on other subjects. As teachers have become responsible for teaching more subjects, the school day has become increasingly fragmented, so that when they schedule, they must think about how some subjects can be integrated. Alternatively, to have enough time to teach a subject in depth, it may be appropriate to teach some subjects for longer periods but for only a quarter or half of the school year. Whatever the problems and whatever the solutions, by creating daily and yearly schedules, teachers establish time limits on literacy instruction, as well as on other subjects.

Teachers determine whether the instructional materials they have been given are appropriate for their students. Should they want to supplement the basal program, they must determine how to do this. Are there monies available for buying tradebooks, for big books, and the like? What kind of joint planning with other teachers at the same grade level is possible? What is the district policy on the basal program tests? Assessment is an issue that directly influences teachers and their use of available curricular materials. But again the point is: Whatever decisions are made by teachers, they have a significant impact on what students read during the year and what they learn.

Most decisions made early in the school year are highly stable and serve to establish the structure of classroom instruction for the remainder. The instructional program, once established, can be refined as the year proceeds. Yet, modifications are typically made within the pattern established at the beginning of the year. They usually represent minor alterations rather than major changes. To the extent that the instructional program proves to have an impact on learning, early decisions about the organization of instruction, materials, and the time scheduling will have substantial consequences for what and how much children learn. Curricular materials in American classrooms, to a great extent, establish what students will learn. The time allocated to instruction typically determines how many of the new concepts presented in the curricular materials are considered. Whether materials are too easy or too difficult will influence how well and how much students learn.

While most of our attention in the field of reading has been devoted to understanding the psychological processes involved and how they can be fostered through alternative instructional strategies, it is also important to remember that classroom instruction involves groups of students and that their instruction is greatly influenced by the set of interwoven decisions made at different levels in school systems. The learning of individuals typically occurs in instructional groups whose instruction is influenced by conditions prevailing in classrooms, as well as by decisions made at the school and district levels.

If the decisions teachers make early in the school year are as important as I have suggested here, what have we learned about making these decisions well? In the next section, I explore the history of ability grouping and consider implications we can draw from the research on ability groups. In this consideration, I draw heavily on earlier materials that I have written (Barr, 1989a, 1989b; Barr & Dreeben, 1991).

Ability Groups and Reading Instruction

Historical Relations between Grouping and Curricular Materials

Teachers can organize their students in many ways for reading instruction, but most prefer to group children on the basis of their reading achievement. They typically form reading groups or ability groups within classes in the primary grades. In the intermediate grades, total class instruction sometimes occurs but almost always after the class itself has been grouped on the basis of ability through departmentalization, cross-grade grouping, or some other form of class grouping.

Ability grouping pervades American schools, particularly for reading instruction at the elementary level. Despite its prevalence, or possibly because of it, most of us have taken it for granted. Ability grouping has an interesting history. The impulse to regularize education goes back at least to the early 1800s in the Lancasterian schools and in the 1930s when Horace Mann advocated graded classes and a well-articulated curriculum following that of Prussian schools (Tyack, 1974). The first American graded school was founded in Boston in 1847 and was adopted in all parts of the nation during the next quarter of a century (Otto, 1932).

Curricular developments accompanied the development of graded schools. The first graded readers were written by Samuel Wood early in the 19th century, probably for the Lancasterian schools (Venezky, 1988); others such as those written by the McGuffeys followed. This grade level articulation of the reading curriculum anticipated and supported the development of graded schools. It was the rapid expansion of schooling during the mid-1800s that led both to graded classes and to the use of graded reading materials.

Later, however, problems with age-graded classes arose because of great differences among students within grades. One response, developed in 1862 by W.T. Harris, the superintendent of the St. Louis schools, was to group students into classes on the basis of their academic progress (Otto, 1932). This was the first example of ability grouping within grade levels.

A second period of expansion in schooling occurred in the late 1800s and early 1900s as new waves of immigration occurred. Early in the 20th century the Progressive Era began in education accompanied by the scientific study of learning, based in part on developments in educational measurement. Because of increased awareness of individual differences among students, this was a period when many new plans were developed, frequently identified with their respective cities: Joplin, Denver, Detroit, Winnetka, Gary, and the like. Each plan attempted in different ways to organize students in grouped settings so that all students could benefit from instruction.

This was also the time when teachers first began to form ability groups within classes for reading instruction. Although it is difficult to date the first appearance of this practice, one of the earliest references found in the 1913 edition of the *Story Hour Readers Manual*[1] suggests separate groups for those who "progress rapidly" and for those who are "slow and need more assistance."

Developments in curricular materials accompanied these changes in grouping. Reading programs became easier at the lower levels through the addition of preprimers. Easier stories were created through word control and repetition (Smith, 1965). Reading programs also became more comprehensive and included both teacher's guides and workbooks for skill practice. For a second time, then, we see shifts in the organization of curricula that paralleled changes in how students are grouped for instruction.

We are currently in a period not unlike that of the early 1900s when our schools were faced with increased cultural and linguistic diversity among students. And similar to this period, we are reconsidering our use of ability grouping and the nature of curricular programs in reading and language arts. Concurrently, our reconceptualization of the processes of reading and writing has stimulated some rethinking about curriculum and instruction, and this in turn has encouraged the reevaluation of ability grouping.

Research on Ability Grouping.

What do we know about ability grouping? Can it be justified? Should we be looking toward other ways to organize our students for instruction? Researchers since the late 1920s have inquired about the consequences of ability grouping for the learning and feelings of students. The typical study compares the learning of students who are grouped in some fashion on the basis of ability or achievement with comparable students who receive instruction in more heterogeneous groups. The literature contains two major waves of reviews, one in the early 1930s and another in the 1960s. Whereas both groups emphasized the inconsistent findings and equivocal results, the earlier reviewers also suggested that ability grouping benefited slow students (e.g., Miller & Otto, 1930; Whipple, 1936), and the later group discerned a tendency for high achievers in homogeneous groups to learn more than comparable students in heterogeneous groups, but for low achievers to do less well in homogeneous than heterogeneous groups (e.g. Eash, 1961; Esposito, 1973; Findley & Bryan, 1971).

One of the more useful summaries of this literature is provided by Robert Slavin (1987) who distinguishes studies in ability grouping *within* classes from various forms of ability grouping *between* classes (see also Barr & Dreeben, 1991). With respect to the former, Slavin found no studies meeting his criteria that compared students' learning in small ability groups within classes with those receiving total class instruction in nonability grouped classes. He therefore found no basis for evaluating this practice in reading.

With respect to ability grouping between classes, Slavin found that classes formed on the basis of ability did not result in more learning than in heterogeneous classes; this might have been because the heterogeneous classes probably employed reading groups within classes. He found no advantage for regrouping students for reading instruction across classes *within* grades, yet he did find a learning advantage for regrouping students *between* grades. Both lower achieving and higher achieving students were found to learn more when instructed in cross-grade groups than similar students instructed in self-contained classrooms.

The main point in thinking about this literature on grouping is the inconclusiveness of the results. Ability grouping has not been shown to be clearly advantageous. Moreover, why we should expect more than inconsistent results is interesting. A social arrangement, of itself, does not lead directly to learning outcomes; rather it is the instructional activities that students experience that influences what they learn and how they feel about it.

Instructional Differences Between Reading Groups

A more recent body of research has posed a different set of questions: Once students are placed in ability groups for reading, does the resulting group composition influence the quality of their instruction? Does the instruction of ability groups differ, and if so, how? Although groups are composed to facilitate differential instruction, the question is whether different instruction constitutes effective instruction. Reviewers such as Allington (1983), Barr (1989a), and Hiebert (1983) describe the findings from this research as follows: The instruction of low group members tends to be characterized by a greater number of intrusions and less time-on-task than students in higher achieving groups. Low group members typically read less material, complete simpler assignments, focus on smaller units of print, and have decoding rather than meaning emphasized. They are given more drill and skill work, read orally more often, and are asked more questions that require recall of information rather than reasoning. Teachers provide them with different prompts and more structure through the provision of advanced organizers for lessons than students in higher achieving groups. While some researchers also claim that low group members receive less instructional time (Hunter, 1978), others have not found differential time allocations (Collins, 1986; Weinstein, 1976).

It is typically concluded on the basis of this evidence that low group members are being treated unfairly. Some observers go further to claim that instruction causes low group members to be poor readers. But there are problems in drawing such conclusions. First, few of the case studies describe student learning in a systematic fashion, and without outcome measures it is difficult to judge the effects of instruction on learning. Second, there are no appropriate instructional contrasts on which to base conclusions. Low groups need to receive and respond positively to the same kind of instruction as high group members before it can be concluded that the same treatment is appropriate. Based on the findings, however, it is reasonable to conclude that low group members receive instruction that differs in some respects from that of high group members and that what they receive may be less acceptable given our current views of best practice (Anderson, Hiebert, Scott, & Wilkinson, 1985).

Although I accept this conclusion, I also want to suggest an alternative, and this concerns the curriculum of instruction. Out of our concern for the lower reading proficiency found among low group members, I believe that we have focused on differences to demonstrate inequality and unfairness in treatment. This focus, however, has blinded us to the important similarities that characterize the instruction of both low and high group members. First, it is well documented that most elementary school students learn from basal programs; both low and high groups read the same stories and participate in many of the same instructional activities.

Figure 2.1. Number of weeks spent by low, middle, and high group. (From R. Barr, R. Chen, & R. Dreeben, The pace of first grade reading groups, submitted for publication, 1991.)

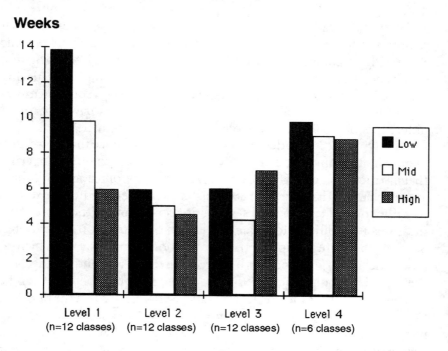

Although the pace of instruction differs among groups, even this is not really true after the first six months of instruction. Figure 2.1 shows, for example, that the low and middle groups in 12 of the first grade classes we studied spent considerably more time than the high groups on level

1 materials (Barr, Chen, & Dreeben, 1992)[2]. The difference between the three groups on level 1 materials is practically and statistically significant [$F(2,33)=5.69$, $p<0.01$]. For levels 2, 3 and 4, however, all three groups

Figure 2.2. Histogram of levels of basal materails read by reading groups. (From R. Barr & M.W. Sadow, Influence of basal programs on fourth-grade reading instruction, *Reading Research Quarter, 24,* 1989, p. 58.

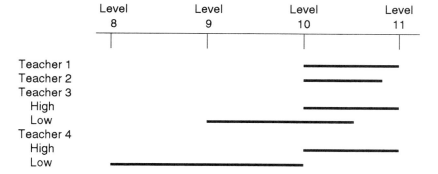

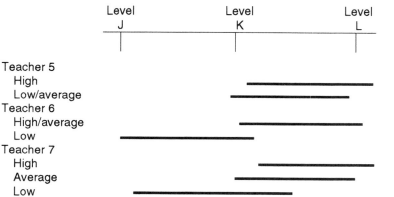

spent about the same number of weeks (the differences do not reach statistical significance). In some classes, the lower groups spent even less time than the high group after the first preprimer. These findings suggest that differences in the level of books that groups read are established early in first grade when the first preprimer is read, and these differences are perpetuated thereafter.

Figure 2.3. Representation of the instructional levels of groups in the basal reading program from Grades 1 to 8. (From R. Barr, *The social organization of literacy instruction, Cognitive and social perspectives for literacy research and instruction,* S. McCormick & J. Zutell, Eds., Thirty-eighth Yearbook of the National Reading Conference, Chicago: National Reading Conference, 1989, p. 27.)

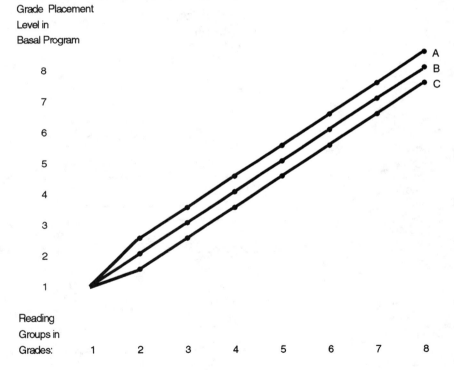

We found similar findings in our study of fourth-grade groups (Barr & Sadow, 1989). As Figure 2.2 shows, low groups read the same or more levels from the basal than did average and high groups. For example, the low group in Teacher 3's class read from one and a half levels of the basal, while the high group completed just one grade level. Even more astounding, Teacher 4's low group completed two levels while the high group completed one.

The results for these groups are characteristic of those in most schools where I have worked: The low groups proceed about a half grade behind and the high group about a half grade ahead of the average group. Thus, differences that come about during the first half of first grade continue to exist between high and low groups for the remainder of elementary schooling. The limited pace of the high group often comes about through informal agreements among teachers as to how far the high group can proceed into the reading materials for the next grade level.

When I work with teachers in schools, we often map the basal placement of their reading groups as they progress from grade to grade; all but a few lower achieving individuals are included in our mapping (Barr, 1989b). I have represented the typical pattern of basal coverage in Figure 2.3, with line A representing the high group, B the average group, and C the low group. Note that I say *pattern of instruction* rather than *pattern of learning.* The variation in learning (reading proficiency) is wider than that in instruction.

Figure 2.3 shows clearly that the difference between low and high group members is really minor. In other words, we choose to label students through membership in low and high group, but then we proceed to offer them instruction that is essentially the same in many respects. It would seem that we should either instruct all students with the same materials in heterogeneous groups or as a total class, offering differential support as necessary, *or* truly individualize instruction so that along with the label of low group member, major benefits are realized through greater instructional support.

Instructional Time and Basal Reading

Consider another set of major decisions teachers make, those pertaining to instructional time. A significant finding from research conducted in the 1970s is the pervasive and significant relation between instructional time and learning (Rosenshine & Stevens, 1984). Obviously, the term instructional time does not mean that any use of time will do, but rather time in which students are engaged in appropriate instructional tasks. Study after study conducted mainly in the 1970s

(Rosenshine & Stevens, 1984) found that in comparison with other instructional variables, the time students spend learning in a content area is closely associated with the level of learning that occurs. What is so interesting about this finding is the extent to which it has been dismissed, as if it were an educational fad whose time had come and gone. To the contrary, I believe that it is something that we need to attend to in a continuing fashion.

How do the differences among students in instructional time come about? One possibility is that they arise from teachers giving preferential treatment to higher reading groups. Yet, the research evidence shows that all children within a class, whether they are poor or good readers, typically receive similar amounts of time for reading instruction and other literacy activities. Figure 2.4 shows the range in the amount of time that different groups in the 13 first grade classes we studied spent in small reading groups.[3] In all these classes, teachers organized children into reading groups for instruction, and almost all reading instruction occurred during small group time. In Class 2, for example, one group received as much as 24 minutes of instruction each day while another group received as little as 15 minutes. This variation of 9 minutes among groups is greater than that for most of the other teachers; only Teachers 1, 12, and 13 show a greater range. The range is greatest for Teacher 12

Figure 2.4. Range in small group time in the 13 classes from 3 districts.

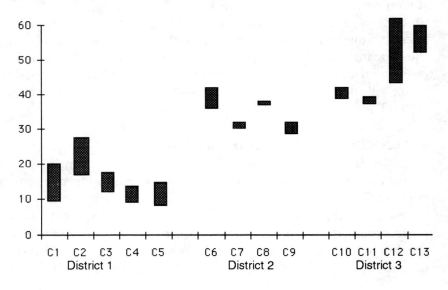

who provided least time for the highest achieving group and more for her two lower groups through a second instructional period in the afternoon. Typically, groups within classes are similar in instructional time. When differences occur, the group receiving the most time is not always the high group; only four of the 13 high groups received the most time in their respective classes. However, only two of the 13 lowest groups received most time. In any case, for most teachers in our sample, the time variations among groups within classes is not great. With the exception of Class 12, most groups in any particular class receive about the same amount of small group time.

More significant, Figure 2.4 shows that there are differences between classes related both to schools and districts in the amount of time that children spend in small group instruction. Consider, for example, the time that students in Class 4 receive as compared to those in Class 13. A student in Class 4 may receive as little as 7 minutes a day in small group reading instruction on the average or as much as 11 minutes a day, depending on the group he or she is in. Further, only two-thirds of this time is used for instructional purposes. By contrast, a student in Class 13 spends a considerable amount of time in small group reading instruction, from 43 to 55 minutes daily, and about 90% of this is used for instructional purposes. These class differences boggle the mind; they represent enormous differences in the opportunity that children have to learn to read and write, and are related to group differences in instruction as well as to conditions tied to the schools and the district.

How do teachers create this opportunity? It is important to realize that the decisions made by teachers and their small group management are only part of the story. Decisions pertaining to time at the school and district level also have a bearing. Consider Figure 2.4 again. District 3 classes typically have more reading instructional time than the other two districts. This is in part because the school day in District 3 is one-half hour longer. The length of the school day can have an enormous bearing on time available for instruction, especially for the availability of blocks of time devoted to combined reading-writing instruction and for giving some groups an additional daily instructional period.

In our study, a longer day represented an opportunity for District 3 teachers. The difference between Classes 12 and 13 in one school and Classes 10 and 11 in a different school in District 3, had to do in part, however, with a school level decision. In the first school, children were allowed to enter the building at 8:50 and instructional activities began at 9:00 a.m., while in the second school, children were not allowed to enter until 9:00. Over the period of a year, this adds up to more than 30 hours of instruction. It also reflects a different attitude on the part of the principal concerning the value of time.

Districts 1 and 2 were similar in the amount of daily time they made available for instruction. Teachers' decisions account for many of the differences you see in Figure 2.4. Teacher 4, for example, decided to group her class into seven groups; though groups were small, no group received much time for instruction. Time was lost in District 1 classes because some teachers spent the first 30 to 40 minutes of each day putting work on the board, collecting lunch money, and taking attendance. Later in the day, they spent long periods of time correcting seat work. That these activities may take some time is expected, but teachers need to find more efficient ways of conducting some activities, while they should consider doing other tasks such as putting work on the chalk board and organizing materials, before children arrive.

Figure 2.5. Pages read by groups of similar ability

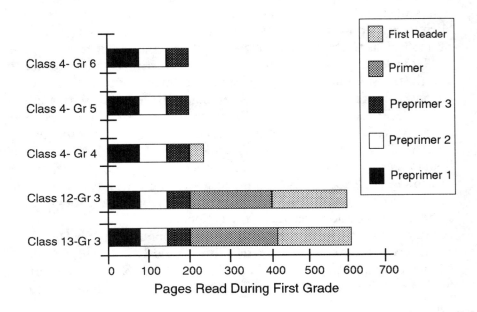

Our research shows that time scheduled for small group instruction is for the most part used productively. However, in this particular sample of teachers, those who realized the least amount of small group time were also those who used it least well. In any case, the amount of time available for small group instruction has a significant impact on the amount of reading that children can accomplish during the first grade. Figure 2.5 shows five groups *of similar ability* learning to read from the same basal materials. The first three groups are from Class 4 where children received limited small group reading time, and the second two are from Classes 12 and 13 where students received considerable reading group time. The first three classes were still reading or had just completed the preprimers at the end of the year, while the latter two were reading in the first grade book. The word learning of the Class 4 groups ranged from 77 to 172 words, in comparison to 543 words for group 3 in Class 12 and 608 words for group 3 in Class 13.

It is not appropriate to conclude from these differences that Teacher 4 should have had her students proceed at a faster pace. In our research, the amount of time for basal instruction and basal coverage is highly related (Barr & Dreeben, 1983; Barr, 1985). The correlation between instructional time and pace in our more recent study was 0.74. Instructional time creates the opportunity for more reading and more learning. Teachers set goals for the reading progress of their children; early in the school year, they can state explicitly how much of the basal they would like each of their groups to complete. They also know that groups who are not achieving the goal cannot simply be encouraged to accomplish more reading in the same time period. Rather, teachers need to extend the time period to enable children to engage in more reading. Proceeding at a fast pace through the basal materials in too little time results in partial learning and frustration. Instructional time and basal coverage must be thought of as a package that creates the opportunity for learning.

Instructional time and basal coverage are strong predictors of learning. In our first study, they accounted for 86% of the variance in word learning and 55% of the variance in general reading achievement (Barr & Dreeben, 1983), and in our second study, they accounted for 83% of the variance in word learning and 49% of the variance in reading achievement (Dreeben & Gamoran, 1986). Small group time considered by itself (see Figure 2.4) does not correlate significantly with the mean aptitude of groups (0.15): it does however, significantly correlate with the average word learning of groups at the end of first grade (0.63) and with their general reading achievement (0.40). In other words, the difference among the reading groups in the duration of the small group activities they experience during first grade (as represented in Figure 5) is strongly associated with their learning.

At the same time, it must be remembered that the relationship between basal coverage and learning is limited in particular ways. If teachers have their students proceed too rapidly through the basal program without sufficient instructional time, and the support it permits, they end up with students who learn relatively little because their level of mastery is low. Thus, if Teacher 4 had simply increased the amount her children read during the same limited time, they would have learned relatively little and been extremely frustrated (Dreeben & Barr 1988).

So far I have argued that teachers' and administrators' decisions have profound implications for students' opportunities to learn. In particular, decisions teachers make early in the school year develop a framework for instruction that greatly influences opportunities to learn. Will this way of thinking about instruction help us to understand the learning of children as we change our forms of social organization and our curricular tasks in the area of literacy? I believe it will. In the next and final section, I discuss some of the current opportunities that face us and discuss them from a sociological perspective.

Current Opportunities

As noted earlier, we are in a period characterized by greater cultural and linguistic diversity among students in our schools. We are also in a period in which our understanding of the relations between reading and writing and the constructive nature of reading has led us to rethink our curricular programs. Given these forces, more and more teachers are beginning to experiment with alternative forms of literacy instruction. New teaching strategies are enabling us to change the way we organize reading instruction. Let me describe just a few of the ways in which I believe that the new strategies will change the way we group children for instruction and use instructional time.

One way is through the use of prereading instruction. During prereading, central concepts are discussed and information about topics is shared; this experience makes the words and concepts in reading selections more accessible to students. Students who without preparation would have had extreme difficulty understanding a selection can, with such preparation, read with comprehension. As a result of this form of preparation for reading, teachers can teacher form more diverse groups or abandon ability grouping entirely.

At the primary level, another way involves using teaching strategies characteristic of literature-based reading programs. One approach, for example, involves a teacher reading and rereading a story aloud to children, followed by discussion of the story. Then with multiple copies of the story or using a big book, children are encouraged to read the story aloud in unison (all children, the boys, the girls, and so forth). Their story reading is supported in two ways: First, the children are already familar with the story, and this familiarity provides clues to word recognition and meaning, and second, since other children are also reading, a child can hear others say unknown words. This format avoids the common problems of round robin reading, particularly for low group members. This format, as well as reading with partners, gives children the opportunity to read entire stories, rather than just a paragraph or two, thereby achieving the goal of having them be directly engaged in reading rather than observing and waiting for their turn. Given such teaching approaches, the same amount of time is better used. Similar to prereading instruction, this more supported form of early reading instruction enables a more diverse group of children to participate jointly in instruction.

Finally, the coordination of reading and writing enables children to learn new concepts through expressive as well as receptive means. This is true for beginning reading where concepts about the nature of the relations between print and speech are being learned. It is also true when new understandings about people and things are being developed. The coordination of reading and writing typically demands longer time periods, and frequently this time can be found only when reading groups are eliminated, and total class modes of instruction are adopted. An advantage of instruction that engages the whole class is that it permits the use of more flexible forms of grouping such as reading partners, book clubs, and peer writing groups.

As we move to literature-based forms of instruction, we may encounter new problems. Teachers may need to address decisions once addressed by basal authors. Take, for example, the sequencing of stories and other selections in terms of difficulty. The purpose of this sequencing is to maintain a balance between challenging new learning and consolidation through practice. The effectiveness of the literature-based first grade tutorial program, Reading Recovery, is often attributed to the extensive education of teachers, the balanced nature of the reading strategies developed, the reading of quality literature, and the holistic nature of the writing tasks. While these are undoubtedly important, at the same time, from a structural perspective, the sequencing of stories in terms of level of difficulty, the pacing of children from one level to the next as they show mastery, and the rigorously effective use of limited time may also have a bearing. We do not yet have the research to evaluate the contributions of these various conditions to learning effectiveness, but these are questions that need to be addressed in the next few years for Reading Recovery and for classroom literature-based programs.

In closing, I argue that a sociological perspective for viewing instruction becomes an even more important conceptual tool as alternatives to traditional forms of instruction emerge. This perspective means that we need to think about current and future changes in reading instruction not simply as alternatives in teaching technique but rather as events that entail the social resources of the whole school system: the division of student populations into groups of varying composition, the allocation and use of time, the types and difficulty of curricular knowledge. In the past, almost all teachers used ability groups in some form and almost all adhered closely to the curriculum provided in basal series. While these structural forms still prevail, we are moving into a time when teachers are becoming much more aware of curricular decisions and their implications for instructional grouping and time use. What was difficult to see before because there was so little variation in decision making is now being brought into sharper relief.

Specifically, in terms of the perspective described earlier, major changes will need to occur in the area of teacher expertise. Teachers who develop their own literature-based literacy programs must possess considerably more knowledge about children's literature and teaching strategies than those who adhere closely to the basal sequence and teaching recommendations. Indeed, in the area of curricular materials, a major shift will occur in decision making as teachers assume more responsibility for book selection and as district adoption committees assume less.

For the two areas that have been the focus of this chapter, time scheduling and student composition, I have described major changes that are occurring at the classroom level. Within existing daily time frames, teachers are beginning to organize longer blocks of time for more integrated forms of literacy instruction. At the same time, grouping patterns are becoming more flexible and ability grouping is disappearing altogether in some classes. Implications from these classroom level changes follow for decisions made higher in school organizations. For example, the need for longer blocks of time in classes has a bearing on the school level scheduling of out-of-class activities and the integration of some of these activities into classrooms. Teacher classroom goals are forcing a rethinking of existing cross-class and cross-grade ability grouping schemes.

The perspective enables us to see how changes at one level in school organization bear on decisions at other levels. Schools are complex organizations where decisions at one level support or constrain what occurs at other levels. As major changes are made in the structural organization of classrooms, adjustments need to be made at other levels in the system as well.

We know that administrative and teacher decisions about grouping, time, and materials will continue to be important. We do not know whether the relationships between group characteristics, time, and amount of reading found for traditional reading instruction will continue to apply to new forms of instruction, for example, whether the amount of time students spend reading and writing will predict their learning in general, or only when teachers give special attention to the sequence and challenge of their reading materials and literacy activities. We are in a period when teachers and administrators are being challenged to make adjustments in the focus and scope of their decision making. It is also a period in which instructional researchers must learn to conceptualize and document the emerging relations among school organizations, teaching, and learning.

End Notes

1. I am indebted to Richard Venezky; for this historical information. The *Story Hours Readers Manual* was published by the American Book Company in 1913.

2. This analysis is based on all groups from 12 of the 13 first grade classes n+36) in the Barr-Dreeben second study completing basal levels 1 and 2, the groups from 11 classes (n=33) completing level 3, and the groups from 6 classes (n=18) who completed level 4. Low groups from one class did not complete level 3 and low groups from 6 classes did not complete level 4 (the primer) and thus they could not be included in those comparisons. The groups from Class 4 were not included in the analysis since many class members were members of two groups and read from two levels in the basal simultaneously.

3. These data were previously reported by Barr; (1985, Table 4, p. 37). In that table, however, basal supervision time (the reading of contextual materials) was reported separately from small group non-instructional time (time allocated to management tasks, intrusions, and waiting). In addition, small group activities focused on letters and decoding are also included in the total number of minutes for small group time reported in Figure 2.2 in this chapter, but not in Table 4 reported earlier. In other words, the range in minutes represented in Figure 2.2 includes all instruction time in the small group setting, and this time was devoted to contextual reading and decoding activities, as well as to activities that were not instructional.

References

Allington, R. (1983). The reading instruction provided readers of differing reading ability. *Elementary School Journal, 83,* 548-559.

Anderson, R. C., Hiebert, E. H., Scott, J. A., & Wilkinson, I. A. (1985). *Becoming a nation of readers.* Washington, DC: National Institute of Education.

Barr, R. (1985). Observing first-grade reading instruction: Instruction viewed with a model of school organization. In J.A. Niles & R.V. Lalik (Eds.), *Issues in literacy: A research perspective* (pp.30-37). Thirty-fourth Yearbook of the National Reading Conference.

Rochester, NY: National Reading Conference.

Barr, R. (1989a). Social organization of reading instruction. In C. Emilhovich (Ed.), *Locating learning across the curriculum: Ethnographic perspectives on classroom research* (pp 57-86). Norwood, NJ: Ablex, 1989.

Barr, R. (1989b). The social organization of literacy instruction. In S. McCormick & J. Zutell, (Eds.), *Cognitive and social perspectives for literacy research and instruction* (pp.19-33). Thirty-eighth Yearbook of the National Reading Conference. Chicago: National Reading Conference.

Barr, R., Chen, R., & Dreeben, R. (1991). The pace of first grade reading groups. Manuscript submitted for publication.

Barr, R. & Dreeben, R. [with Wiratchai, N.] (1983). *How schools work.* Chicago: University of Chicago Press.

Barr, R. & Dreeben, R. (1991). Grouping students for reading instruction. In R. Barr , M. Kamil, P. Mosenthal, & P.D. Pearson (Eds.), *Handbook of Reading Research. Volume II* (pp.885-910). New York: Longman.

Barr, R. & Sadow, M. W. (1989). Influence of basal programs on fourth-grade å. *Reading Research Quarterly, 14,* 44-71.

Collins, J. (1986). Differential treatment in reading instruction. In J. Cook-Gumperz (Ed.), *The social construction of literacy* (pp.117-137). Cambridge, England: Cambridge University Press.

Dreeben, R. & Barr, R. (1987). An organizational analysis of curriculum and instruction. In M.T. Hallinan (Ed.), *The social organization of schools. New conceptualizations of the learning process* (pp.13-39). New York: Plenum.

Dreeben, R. & Barr, R. (1988). The formation and instruction of ability groups. *American Journal of Education, 97,* 34-61.

Dreeben, R., & Gamoran, A. (1986). Race, instruction, and learning. *American Sociological Review,* 51, 660-669.

Eash, M. J. (1961). Grouping: What have we learned? *Educational Leadership, 18,* 429-434.

Esposito, D. (1973). Homogeneous and heterogeneous ability grouping: Principal findings and implications for evaluating and designing more effective educational environments. *Review of Educational Research, 43,* 163-179.

Findley, W. & Bryan, M.C. (1971). *Ability grouping: 1970-II. The im-*

pact of ability grouping on school achievement, affective development, ethnic separation, and socioeconomic separation. Athens, GA: University of Georgia, The Center for Educational Improvement. (ERIC Document Reproduction Service No. ED 048 382).

Hiebert, E.H. (1983). An examination of ability grouping for reading instruction. *Reading Research Quarterly, 18,* 231-255.

Hunter, D. (1978). Student on-task behavior during second grade reading group meetings (Doctoral dissertation, University of Missouri-Columbia). *Dissertation Abstracts International, 39,* 4838A.

Miller, W. S. & Otto, J. (1930). Analysis of experimental studies in homogeneous grouping. *Journal of Educational Research, 21,* 95-102.

Otto, H. J. (1932). *Current practices in the organization of elementary schools.* Evanston, IL: Northwestern University, School of Education.

Rosenshine, B. & Stevens, R. (1984). Classroom instruction in reading. In P.D. Pearson, R. Barr, M. Kamil, & P. Mosenthal (Eds.) *Handbook of reading research* (Vol. 1, pp. 745-798). New York: Longman.

Slavin, R.E. (1987). Ability grouping: A best-evidence synthesis. Review of *Educational Research, 57,* 293-336.

Smith, N.B. (1965). American reading instruction. Newark, DE: International Reading Association.

Tyack, D. (1974). *The one best system.* Cambridge, MA: Harvard University Press.

Venezky, R.L. (1988). *The American reading script and its nineteenth century origins.* Unpublished manuscript, University of Chicago, The First Marilyn Sadow Memorial Lecture, Department of Education, Chicago.

Weinstein, R.S. (1976). Reading group membership in first grade: Teacher behaviors and pupil experience over time. *Journal of Educational Psychology, 68,* 103-116.

Whipple, G.M. (1936). *The grouping of pupils.* Thirty-fifth Yearbook, Part 1, National Society for the Study of Education. Chicago: University of Chicago Press.

3

Emergent Literacy: Alternative Models of Development and Instruction

Jana M. Mason
Carol L. Peterman
David D. Dunning
Janice P. Stewart

In the field of beginning reading, there appear to be dissimilar explanations about how children learn to read, resulting in disagreements about appropriate instructional practice in reading. The goal of this chapter is to present three different models of reading, representing developmental, cognitive processing, and social cognition perspectives. What we hope to show is that these models of reading are not as disparate as they appear to be, that they can be useful to educators, and indeed, that they offer practical advice about what, how, and when to teach beginning reading.

These three perspectives are presented to some extent in recently published reviews of reading research by Ehri (1991) and Juel (1991) who present developmental perspectives, Stanovich (1991) who describes a cognitive processing position, and Sulzby and Teale (1991) who suggest a social cognition perspective. Although these models seem to lead to dissimilar guidelines for instruction, each actually serves a role in explaining different aspects of reading and of learning to read. After describing each type of model, we compare them and then discuss a research study which clarifies some of the similarities, differences, and instructional implications of these models.

Models of Reading Development
Developmental Models of Reading
A developmental model of reading draws on information about the concepts children acquire as they learn about how to read. A number of similar models have been proposed that evolve from research with young children. These models are based principally on observations of strategies children use as they attempt to read and on analyses of children's responses to word recognition, reading, writing, and spelling tasks (e.g., Biemiller, 1970; Chall, 1979, 1983; Ehri, 1987, 1991; Ferreiro & Teberosky, 1982; Juel, 1983, 1991; Mason, 1975, 1980). The beginning steps of reading are depicted in terms of ability to read and spell printed words in or out of context.

In these models, reading development is usually expressed in terms of key changes that a child makes in understanding how to read. These models rely in large part on the Piagetian notion of levels or stages of development in which sets of insights lead learners toward coordination or reorganization of strategies for effective reading. For example, focusing on the insight regarding the letter and letter-sound connections, I pointed out this shift in perspective:

> When a child can unlock the pronunciation of unfamiliar printed words, this marks a transition from a knowledge of the word achieved by recognizing each word as a unique object to a knowledge of the word achieved by realizing that letters are symbols for predictable sounds. From that point on the child is not restricted to reading familiar words; any words that have regular letter-sound patterns can be decoded. With the acquisition of decoding skills, a child realizes the power inherent in generalization" (Mason, 1975, p.195).

Figure 3.1 presents a model that highlights the notion of stages of development in word reading ability. This model, suggested by Ehri's research review (1991), depicts three stages. The first stage is referred to as logographic because children first read by relying on unique visual characteristics of words, not letters, much like remembering pictures or Chinese characters. Children might, for example, remember the word, *look*, because it appears to have two eyes. First names are often the first-read words (Ferreiro, 1986; Mason, 1980), though many children have misconceptions about the appearance of their names. Clay (1979), for example, reported a child who said he saw his name, IAN, on a book cover in the word, GIANT. During this first stage, children typically learn words in context, such as signs, labels and other environmental print, and some sight words, such as names of favorite people and familiar objects. But remembrance is transitory, and they seldom learn and remember printed words out of context or recognize old words in new contexts (Mason, 1980).

Figure 3.1. A Schematic Model of Word Reading Development*

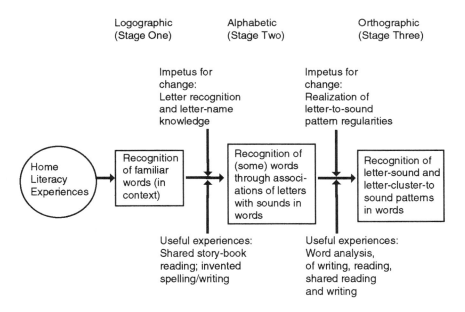

* Drawn principally from Ehri's (1991) review

As children begin to recognize letters and learn the names of these letters, they move toward stage two, or the alphabetic stage. In this stage, children begin to apply letter-sound associations to reading and they remember and spell some words. They also attend to first letters and consonants in words because these letters have more dependable sounds and cue the more obvious letter-sound relationships in words. At this stage, children are quite inventive when they try to read or write. They might, for example, spell words using only consonants or the first consonant (Bissex, 1980); they might start reading a word correctly and then guess one that fits the context or is a well-known printed word to them.

When children reach the third, orthographic stage, they realize that spelling patterns recur across words. This major insight, which some teachers refer to as "cracking the code," enables children to decode words using letter-sound rules and analogies to similar letter patterns. Children at this stage are also able to memorize and quickly recognize common and uniquely spelled sight words. Knowledge of varied word recognition strategies means that children can now acquire the necessary conceptual understanding to learn words on their own.

A developmental word reading model assumes that children can easily apply their knowledge about oral language features to the writing system. This assumption means that knowledge of letter and letter-cluster sounds within words (i.e., phonemic awareness) becomes paramount in learning to read. As such, the model offers suggestions about how and when phonological awareness could be acquired (Ehri, 1991), and the use of such models has led to findings that attaining phonological concepts can improve children's reading (Bradley & Bryant, 1983; Lundberg, Frost, & Peterson, 1988). Although many children acquire some insights about written language in the preschool years through informal experiences of labeling objects, scribbling and writing and hearing stories that have been read to them, these experiences are not uniform and do not necessarily make children aware of the alphabetic system (Adams, 1990). However, the model does not include descriptions of the connections to oral language competencies nor to guidelines for instruction of concepts related to books or text and story. Even though the model was not intended to be extended to comprehension, it can be questioned whether young children intuitively understand that print is encoded speech, that their messages can be written down, that they can communicate by drawing, telling, or writing about their ideas, or that they can listen to and remember stories read or told to them.

In summary, a developmental model of word reading uncovers a need for understanding letter-sound correspondence which leads to recommendations that beginning reading instruction focus on the recognition of letters and phonemes and the coding of letters as sounds, particularly the synthesis (blending) of sounds into words (Lesgold, Resnick, & Hammond, 1985). The model is generally silent about other print concepts, and about listening comprehension and the broader oral-written language relationships.

Cognitive Processing Models of Reading

Cognitive processing models depict the ongoing, stage-like changes in mental activity that are involved in recognizing and understanding text. These models are based principally on research on skilled readers' processing of words and brief texts. The research, mainly regarding word recognition, has been carried out for most of this century (e.g., Gough, 1972; Kolers, 1970; Lesgold & Perfetti, 1981; Wheeler, 1970), with current research involving computer-directed tracking of eye movements (e.g., McConkie et al., 1987). Recent reviews of cognitive processing models have been written by in Adams (1990), Rayner and Pollatsek (1989), and Stanovich (1991).

Figure 3.2 shows one such model in which the processing mechanism includes recognition of letter forms, encoding, identifying plausible meanings, and fitting recognition of text features with comprehension. The model depicts both working and long term memory as well as both lexical processes and text comprehension processes. Lexical processing refers to analysis of words, letters, and letter feature information. Comprehension refers to aspects of text understanding and interpretation. As the two-way arrows illustrate, the process is interactive (Rumelhart & McClelland, 1981; 1987) in the sense that word features provide evidence for letters, and letters provide evidence for words (Perfetti & Curtis, 1986). Comprehension is assumed to occur during all phases of the reading act, and analysis of the text occurs at several levels so that lexical information is connected with sense-making and text interpretation.

Figure 3.2. Schematic Model of Word Recognition Processing*

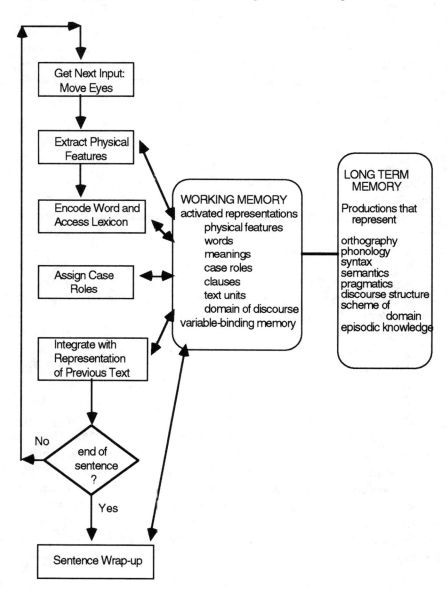

* The Just and Carpenter (1987) model of reading. Source: From *A Theory of Reading: From Eye Fixations to Comprehension* by Marcel Just and Patricia Carpenter 1980. *Psychological Review, 87,* p. 331. Copyright 1980 by the American Psychological Association. Reprinted by permission.

Some of the research on which cognitive processing models draw has compared word recognition processing strategies of more and less proficient readers. This research has uncovered processing deficits in poor readers and has led to suggestions about beginning reading instruction as well as remedial instruction. For example, research of this nature has indicated that poor readers process letters and words slowly, are overreliant on context, and have an inadequate understanding of complex letter-cluster-to sound patterns. This research also indicates that poor readers' written vocabulary knowledge is more limited than that of good readers, and that both poor readers' reading and listening comprehension skills are weaker than good readers.

Consequently, instructional recommendations springing from models such as shown in Figure 3.2 have given priority to processing letters and letter patterns quickly and encoding them into sounds. Moreover, stress is placed on phonological awareness as a precursor to knowledge of letter-pattern rules and analogies to letter patterns of other words (Perfetti & Curtis, 1986; Stanovich, 1986). Moreover, because language competencies are assumed to be adequate for beginning reading, differences in ability to read are explained principally by differences in word recognition ability. As Stanovich (1991) explained, "While it is quite possible for an adult to have poor reading comprehension ability despite adequate word-decoding skills–probably due to deficient general listening comprehension skills–it is highly unlikely that excellent reading comprehension will be observed in the face of deficient word recognition skills" (p. 419). So, even though cognitive processing models lack information about the developmental progression of printed word processing and encapsulate comprehension as an ongoing part of the reading process, phonics instruction is recommended to help initiate reading, and not learning how to use phonetic information is assumed to explain reading failure (Stanovich, 1991).

Social Cognition Models of Reading

A model of reading can be drawn from Vygotsky's theory of cognitive development (Vygotsky, 1929, 1978, 1934/1986). This model places learning and development within a social or cultural setting. According to Wertsch (1985), Vygotsky based his theory on the notion of joint construction of concepts. Children begin learning about a concept through exploration and with assistance from others. Eventually, they are able to embed the concept within their own personal framework. Vygotsky argued that what children learn appears twice, or on two planes.

> First it appears on the social plane, and then on the psychological plane. First it appears between people as an interpsychological category, and then within the child as an intrapsychological category. This is equally true with regard to voluntary attention, logical memory, the formation of concepts, and the development of volition. (cited by Wertsch, 1985, p. 11)

Drawing on Vygotsky's (1929) four stages of social-cultural development, Mason and Sinha (in press) have proposed a model of reading from a social cognition perspective. First, in the natural development stage, children engage in spontaneous play and so create "associative or conditional reflexive connections between the stimuli and reactions" (Mason & Sinha, in press, p. 419). Thus, as children explore literacy concepts, they scribble, imitating the form of the written language they see. They also interweave words and phrases from stories into their speech, they imitate characters from stories they have heard, and they sing and play rhyming and other word-sound games. Little may seem to be accomplished because children are limited by attention, interest, and memory. However, this activity sets the stage for learning to read through interaction with knowledgeable others.

As they move into the second stage, children begin to see patterns, structures, and relationships. Learning can be child-instigated as a result of continued exploration, but when the domains are complex it is more likely to occur through assistance by an adult; that assistance may be direct and planned or informal and spontaneous. According to Vygotsky, the adult responds to the child's attempts to understand by operating within the child's range of understanding. Using symbolic or concrete representations, akin to the use of tools, the adult provides whatever sign, symbols, or tools the child needs to make connections between and among the new constructs, and to help him or her maintain interest, and handle memory demands.

In the arena of literacy, adults establish routines for literacy activities by reading to children on a regular basis, talking about story ideas or telling stories at bedtime, engaging in a joint recounting of daily events, arranging for children to help cook, fix, or make things, and participating in board or card games. Adults also reread stories to children until the children have memorized them and can recite the texts back to the adults. Adults instigate attention to the elements of print by providing and reading ABC books and signs and labels to children. They also help children see connections between letters and the pictured words and they give children writing materials and encourage them to draw, label, write their names, and construct messages. Through these wide-ranging activities, children begin to construct the critical features of the literate environment, connecting letters and sounds, realizing how to identify some words, recognizing the importance of meaning and communicating in printed messages, and so on.

In the third stage children figure out how to make effective and independent use of the new concepts with tools or symbols as props, and so practice their discoveries in supported ways. In the literacy domain, teachers and parents report children "writing up a storm," writing messages using their peculiar form of invented spelling, copying words, sending messages, telling and dictating stories, and embedding print within their drawings. Often they begin writing by adding a new word to known sentences, a kind of theme and variation. They begin to attend closely to print in books that have been read to them. On their own, they try to read signs and words in context and easy books that contain useful pictures, words they have learned, and predictable story ideas.

In the fourth stage children are freed from the need for external tools or props, such as enabling plans, concrete examples, or other learning aids. They have now internalized the process of thinking and working with such props. The physical presence of the tool is no longer needed as the child "starts to use the inner schemes, tries to use as signs his remembrances, the knowledge he formerly acquired" (Vygotsky, 1929, p. 427). In the case of reading, we see children moving away from dependency on pictures and limited letter information for letter-sound clues to printed words, toward multiple strategies for reading (Clay, 1979), and in the process, toward reading more widely (Soderbergh, 1979). In the case of writing, having mastered basic spelling and sentence patterns, children become able to analyze words into constituent phonemes (Ehri, 1989) and to construct messages and other texts more or less independently (Bissex, 1980).

As noted, Mason and Sinha based these four stages in their social cognition model on Vygotsky's work. Brown, Collins, and Duguid (1989) have also proposed a model employing constructs similar to

Vygotsky's. Their model, presented in Figure 3.3, is a more general social cognition model than Mason and Sinha's. But Figure 3.3 is useful in summarizing the stages in a social cognition view of reading development. The connections between Figure 3.3 and Vygotsky's ideas are apparent if "world/activity" is replaced with "natural involvement" and each of the next stages with the three succeeding stages of cultural development. Cultural reasoning, the final stage in Vygotsky's scheme, includes concepts of reflection and generality.

Figure 3.3. A Social Cognition Model of Development

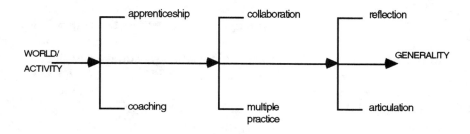

Applying either the Mason and Sinha social cognition model or the more general model in Figure 3.3 to literacy development would suggest that children become involved in reading activities before they can read, as a social-cultural activity. Adults assist children in acting like readers by reading to children and by helping them discuss the text ideas. Adults might reread stories until children can recite them, as well as point out and identify words on signs and labels. Children then begin to understand more about reading concepts, through natural exploration, under adult guidance, and in collaboration with more capable peers. Thus, adults support the learning by providing a scaffolding of concepts which enables children to engage in reading tasks that are too difficult to accomplish alone. Through supported and shared reading activity, children eventually move to a higher psychological plane and so to a new awareness about how to read. This conception explains why

Vygotsky argued that instruction proceeds ahead of development: "It awakens and rouses to life those functions that are in the process of maturing or in the zone of proximal development. It is in this way that instruction plays an extremely important role in development" (Vygotsky, cited by Wertsch & Stone, 1985, p. 165).

A great deal of instruction on literacy that "rouses to life" occurs in home and early school settings, in routinized, contextualized settings. Storybook readings, alphabet book and block activities, language games, and shared writing activities are a few prominent examples. In such activities, according to Bruner (1985), the adult and child are fully engaged, there are fairly easily recognized intentions, and the adult can easily adjust his or her hypothesis about what the child understands in order to provide effective scaffolding.

By focusing on learning in terms of interactional stages, and in which there is movement through language interaction on the social plane to internalized language use on the psychological plane, a social cognition model leads to the assumption that learning to read requires wide-ranging support of others in settings in which the child is the initiator or the willing and involved participant. Literacy is embedded in social construction of knowledge, with reading being fostered through collaboration. In school settings, literacy is fostered through discussions with teachers and classmates, and through solving problems together about how to read, comprehend, write, and communicate ideas. Support for this notion was demonstrated with regard to beginning reading some 40 years ago (MacKinnon, 1959), and is central to current whole language programs (e.g., Newman, 1985) and emergent literacy approaches (Mason & Au, 1990; Mason, Kerr, Sinha, & McCormick, 1990; McGee & Richgels, 1990; Phillips, Norris, Mason, & Kerr, 1990; Schickedanz, 1986; Strickland & Morrow, 1989; Sulzby & Teale, 1991). It is also viewed as critical to learning in general (Brown, Collins, & Duguid, 1989; Rogoff, 1991; Wertsch, 1985).

Thus, the social cognition model suggests that knowledge about how to read words and comprehend texts is socially constructed, progressing from stages of exploration and support and guidance of knowledgeable others to independent and personal constructions of ways of reading and comprehending written information. "Groups are not just a convenient way to accumulate the individual knowledge of their members. They give rise synergistically to insights and solutions that would not come about without them" (Brown, Collins, & Duguid, 1989, p. 40).

Comparison of the Models and Their Implications for Instruction

Before discussing the three models together, we should point out that the phrase, "stages of development," which is used to depict characteristics of all three models, does not have the same meaning across them. In the word reading model, stages of development describes well-defined phases of children's understanding about how to read and write. In the cognitive processing model, it indicates aspects of the internal process of recognizing and understanding a phenomenon. In the social cognition model, it represents changes both in the learner-tutor relationship and in the learner's understanding.

Developmental models of learning to read feature the perspective of individual differences in the course of learning to read words. Because an ability to recognize printed words is obviously needed in order to read, developmental models have focused on the emergence of word reading and spelling as well as on changes in the ability to figure out how to read and spell words. Questions are asked about what the child knows at any given time rather than how the child is learning, and so scant attention has been paid to collaboration between children and adults in learning. Similarly, only recently with the replacement of the term reading readiness with the term, emergent literacy, has there been much research on the acquisition of concepts that are needed before a child can read (Mason & Sinha, in press; Teale & Sulzby, 1986).

Developmental models have been interpreted to suggest how to teach children letters and words and how to organize phonics for first grade beginning reading instruction. Recommendations have centered on how to teach phonemic awareness, letters, and letter sounds because these elements are obviously required in order for children to learn to read. However, in their zeal to accurately reflect the components of developmental models and to be instructionally efficient, some educators have overinterpreted these model by requiring that letters and words be taught before allowing children to use books. One unfortunate result is that some teachers then assume that letter elements must be mastered before children can effectively read connected text. Such an assumption means that these teachers do not help children to learn about how to read in other ways, such as by listening to stories in books, reciting stories, or writing. Another unfortunate result of overinterpretation of developmental models is that recommendations for a kindergarten reading curriculum are sometimes unnecessarily restricted to having children focus on recognizing and forming upper and lower case letters and connecting letters to sounds and printed words.

Cognitive processing models have also influenced reading instruction. Because they highlight the importance of rapid recognition of the elements of print, these models have led to an emphasis on decoding automaticity, that is, the rapid recognition of high frequency printed words. Another central construct is the importance of integration of letter with word and text meaning to form text understandings. These models have also led to comparisons of good and poor readers' texts processing in which it has been found that poor readers suffer from letter-sound processing deficiencies. As a result, instructional guidelines have generally recommended that attention be paid in beginning reading instruction to rapid early acquisition of phonetic principles, and the same overinterpretations for instruction have occurred as were described for the developmental model.

A cognitive processing model is particularly well-tuned to the first grade curriculum where rules for recognizing letters in words and word drill and practice to achieve reading fluency are stressed. Although comprehension processing is an inherent part of the model, little is made of comprehension in recommendations for beginning reading instruction probably because of the assumption that the first reading texts are so easy to comprehend that the process of comprehension can be taken for granted.

In contrast, the social cognition model of literacy development highlights the notion that children are involved in reading activities before they can read, that adults foster learning by engaging children in meaning-oriented literacy activities, that children begin learning to read through listening to and engaging in book reading and story telling, and that adults help children by focusing on text connections and text elements within a meaningful context. Reading, then, is initiated by children and adults together through child-directed exploration as well as through adult guidance and collaboration. Thus, unlike the other two models, the social cognition model assumes that a confluence of home and school activities and events helps children begin to read; adult-child talk about literacy and language in contexts that are meaningful to the child is the central characteristic. In other words, social cognition models of learning to read focus on the process of learning in terms of social, or joint, construction of knowledge about reading. This attention to the process of learning through social interaction departs markedly from either the developmental or cognitive processing models.

One problem, however, with social cognition models is their lack of specificity regarding the order of development of concepts, as well as their inability to depict the process of reading or changes in the process. As a result, when a social cognition perspective is the basis for designing an early reading curriculum, the instructional suggestions have often been quite vague. This vagueness has led to the misinterpretation that learning is a purely natural process, or to an assumption that written language is not learned through modeling but is dependent on child-initiated interpretation of particular social contexts, or even to a belief that children merely need to be provided with materials for exploration of reading and writing on their own and with peers.

The social cognition model features language interactions. It highlights goals, actions, and the shift of responsibility for thinking, solving, and remembering task information that takes place within dyadic and group learning situations. The word and cognitive processing models, by contrast, emphasize internal processing at the individual response level. Social cognition models emphasize how learners collaborate with tutors to construct the information to be learned; the other two models emphasize what should be taught. Thus, emphasis on the context and function of reading is depicted in social cognition models while the other models emphasize acquisition of the items or elements of print in the others. The social cognition models lead to guiding a child's exploration of print instead of having the child practice what has been told or explained. Instead of outcome variables (e.g., reading fluency, proportion of words learned based on number taught, ability to generalize from words learned to new words), adult-child talk surrounding planning, joint participation, initiations by the learner, and attempts by the learner to regulate his or her own learning activity is stressed.

Implications drawn from the developmental and the cognitive processing models emphasize learning how to recognize letters and sounds so that words can be figured out. No single procedure is suggested, though a frequently mentioned recommendation is to link letter forms with letter names and to help children hear ending patterns (rhymes) and the initial sound of familiar words. As letters and sounds are learned, words and then texts are given for children to read. With the social cognition model, exploration of literacy materials by children is thought to initiate reading and writing. This exploration would include scribble-writing, playing with alphabet block letters, and reciting previously read books. As adult-child shared story reading and writing activities take place, letters, letter-sounds, and words are learned in an incidental way. Such activities arouse children's interest in literacy, and leads them to practice and extend these joint activities on their own activities. As a result, independent reading and writing practice is mingled with adult-supported analysis that enables children to reflect about how letters and other cues help in figuring out words and understanding texts.

Thus, a comparison of the three models indicates that they differ in their instructional implications. But this comparison does not show that one model is better than the others. Indeed, while the developmental and the cognitive processing models have an advantage in that they provide clearer pictures of reading development and the processes involved in reading, the social cognition model provides a more detailed explanation of how adults could lead children to become good readers. Consequently, all three models are important in obtaining a clear picture of what and how to teach.

The results of a longitudinal study illustrate the importance of all three perspectives. Mason, Dunning, Stewart, and Peterman (1991) examined children's word recognition and comprehension development as they moved from kindergarten to third grade. The study focused on the early influences of language understanding, early reading knowledge, and home background characteristics on children's later decoding and comprehension abilities. Mason et al. tested entering kindergarten children's knowledge about language and literacy and used a home questionnaire for parents to evaluate children's interest and involvement in literacy and characteristics of the family. The purpose was to determine whether these early literacy-related measures predicted the children's reading performance at the end of kindergarten, the beginning and end of grade one, and the end of grades two and three.

The analyses revealed that early language understanding had a sustained effect first on decoding and word recognition, and then on comprehension. Moreover, children's early reading interest and ability before they learned to read had a significant influence on their early language and literacy knowledge and on later reading ability. A problematical home environment had a negative influence on later reading.

The results of the study indicated that both language understanding and early reading interest and knowledge strongly predict children's later reading. Language understanding at the end of kindergarten and the beginning of first grade predicted both decoding and comprehension. But by the end of first grade early language understanding predicted primarily comprehension. Early reading ability predicted kindergarten and first grade decoding, but its importance faded in second and third grade as reading tests begin to emphasize comprehension more strongly. Home characteristics had both an early and later effect, affecting both the language and early reading measures as well as later reading comprehension. The home influence measure with the strongest sustained effect was children's early literacy interest and involvement at home.

Each model of reading is useful in understanding the results of this study. The developmental word reading model correctly predicts the change in children's knowledge from letters to letter-sounds and short words, to more complex words. However, the developmental model ignores three important factors in predicting decoding ability: the supportive role of the family, the child's early reading and writing interest, and the child's language understanding. The cognitive processing model correctly predicts the importance of an ability to decode and read words quickly and it correctly predicts the role of language understanding in comprehension. However, the cognitive processing model leaves out development and the roles played by others in fostering interest and involvement in reading. The social cognition model features explanations about the roles played by the family and child by drawing on language interactions; but it lacks the detail about letter and word understanding that are identified in the first two models.

Conclusion

The social cognition model helps to explain how language, culture, and communication experiences and children's home literacy experiences affect reading development; it provides needed explanations about how to foster effective literacy-related social interactions at home and in school. But the developmental and cognitive processing models are also helpful because they indicate what aspects of reading are important for children to learn. Together, the three models provide essential information about how children learn to read and about how they might effectively be taught.

Together the three models suggest that constructs for recognition of letters, sounds, and printed words need to be learned and that they are best learned through the support and under the direct guidance of more expert family members and teachers. Children begin to apply oral language to meaningful aspects of printed language and written language structures and thence to elements of language, particularly letters and printed words. With the help of significant adults and knowledgeable older children, children extend those concepts by reading many books, practicing, and as the children themselves report, by reading and figuring out words in books. Thus, early home involvement in literacy and parent and teacher support for literacy need to be studied in conjunction with reading and language development. Grade-to-grade changes in reading should extend beyond tracing the development of decoding ability and reading comprehension skill. Recommendations for reading instruction should include ways to foster all children's involvement in letters, sounds, words and book reading activities.

In short, the cognitive and developmental models are important for their characterization of the elements of print, the initial steps in learning to read, the role of language, and the process of reading. The social cognition model suggests how learning to read can be facilitated by making that learning a shared enterprise with concepts about letters, sounds, written words, and texts acquired at first through meaningful contexts. Thus, consideration of all three models will help teachers and researchers to unravel and understand unanswered questions and and to address problems about how children learn to read and how their progress toward achievement of a literate stance can best be supported by others.

References

Adams, M. (1990). *Beginning to read: Thinking and learning about print.* Cambridge, MA: MIT Press.

Biemiller, A. (1970). The development of the use of graphic and contextual information as children learn to read. *Reading Research Quarterly, 6,* 75-96.

Bissex, G. (1980). *GYNS AT WRK A child learns to write and read.* Cambridge, MA: Harvard University Press.

Brown, Collins, & Duguid (1989).

Bradley, L. & Bryant, P. (1983). Categorizing sounds and learning to read: A causal connection. *Nature, 301,* 419-21.

Bruner, J. (1985). Vygotsky: A historical and conceptual perspective. In J. Wertsch (Ed.), *Culture, communication, and cognition: Vygotskian perspectives* (Chapter 1). New York: Cambridge University Press.

Chall, J. (1979). The great debate: Ten years later, with a modest proposal for reading stages. In P. Weaver & L. Resnick (Eds.), *Theory and practice of early reading* (Vol. 1, pp. 29-56). Hillsdale, NJ: Erlbaum.

Chall, J. (1983). *Stages of reading development.* New York: McGraw Hill.

Clay, M. (1979). *Reading: The patterning of complex behavior.* Portsmouth, NH: Heinemann.

Ehri, L. (1987). Learning to read and spell words. *Journal of Reading Behavior, 19,* 5-31.

Ehri, L. (1989). Movement into word reading and spelling: How spelling contributes to reading. In J. Mason (Ed.), *Reading and writing connections* (pp.65-82). Boston: Allyn & Bacon.

Ehri, L. (1991). Development of the ability to read words. In R. Barr, M. Kamil, P. Mosenthal, & P.D. Pearson (Eds.), *Handbook of reading research* (Vol II, pp. 383-417). New York: Longman.

Ferreiro, E. (1986). The interplay between information and assimilation in beginning literacy. In W. Teale, & E. Sulzby (Eds.), *Emergent literacy: Writing and reading* (pp.15-49). Norwood, NJ: Ablex.

Ferreiro, E., & Teberosky, A. (1982). *Literacy before schooling.* Portsmouth, NH: Heinemann.

Fries, C. (1963). *Linguistics and reading.* New York: Holt, Rinehart, & Winston.

Gough, P. (1972). One second of reading. In J. Kavanagh & I. Mattingly (Eds.), *Language by ear and by eye: The relationship between speech and reading* (pp. 331-358). Cambridge, MA: MIT Press.

Juel, C. (1991). Beginning reading. In R. Barr, M. Kamil, P. Mosenthal, & P.D. Pearson (Eds.), *Handbook of reading research* (Vol. 1, pp. 759-788). New York: Longman.

Kerr, B., Mason, J., & McCormick, C. (in progress). *Literacy discourse in shared reading events.*

Kolers, P. (1970). Three stages of reading. In H. Levin & J. Williams (Eds.), *Basic studies on reading* (pp. 90-118). New York: Basic Books.

Lesgold, A., & Perfetti, C. (1981). *Interactive processes in reading.* Hillsdale, NJ: Erlbaum.

Lesgold, A., Resnick, L., & Hammond, K. (1985). Learning to read: A longitudinal study of word skill development in two curricula. In G. Mackinnon & T. Waller (Eds), *Reading Research: Advances in theory and practice* (Vol. 4). New York: Academic Press.

Lundberg, I., Frost, J. & Peterson, O. (1988). Effects of an extensive program for stimulating phonological awareness in preschool children. *Reading Research Quarterly, 23,* 263-284. MacKinnon, A. (1959). *How do children learn to read.* Vancouver, BC: Copp Clark.

Mason, J. (1975). The acquisition of reading skills: A developmental stage processing model. *Reading Improvement, 12,* 195-202.

Mason, J. (1980). When do children begin to read?: An exploration of four-year-old children's letter and word reading competencies. *Reading Research Quarterly, 15,* 203-227.

Mason, J. & Au, K. (1990). *Reading instruction for today,* Second Edition. New York: HarperCollins.

Mason, J. & Sinha, S. (in preparation). Emerging literacy in the early childhood years: Applying a Vygotskian model of learning and development. To appear in B. Spodek (Ed.), *The handbook of research on the education of young children.* New York: MacMillan.

Mason, J., Dunning, D., Stewart, J., & Peterman, C. (in preparation).

McConkie, G., Kerr, P., Reddix, M., & Zola, D. (1987). *Eye movement control during reading: I. The location of initial eye fixations on words* (Tech. Rep. No. 406). Urbana-Champaign: University of Illinois, Center for the Study of Reading.

McGee, L., & Lomax, R. (1990). On combining apples and oranges: A response to Stahl and Miller. *Review of Educational Research, 60,* 133-140.

McGee, L., & Richgels, D. (1990). *Literacy's beginnings: Supporting young readers and writers.* Boston: Allyn & Bacon.

Newman, J. (Ed.) (1985). *Whole language: Theory in use.* Portsmouth, NH: Heinemann.

Perfetti, C., & Curtis, M. (1986). Reading. In R. Dillon & R. Sternberg (Eds.), *Cognition and instruction.* New York: Academic Press.

Phillips, L., Norris, S., Mason, J., & Kerr, B. (1990). *Effect of early literacy intervention on kindergarten achievement* (pp. 199-208).

Rayner, K., & Pollatsek, A. (1989). *The psychology of reading.* Englewood Cliffs, NJ: Prentice Hall.

Rumelhart, D., & McClelland, J. (1981). Interactive processing through spreading activation. In A. Lesgold & C. Perfetti (Eds.), *Interactive processes in reading* (pp. 37-60). Hillsdale, NJ: Erlbaum.

Rumelhart, D., & McClelland, J. (1987). Learning the past tenses of English verbs: Implicit rules or parallel distributed processing? In B. MacWhinney (Editor), *Mechanisms of language acquisition.* Hillsdale, NJ: Erlbaum.

Schickedanz, J. (1986). *More than the ABCs: The early stages of reading and writing.* Washington, DC: NAEYC.

Schickedanz, J. (1990). The jury is still out on the effects of whole language and language experience approach for beginning reading: A critique of Stahl and Miller's study. *Review of Educational Reseach, 60,* 127-131.

Soderbergh, R. (1977). *Reading in early childhood: A linguistic study of a preschool child's gradual acquisition of reading ability.* Washington, DC: Georgetown University Press.

Stahl, S. (1990). Riding the pendulum: A rejoinder to Schickedanz and McGee and Lomax. *Review of Educational Research, 60,* 141-151.

Stahl, S., & Miller, P. (1989). Whole language and language experience approaches for beginning reading: A quantitative research synthesis. *Review of Educational Research, 59,* 87-116.

Stanovich, K. E. (1986). Matthew effects in reading: Some consequences of individual differences in the acquisition of literacy. *Reading Research Quarterly, 21,* 360-407.

Stanovich, K. E. (1990). Word recognition: Changing perspectives. In

R. Barr, M. Kamil, P. Mosenthal, & P.D. Pearson (Eds.), *Handbook of reading research* (vol. II, pp. 418-452). New York: Longman.

Stanovich, K. E. (1991). Discrepancy definitions of reading disability: Has intelligence led us astray? *Reading Research Quarterly, 26,* 7-29.

Strickland, D., & Morrow, L. (1989). *Emerging literacy: Young children learn to read and write.* Newark, DE: IRA.

Teale, W., & Sulzby, E. (1986). Emergent literacy as a perspective for examining how young children become writers and readers. In W. Teale & E. Sulzby (Eds.)., *Emergent literacy: Writing and reading* (pp. vii-xxv). Norwood, NJ: Erlbaum.

Vygotsky, L. (1929). The problem of the cultural development of the child. *Journal of Genetic Psychology, 26,* 415-434.

Vygotsky, L. (1978). *Mind in society.* Cambridge, MA: Harvard University Press.

Vygotsky, L. (1934/1986). *Thought and language.* Cambridge, MA: MIT Press.

Wertsch, J. (Ed.) (1985). *Culture, communication, and cognition: Vygotskian perspectives.* New York: Cambridge University Press.

Wertsch, J., & Stone, C. (1985). The concept of internalization in Vygotsky's account of the genesis of higher mental functions. In J. Wertsch (Ed.) (1985). *Culture, communication, and cognition: Vygotskian perspectives* (Chapter 7). New York: Cambridge University Press.

Wheeler, D. (1970). Process in word recognition. *Cognitive Psychology, 1,* 59-87.

4

Longitudinal Research on Learning to Read and Write with At-risk Students

Connie Juel

Two children are about to begin first grade. They have the same teacher. They come from similar backgrounds and have similar scores on IQ tests. During the school year, one child learns to read with relative ease. The other child is barely able to read a preprimer by the end of first grade. What accounts for the success of one and the relative failure of the other? Will the child who soared in first grade continue to fly? Will the child who got off to a poor start overcome it?

The answers to these questions are, of course, complex. They depend on family, child, teacher, school, and society–to name but a few of the factors which influence the answers. The study described in this chapter followed the reading and writing development of the same group of children as they progressed from the beginning of first grade until the end of fourth grade. It began with a conceptualization of the development of reading and writing (Juel, Griffith, & Gough 1986; Juel, 1988). The development of those cognitive factors that were thought to be most responsible for literacy development within this conceptualization were closely monitored in the children.

The conceptualization that guided the study is shown in Figure 4.1. Reading comprehension is seen from the Simple View (Gough & Tunmer, 1986; Juel, Griffith, & Gough, 1986). From this view reading is composed of (a) word recognition (i.e., decoding) and (b) listening comprehension. That is, while neither factor in itself is seen as simple, the two factors are viewed as the two basic components that enable reading comprehension.

To illustrate these two components, one of my favorite books is *En Biodlares Død* (Gustafsson, 1978). Unless you read Swedish, one immediate problem you have with the above statement is word recognition. In fact this is the sole problem I had with the book until its English translation appeared (Gustafsson, 1981). If we assume your word recognition in Swedish is perfect (or you are reading the translation), then your comprehension of the book will depend upon your listening comprehension. That is to say, your reading comprehension will depend on the same basic factors that would enable you to comprehend the book if it were read to you. Such factors include your vocabulary, world knowledge, interest, and so forth. Here's a passage from the Gustafsson (1981) translated book:

> People now look in a bit more frequently, they say very openly that I should go to the hospital. They are practical,the people in northern Västmanland. One never says in Västmanland: "He has died." One says: "He is gone dead." They are afraid that I "will go dead." (p. 151)

The sense you make of the above passage will depend upon the same basic factors, regardless of whether you have just read it or heard it spoken: Factors such as (but obviously not limited to) your prior knowledge of the story, your knowledge of Gustafssons' novels, what you know about people in Västmanland, your reasoning, and your feelings about death. If your word recognition (i.e., of the book in Swedish) is nil, you will not comprehend. If your word recognition is perfect, your reading comprehension will depend on factors such as those listed above.

Writing may be also considered the product of two basic factors (a) spelling and (b) ideation (defined as the generation and organization of ideas). Without reasonably transparent spelling, Gustafsson's novel would be unintelligible. Without ideas, it would be uninteresting and/or devoid of content.

Most children entering first grade are relatively rich in the higher-level factor (i.e., listening comprehension or ideas) compared to the lower-level factor (i.e., word recognition or spelling). It was the children's development of the lower-level skills in first and second grade that most interested us in looking at literacy development in first and second grade (Juel, Griffith, & Gough, 1986). It was the developing relationship between the lower and higher-level factors that most interested me as I followed these children from first through fourth grade (Juel, 1988). Both studies will be described below.

The Development of Literacy in First and Second Grade

The Model

We (Juel, Griffith, & Gough, 1986) hypothesized that in first and second grade children's reading comprehension and writing development would be influenced primarily by their growth in word-level skills (e.g., word recognition and spelling) rather than their growth in higher-level skills (e.g., listening comprehension or ideas). This was based on the assumption that automatic lower-level skills are critical to higher order cognitive processes. With automatic word recognition, attention can be more fully focused on comprehension (LaBerge & Samuels, 1974). Early efficient word recognition seems to lead to better comprehension than does the reverse order (Calfee & Piontkowski, 1981; Lesgold, Resnick, & Hammond, 1985; Shanahan, 1984).

The directionality of the lower order skill, spelling (whether invented or standard), to the higher order skill of writing is less clear. Shanahan (1984) provides some evidence that writing, like reading, is initially dependent on the word-level factor. Several theorists, including Bereiter (1980), Gundlach (1981), and Scardamalia (1981), have commented on the necessity for many aspects of the writing process (e.g., spelling) to become automatic so that the attention of the writer is available for composing (e.g., for organizing ideas). We expected, therefore, that as in reading, we would find early writing influenced more by growth in the word-level factor (i.e., spelling).

Figure 4.1. Proposed model of literacy acquisition. (After Juel, Griffith, & Gough, 1986)

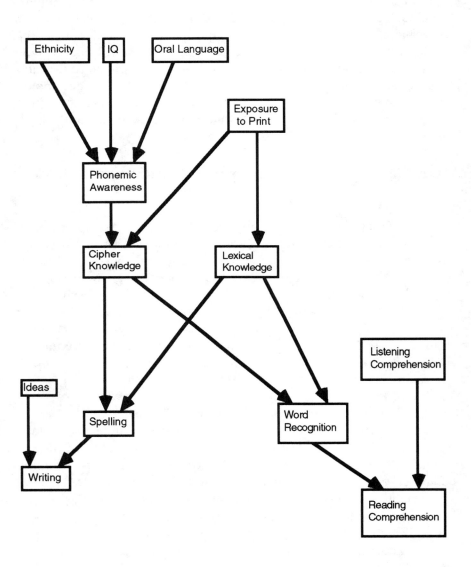

We further hypothesized that word recognition and spelling skill would be highly correlated as both abilities appear to depend on the same sources of knowledge (Figure 4.1). Both critically involve cipher knowledge, or knowledge of the spelling-sound correspondences of the language. Knowledge of the English cipher is what enables you to pronounce, with considerable speed, such pseudowords as: cleef, nuv, yode, bufwix. You might also think about how you spell a word you don't readily recall. You often hear yourself slowly saying the word as you write letters which are likely to correspond to the sounds you say. Knowing the orthographic cipher of English, it would be difficult to either misspell or mispronounce regular and unequivocal words like "dish" and "gun" and "lamp," that is, those words where the phonemes typically map to specific letters. But there are at least two sets of words where cipher knowledge alone will let you down. First, there are irregular words like "pint." Second, there are words which incorporate letter sequences with equivocal pronunciations, such as the "ea" in "steak," "area," "leak," and "head." Thus, the decoder must learn which pronunciation of EA applies in "beak" and which in "break," the speller must learn that /i/ is spelled "ea" in "bean" but "ee" in "green." Thus word recognition and spelling require, in addition to the cipher, considerable specific lexical knowledge, that is, knowledge of which specific letter combinations belong in particular words. The primary way to gain this type of word specific knowledge seems to be through exposure to printed words; through reading itself. The most likely way to learn the correct spelling of "green" is to see it in print.

To further understand the distinction between cipher and lexical knowledge, it might help to know how we assessed them. The assessment of cipher knowledge used in the study was the Bryant Test of Basic Decoding Skill (Bryant, 1975). This test consists of 50 pseudowords, which children read aloud. The first 20 pseudowords are CVCs (consonant-vowel-consonants, e.g., buf, dit, nuv). The next 20 items are more complex single syllable pseudowords (e.g., yode, shi, fler, cleef). Only the last 10 items have more than one syllable (e.g., cosnuv, uncabeness). For the assessment of lexical knowledge we used the spelling subtest of the IOWA. In this subtest the children are told three words that will be in a sentence (e.g., mother, drive, traffic), then the sentence is read to the children (e.g., Shirley's *mother* will not *drive* in heavy *traffic*). There is an oval under each of the three words, and one of the words is misspelled. The child fills in the oval under the misspelled word. "Mother," for example, might be misspelled "muther."

The beginning reader is limited in ability to read printed texts because this reader is assumed to lack much lexical or cipher knowledge. The child often begins to recall and reproduce words based on partial lexical knowledge. The child may recall first letters, approximate number of letters, distinctive letters, and so forth (Gough & Hillinger, 1980; Juel, 1991). Gradually, however, as the child wants to read or spell numerous words, reliance on somewhat random lexical knowledge (e.g., the first letter for one word, the first and last for another), becomes increasing difficult. It becomes harder to find features which distinguish one word from another as printed words in English are not particularly visually distinctive. Recalling the word "cat" by the letter "c", or its length, will not suffice reliably to distinguish it from "cap" or "can" or "cot." We assumed that the development of cipher knowledge keeps the task of word recognition from becoming insurmountable for the beginning reader. Knowledge of spelling-sound relationships can be applied to any word which is not instantaneously recognized, providing a more systematic and reliable tool to use than random recall of letters.

With some cipher knowledge a child can also more easily write words. The child can say the word, listen to its sounds, and spell it, based on some notion of how the sounds s/he hears map to letters. Early cipher knowledge may: 1) lead to invented spellings, such as "KT" or "KAT" for "cat;" 2) provide the child sufficient letter-sound cues to pronounce the printed word "cat," and 3) facilitate the increased reading of texts. With further text exposure, we assumed, the child will recognize and spell more and more words based on direct lexical knowledge of *all* the letters in a word. Initially, however, using sound-letter cues provided by patterns of letters facilitates access to both the recognition and production of printed words.

A critical prerequisite to gaining cipher knowledge is being able to "hear" the sounds in words, or what is known as phonemic awareness. Until the child can perceive words as somewhat distinctive sounds, it is difficult if not impossible to attach letters to the sounds within words. Phonemic awareness allowed Bissex's five-year-old son, Paul, to engage in the following dialogues with his mother:

PAUL: What makes the /ch/ (in TECH)?
MOTHER: c-h (p. 12)

PAUL: What makes the "uh" sound?
MOTHER: In what word?
PAUL: "Mumps"
MOTHER: "u" (p. 13)

To be able to ask these questions, it is clear Paul has phonemic awareness—or he would not perceive the /ch/ in "teach" or the "uh" in "mumps." Invented spelling (as in TECH for "teach") combines phonemic awareness, knowledge of the alphabet, and developing, but incomplete, cipher knowledge.

Armed with phonemic insights, a child like Paul can slowly acquire cipher knowledge through print exposure. As this child connects printed words like "oatmeal," "toad," "boat," and "float," with their spoken counterparts, he will either consciously or unconsciously begin to connect their letters to spoken sounds. He can perceive where in the word the long "o" sound occurs, and which letters are used to write it. He can learn which letters connect to the /b/ and /f/ sounds he hears in some words. It is this cipher knowledge which would allow him to pronounce or spell a word he has never seen before, or allow him to pronounce a pseudoword such as "boaf." Exposure to print, then, can contribute to growth in cipher knowledge for children with phonemic awareness.

On the other hand, a child without phonemic awareness and/or cipher knowledge depends wholly on lexical knowledge to spell or read. The misreadings and misspelling of such a child are quite distinctive. Misreadings often yield a real word which shares some features of the unidentifiable word (e.g., first letters, approximate length). These misreadings are often good "guesses" as they are words the child has encountered in prior readings. In response to "rain," the misreadings of first grade children without cipher knowledge (as determined by their inability to read pseudowords like "buf") were: "ring," "in," "runs," "with," "ride," "art," "are," "on," "reds," and "running" (Juel, Griffith, & Gough, 1985). Without cipher knowledge, these children correctly spell by recalling all of the letters in a given word in order. They misspell when they can't recall some or all of the letters. The child may recall the approximate length of a word and some letters, and then fill in the missing letters with random letters. Since the child can't "sound out" a word as an aid in sequencing the letters, the order of the letters is easily reversed. Here are some misspellings of the word "rain" by the children discussed above: "weir," "rach," "yes," "uan," "ramt," "fen," "rur," "Rambl," "wetn," "wnishire," "rup," five "ran'"s and one drawing of raindrops. These misspellings clearly represent a range in orthographic understandings. The five children who spelled "rain" as "ran" may have had incomplete lexical knowledge or they may have had some phonemic awareness and used the long "a" name sound of the letter "a" in an invented spelling of "rain." Invented spelling may mark the beginning of reading and writing using cipher knowledge.

Finally we were concerned with some factors which might contribute to phonemic awareness. We examined three possible factors: ethnicity, oral language, and IQ. We thought that phonemic awareness of the sounds in spoken school English might be affected by the language (i.e., Spanish) or dialect spoken at home, the child's knowledge of spoken English, and/or the child's reasoning ability and verbal growth as assessed by an IQ test.

Phonemic Awareness

A detailed evaluation of the model in Figure 4.1 (p. 76) is presented in Juel, Griffith, and Gough (1986). Overall, the model held up well. Of the three factors related to phonemic awareness, the most potent predictor was ethnicity. It could be that: 1) hearing different languages at home than at school slows the general insight of phonemic awareness (hearing words as sequences of somewhat distinctive sounds); 2) phonemic awareness in one language does not necessarily transfer to another language; and/or 3) differences exist between the ethnic groups in home language play, story reading, and other factors likely associated with the development of phonemic awareness (Hall, 1990; Maclean, Bryant, & Bradley, 1987). While all three predictors in our model were related to phonemic awareness, none were overly powerful predictors.

Phonemic awareness was both strongly predictive of cipher knowledge and considerably more predictive than exposure to print (how many words the child had seen in running text in the basal reader). That strongly suggests that print exposure alone does not produce cipher knowledge until the child has the insight of phonemic awareness. To illustrate this point, at the end of first grade we examined two groups of children, both of whom had been exposed to fairly large amounts of print in their first grade readers. One group had considerable phonemic awareness; the other did not. We tested them for a possible difference in their ability to read the pseudowords on the Bryant test. We found a significant difference between the two groups. For the low phonemic awareness group the mean score on the Bryant was only 3.7 and the modal score was zero. Despite having been exposed to large amounts of print and a year of phonics instruction, many children with poor phonemic awareness could not read a single pseudoword (e.g., "buf") at the end of first grade. The mean score for the high phonemic awareness group was 27.9 and the mode was 21.

Phonemic awareness had a powerful relation to word recognition. After removing the relatively minor influence of IQ and listening comprehension on end-of-year word recognition in first grade, phonemic awareness accounted for 49% of a child's ability to read real words (Juel, Griffith, & Gough, 1986). We assumed that this is true because first grade children are quite dependent on cipher knowledge to read words. Cipher knowledge, of course, is largely dependent on phonemic awareness.

Word Recognition and Spelling
We predicted that because word recognition and spelling depend on the same sources of knowledge–cipher knowledge and lexical knowledge– overall performance in the two skills should be highly correlated. Indeed, the correlation between WRAT word recognition and spelling was .84 (N=108, p < .001) in first grade and .77 (N=83, p < .001) in second grade. The WRAT tests are both production tests where the child actually write or read words. In first grade cipher and lexical knowledge together accounted for 75% of word recognition on the WRAT and 72% of spelling performance on the WRAT, whereas in second grade they accounted for 54% of performance in both word recognition and spelling. For both spelling and word recognition, cipher and lexical knowledge accounted for both a large and similar amount of variance within each grade.

The influence between cipher knowledge and lexical knowledge did appear to shift between the grades, however. Cipher knowledge was much more related to growth in word recognition and spelling skill in first grade than was lexical knowledge. In first grade cipher knowledge accounted for 21% of performance on the WRAT word recognition test (over and above the contribution it shared with lexical knowledge), while lexical knowledge uniquely accounted for only 3% of performance. In first grade cipher knowledge independently accounted for 15% of performance on the WRAT spelling test, while lexical knowledge accounted for 7%. The predominance of cipher knowledge probably reflects the successful beginning reader and writer's heavy use of letter-sound relationships to both decode and encode written words.

By second grade, however, lexical knowledge predominated. In second grade cipher knowledge accounted for only 4% of performance on the WRAT word recognition test (over and above the contribution it shared with lexical knowledge), while lexical knowledge uniquely accounted for 20% of performance. This suggested that more and more words were now being processed automatically on the basis of their orthographic features, rather than by actively using spelling-sound information. In second grade cipher knowledge independently accounted for 8% of performance on the WRAT spelling test, while lexical knowledge accounted for 15%. The dominance of lexical knowledge was not as pronounced in spelling as in word recognition. This probably reflects the more difficult nature of a production task like spelling over simple word recognition. Recognition of specific words likely becomes automatic sooner than spelling those same words since spelling requires more active decisions of which letter sequences actually correspond to the sounds heard in a particular word (e.g, a child may recognize "rain" but later spell it "rane").

Reading Comprehension

Reading comprehension in first grade was considerably more influenced by the lower-level skill of word recognition than the higher-level skill of listening comprehension. Reading comprehension at the end of first grade increased .71 standard deviation for each standard deviation increase in word recognition. Listening comprehension had a nonsignificant statistical impact on reading comprehension in first grade.

The relations among first-grade students' skill at the end of first grade in phonemic awareness, cipher knowledge (Bryant decoding test), and reading comprehension, is depicted in Figure 4.2. Children indicated with an X scored at or above grade level on the IOWA reading comprehension subtest. Children indicated with a 0 scored below grade level on this subtest. Children with good reading comprehension cluster in the upper right-hand quadrant. That means they were children with good cipher knowledge. In first grade, of course, good cipher knowledge generally meant good word recognition.

Figure 4.2. The relationships among end-of-year first-grade children's phonemic awareness, cipher knowledge (Bryant Decoding Test), and reading comprehension. Children indicated with an X scored at or above grade level on the IOWA reading comprehension subtest.

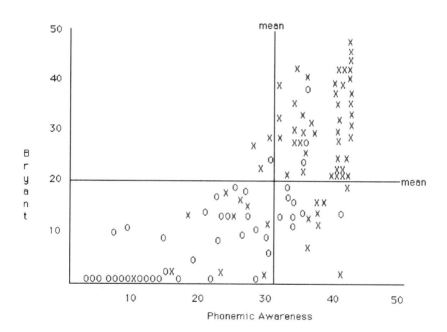

Children indicated with an O scored below grade level on this subtest. (After Juel, Griffith, & Gough, 1986)

Notice that there are virtually no children in the upper left-hand quadrant in Figure 4.2. There were no children with poor phonemic awareness who had strong cipher knowledge. There are, however, many children in the lower left-hand quadrant of Figure 4.2. These are children with good phonemic awareness, but weak cipher knowledge. Taken together these two findings suggest that phonemic awareness is a necessary, but not sufficient, condition for development of cipher knowledge.

Children who either entered first grade with phonemic awareness, or developed it relatively early in first grade, advanced considerably more rapidly in cipher knowledge. These same children then increased their word recognition dramatically. In first grade, word recognition was the determining factor in reading comprehension; these children were also the good comprehenders. A question to be addressed in the study which followed the children over several more years was whether these children would retain their edge. The answer will be discussed later.

In second grade, word recognition was by far the strongest predictor of reading comprehension. Listening comprehension, however, made a marginally significant contribution–beginning a trend that increased in subsequent grades.

Writing

In each grade we had the children tell an oral story about a colorful picture which showed animals in a schoolroom setting. At a different time we also had the children write a story about the picture. The oral story was used as an assessment of children's story ideas, when freed from the mechanics of writing. The oral stories were tape recorded and transcribed. The oral and written stories were holistically rated. Raters were asked not to evaluate the writing samples based upon how the children had spelled words. Rather they were asked to rate the written stories in the same way they rated the oral story, considering: level of story development, syntactic maturity, and richness of vocabulary.

In first and second grade, spelling (as assessed by the WRAT spelling test) and ideas (as assessed by the oral story telling) both made significant contributions to children's story writing. As with reading comprehension, in first grade the word-level factor (i.e., spelling) held sway. In first grade spelling accounted for 32% of story writing performance (over and above the variance it shared with ideas). Ideas yielded a unique contribution to story writing of only 5% in first grade.

In second grade, however, ideas (as demonstrated by the child's ability to tell an oral story) made a unique contribution of 30% to story writing, while spelling uniquely only contributed 9% (Juel, Griffith, & Gough, 1986). As with reading comprehension, higher level skills apparently become more involved when word-level processes are more automatic.

"Ideas" contributed to story writing over and above the assessments of the children's IQ and oral language. In a hierarchical regression analysis, IQ (combined WISC-R block design and vocabulary subtests) was entered first, and accounted for only 8% of second grade story writing performance. A child's "listening comprehension" was entered next and it accounted for an additional 6% of performance (that was over and above what it shared with the IQ assessment). Finally the child's "Idea" score was entered. Ideas contributed a robust additional 25% to explaining writing performance. These data suggest that the generation of ideas stems from somewhat distinct roots than those assessed by IQ and listening comprehension tests.

The Development of Literacy from First through Fourth Grades

Fifty-four children remained at the school from the beginning of first grade until the end of fourth grade. I continued to follow these children and examine whether those children who had achieved early reading and writing success continued to flourish and whether the slow starters continued to trail (Juel, 1988). I was particularly interested in determining factors that contributed to the growth or lack of growth of the children. Some of what I discovered follows.

Does How Well a Child Reads in First Grade Predict How Well that Child Will Read in Fourth Grade?

In a school without a strong intervention program, the answer was yes. Children who were reading poorly at the end of first grade almost always remained poor readers through the next three years. My study (Juel, 1988) showed that there was a .88 probability that a child who scored in the bottom quartile on the IOWA reading comprehension subtest (IOWA; Hieronymous, Lindquist, & Hoover, 1980) at the end of first grade would still be reading at least 6 months below grade level at the end of fourth grade.

The child who was at least an average reader at the end of first grade tended to remain at least an average reader through the next three years. The probability that a child would become a poor reader in fourth grade if he or she had at least average reading skills in first grade was only 12. Those children in Figure 4.2 (page 83) who were represented as X's at the end of first grade almost invariably remained good readers through the next three years of school, while the children who were not reading well at the end of first grade mainly remained poor readers through fourth grade.

Why Do Poor Readers Stay Poor Readers?

This is a multi-faceted question, as previously stated. In my study (Juel, 1988) I focused on: (1) Those reading abilities that may not have developed in time to support the child's literacy growth and (2) Certain classroom factors that might have contributed to the poor development. Some of the reasons found in this study why poor readers stay poor readers are described below.

Reason One: Poor readers are slow to develop phonemic awareness. Word recognition was a severely limiting factor upon reading comprehension in all four grades, but particularly in first grade. For most children in this study, if they could read the words they could comprehend the text. Word recognition can be traced to both cipher and lexical knowledge (See Figure 4.1, page 76). As mentioned earlier, in first grade word recognition is more dependent upon cipher knowledge. Cipher knowledge was particularly dependent upon phonemic awareness. It may be fairly said that one reason children failed to learn to read well in first grade was that they were slow to gain phonemic awareness. Indeed, the children who entered first grade with little phonemic awareness became poor readers. The modal score for this group on the phonemic awareness test administered at the beginning of first grade was 0. The mean score on this test for the children who became good readers (21.7) was considerably higher than that of the poor readers (4.2). By the end of first grade, the good readers had a mean score on the phonemic awareness test that approached ceiling (37.5). The poor readers made considerable gains in phonemic awareness in first grade, ending the year with a mean score of 18.6. Notice, however, that this score is less than that which the children who became average or good readers scored at the beginning of first grade.

Reason Two: Children with little or no phonemic awareness cannot benefit from phonics instruction. Without phonemic awareness children could not benefit much from the direct phonics instruction provided in the classroom. A statement, such as, the letter "f" makes the sound you hear at the beginning of the word "fish," makes no sense to a child who does not perceive the /f/ in "fish." Such a child can memorize the statement, can parrot back to you that the letter "f" makes the /f/ sound, and even tell you that you are to sound out words. Such a child, however, cannot apply this information and cannot use it to actually sound out words. By the time the poor readers were ready to benefit from the first grade phonics instruction they were going into second grade.

Reason Three: Poor readers lag behind good readers in word recognition. At the end of fourth grade, the majority of the poor readers still could not decode all the monosyllabic pseudowords (e.g., "buf," "dit," "yode") on the Bryant decoding test. At the end of fourth grade the poor readers were displaying cipher knowledge which was only slightly advanced from that which the children who were good readers displayed at the end of first grade. This meant the poor readers were more dependent on lexical knowledge to identify words than were the good readers. Since reading was difficult for the poor readers, however, they did not read as much (as we shall see) and therefore they also lagged behind the good readers in lexical knowledge. Given that the poor readers were lacking in both cipher and lexical knowledge it is not surprising that their word recognition skill was considerably less than the good readers. The good readers correctly read more words on the WRAT at the end of second grade than the poor readers correctly read at the end of fourth grade.

Reason Four: Poor readers are inappropriately placed in basal readers. The school used basal readers as the primary texts for reading period. After a child had read a particular basal in class (e.g., the primer) the child was individually asked to read a list of core vocabulary words from that book. On average, from the primer (i.e., the book usually read about the middle of first grade) on, the good readers failed to read about 8% of the words. On average, from the primer on, the poor readers failed to read 23% of these words.

Now think what it would be like to not be able to recognize 20% of the words in this chapter. Of the 80% of the words you could read, many would be the function words and very common nouns. In the above sentence, for example, that would mean you would fail to recognize about eight words. These eight words are likely to be the rarer words; words like "recognize," "chapter," "function," "common," and "noun." In other words the words you are least likely to recognize would be exactly the words that carry the meaning of what you are reading.

Reason Five: Poor readers hate reading. Imagine that in each grade you had to read out of books that are too difficult for you. Imagine too that you have often had to read these books aloud in class in front of your peers. It is not surprising that by fourth grade 20 out of 25 poor readers said they don't like to read (Juel, 1988). Several poor readers mentioned they didn't like to read because it was boring. Indeed, it would be boring if you couldn't recognize the more meaty (i.e., content) words. Even more revealing might be that when asked, "Which would you rather do, clean your room or read?" Only 5% of the good readers said they would choose to clean their room, whereas 40% of the poor readers chose to clean. One poor reader stated, "I'd rather clean the mold around the bathtub than read."

Reason Six: Poor readers read less than good readers both in and out of school. If reading has not been very pleasant in school it is not very likely a child will voluntarily read at home. In fourth grade the poor readers reported reading at home about once a week; the good readers reported reading nearly four nights a week. The good readers were also able to tell us what they were reading, whereas few poor readers could supply such information. Again why would anyone read when it's so difficult? In the words of some of the poor readers as to why they don't read: "It takes too much time and I'd rather do something else;" "It's boring;" "I'd rather play cause I read all day at school" (or maybe it just seems like it); or simply, "I hate it."

Even though most poor readers are reading from too difficult books in their reading instruction, they are still not reading as many books during reading instruction as the good readers. By the end of fourth grade several poor readers hadn't completed the last third grade reader or the fourth grade reader. The good readers, on average, had seen about 178,000 word in running text in their basal readers by the end of fourth grade, whereas the poor readers had seen less than half of that–about 80,000 words.

It's fairly obvious that exposure to fewer words means less opportunity to develop lexical or cipher knowledge. Weaker lexical and cipher knowledge means weaker spelling and word recognition. There are other ramifications of less reading that will affect both reading comprehension and writing. I'll discuss these ramifications next.

Reason Seven: Poor readers fall behind their peers in listening comprehension. Every year listening comprehension began to have more of an impact upon reading comprehension (Juel, 1988). Every year the children who were making good progress in word recognition also made considerable growth in listening comprehension. The good readers in fourth grade, however, did not enter the school strong in listening comprehension. At the beginning of first grade the means of both the group of children who would become good readers in first grade and those who would become poor readers were below the 39th percentile on the Metropolitan Readiness Test School Language and Listening Comprehension subtest. At the end of first grade, the children were given the IOWA Listening Comprehension subtest. This subtest involves marking pictures which depict a sentence or passage about which the teacher reads. Perhaps given the large population of first language Spanish and the low socio-economic-status (SES) of the neighborhood, it is not too surprising that the mean score on this test at the end of first grade for both the children who became good readers and the children who became poor readers was low average. At the end of first grade the group of children who were poor readers scored a mean grade equivalent of 1.4 on this subtest while the good readers had a mean grade equivalent of 1.5. By the end of fourth grade the children who remained good readers scored a grade equivalent of 5.2, while the children who remained poor readers scored a grade equivalent of only 2.6. In what is perhaps both the most surprising and the saddest finding of my study, the poor readers made very little growth in listening comprehension through the next three grades. One of the more positive findings of the study, however, was that the children who became good readers made considerable growth in listening comprehension after first grade.

This study may suggest that the lack of growth in listening comprehension (i.e., in meaning vocabulary, world knowledge) shown by the poor readers was connected to the lesser amount of reading these children did both in and out of school compared to the good readers. The finding is consistent with the view of Nagy and Anderson (1984) that "beginning in about third grade, the major determinant of vocabulary growth is amount of free reading" (p. 327). Stanovich (1986) describes the same phenomenon likely found in this study and calls it the "Matthew Effect":

> The effect of reading volume on vocabulary growth, combined with the large skill difference in reading volume, could mean "a rich get richer" or cumulative advantage phenomenon is almost inextricably embedded within the developmental course of reading progress. The very children who are reading well and who have good vocabularies will read more, learn more word meanings, and hence read even better. Children with inadequate vocabularies–who read slowly and without enjoyment–read less, and as a result have slower development of vocabulary knowledge, which inhibits further growth in reading ability. (p. 381)

According to the Simple View of Reading, reading comprehension is the product of word recognition and listening comprehension (Figure 4.1, page 76). By the end of fourth grade all the poor readers were lacking in either one of these two areas, or more likely in both. In my study, a vicious cycle seemed evident. Children who did not develop good word recognition skills in first grade began to dislike reading and read considerably less both in and out of school. They thus lost the vehicle as well as the desire to develop vocabulary, concepts, ideas, and so forth through wide reading. By the end of fourth grade the children who were good readers had a mean score of grade equivalent 5.9 on the ITBS reading comprehension subtest. The poor readers had a mean score of 3.5 on this subtest. The good readers were more than two grade levels ahead of the poor readers on this subtest.

It is likely that the gap between the poor and good readers will continue to widen in the years to come. The good readers will continue to read more and continue to outdistance the poor readers in the two primary components of reading comprehension. In later years the gap will be particularly striking in listening comprehension (Curtis, 1980; Singer, 1976). Assuming the poor readers eventually overcome their word recognition problems, over the years they will have fallen behind their good reader peers in listening comprehension as they were reading considerably less both in and out of school. The longer a child remains a poor reader (e.g., due to poor word recognition), the less the child will read, which will provide fewer opportunities for growth in listening comprehension.

What Is the Relation Between Early Reading Ability and Early Writing Ability?

Writing in the Simple View (Figure 4.1, page 76) is seen as primarily the product of spelling and ideas. Spelling had more of an impact on the first grade children's story writing than it did on fourth grade student's writing. In a hierarchical regression predicting written animal stories in first grade, spelling accounted for 29% of the variance (after controlling for the influence of ideas), whereas in fourth grade spelling accounted for 10% of the variance. The influence of ideas, however, increased with each grade level. In first grade ideas accounted for 8% of the variance (after controlling for the influence of spelling); by fourth grade the impact of ideas had increased to account for 30% of the variance.

Poor readers appear to become poor writers. The correlation between reading comprehension and story writing rose each year. It ranged from a low of .27 in first grade to .52 in fourth grade. By fourth grade 17 of the 25 poor readers were also poor writers, whereas only 4 of the 29 good readers were poor writers. Of the 17 poor readers who were also poor writers, 11 could neither write nor tell a good story. They lacked what I called story ideas (i.e., knowledge of story structures and the delivery of interesting story episodes). Of these 11 children, 7 were also poor spellers. The 6 poor readers who had good ideas were all poor spellers.

Through the years the good readers, as a group, told increasingly more interesting stories, whereas poor readers did not. Most poor readers were still telling and writing descriptions rather than stories in the fourth grade. These descriptions usually amounted to little more than an expanded list of what was seen in the animal picture.

I'd like to make the case that just as the good readers grew in listening comprehension through reading, they also grew in ideas for stories (as well as knowledge of story structures and vocabulary with which to express those ideas). A hierarchical regression predicting the children's oral stories in each grade supports the case. IQ scores (the vocabulary and block design subtests of the WISC-R) were entered first in the regression, accounting for from 16% of the variance in first grade to 10% of the variance in fourth grade. Place in series (how far a child was in the basal reading series) was then entered. After controlling for IQ, place in series still accounted for a significant amount of variance in each grade. Place in series contributed 6% to the variance in first grade, but its impact rose with each grade level–accounting for a substantial 30% of the variance in fourth grade. Thus, as a general rule, the more children read in school, the more interesting stories they both told and wrote.

The differential growth in writing ability between the good and poor readers is highlighted by comparing the actual written stories of these two groups. In Table 4.1 (page 97) are the written stories about animals by two girls. These two girls were in the same classrooms for four years and they had identical IQ scores in second grade, as assessed by the combined WISC block design and vocabulary subtests. Neither child entered first grade as a reader, but Missy made rapid progress in reading in first grade and continued to be a strong reader in subsequent grades. Missy liked to read and indicated she frequently checked books out of the school library to read by herself at home. Shayna, on the other hand, was a poor reader in each grade. She indicated she "hated" reading and did not read at home.

Differences in their writings clearly emerge by the end of first grade, and they reflect the differences found between other poor and good readers. By the end of first grade, Missy is attempting to say something that is not directly portrayed in the animal picture stimulus, while Shayna describes just what she sees in the picture. Early on Missy branched out in her syntax, while Shayna used very limited and repetitive forms of sentence structure. For most good readers, elements of story structure began to appear in second or third grade. Such elements are apparent in Missy's writing by third grade, but like most other poor readers, Shayna was still writing a description of the picture in fourth grade. Differences in vocabulary also appeared by at least fourth grade. Words like "arrangements," "chattering," and "sandstorm" appear in Missy's writing in fourth grade, while vocabulary growth is not as evident in Shayna's writing.

Figure 4.3. Model of how early reading affects later reading and writing.

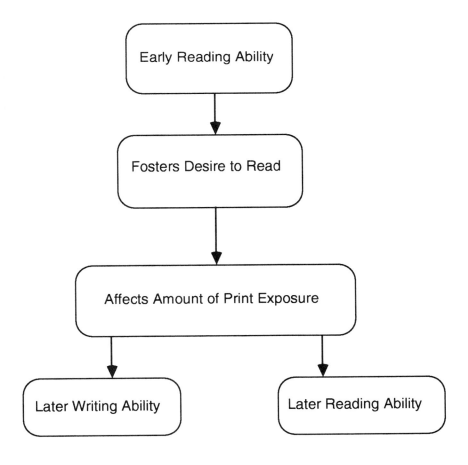

Conclusions

The Simple Views of reading and writing received support in this longitudinal study. Poor readers were either behind in word recognition, in listening comprehension, or in both areas. Poor writers were either lagging in spelling, in the generation of ideas for stories, or in both areas.

Results of the study can be summarized in the model presented in Figure 4.3, page 93. The directionality of the model (i.e., that reading enhances writing rather than vice versa) may reflect the rather typical school experiences of the children in our study: The early curricular focus was on reading rather than on writing. It may be that the directionality would be reversed in other contexts.

Although the model may seem simplistic, it reflects two important processes. First, the early attainment of reading skills in the primary grades appeared critical for later success in reading. Second, the early attainment of reading skill was important for later writing success. Print exposure fosters both word-level and higher level skills. Children who have a relatively smooth transition into reading like to read, read more both in and out of school, and have more opportunities to grow through reading in ideas, concepts, vocabulary, and other higher-level skills that will help them become even better readers and more accomplished writers.

References

Bereiter, C. (1980). Development in writing. In L. W. Gregg & E. R. Steinberg (Eds.), *Cognitive processes in writing* (pp. 73-96). Hillsdale, NJ: Erlbaum.

Bissex, G. L. (1980). *Gnys at wrk*. Cambridge, MA: Harvard University Press.

Bryant, N. D. (1975). *Diagnostic test of basic decoding skills*. New York: Teachers College, Columbia University.

Calfee, R. C., & Piontkowski, D. C. (1981). The reading diary: Acquisition of decoding. *Reading Research Quarterly, 16*, 346-373.

Curtis, M. (1980). Development of components of reading skill. *Journal of Educational Psychology, 72*, 656-669.

Gough, P. B., & Hillinger, M. L. (1980). Learning to read: An unnatural act. *Bulletin of the Orton Society, 30*, 179-196.

Gough, P. B., & Tunmer, W. E. (1986). Decoding, reading, and reading disability. *Remedial and Special Education, 7(1),* 6-10.

Gundlach, R. A. (1981). On the nature and development of children's writing. In C. H. Frederiksen & J. F. Dominic (Eds.), *Writing: The nature, development, and teaching of written communication (Volume 2, Writing: Process, develoment and communication,* pp. 133-152). Hillsdale, NJ: Erlbaum.

Gustafsson, L. (1978). *En biodarles død.* Stockholm: P. A. Norstedt and Söners Förlag.

Gustafsson, L. (1981). *The death of a beekeeper* (J. K. Swaffar & G. H. Weber, Trans.). New York: New Directions Books. (Original work published 1978).

Hall, E. A. (1990). *Correlates of phonemic awareness in preschool children.* Unpublished doctoral dissertation, University of Texas, Austin.

Hieronymous, A. N., Lindquist, E. F., & Hoover, H. D. (1980). *IOWA Test of Basic Skills.* New York: Houghton Mifflin.

Jastak, J., Bijou, S., & Jastak, S. (1978). *Wide Range Achievement Test.* Wilmington, DE: Jastak Associates.

Juel, C. (1988). Learning to read and write: A longitudinal study of fifty-four children from first through fourth grades. *Journal of Educational Psychology, 80,* 437-447.

Juel, C. (1991). Beginning reading. In R. Barr, M. L. Kamil, P. B. Mosenthal, & P. D. Pearson (Eds.), *Handbook of reading research: Vol. 2* (pp. 759-788). New York: Longman.

Juel, C., Griffith, P. L., & Gough, P. B. (1985). Reading and spelling strategies of first grade children. In J. A. Niles & R. Lalik (Eds.), *Issues in literacy: A research perspective* (pp. 306-309). Rochester, NY: The National Reading Conference.

Juel, C., Griffith, P. L., & Gough, P. B. (1986). Acquisition of literacy: A longitudinal study of children in first and second grade. *Journal of Educational Psychology, 78,* 243-255.

LaBerge, D., & Samuels, S. J. (1974). Toward a theory of automatic information processing in reading. *Cognitive Psychology, 6,* 293-323.

Lesgold, A., Resnick, L. B., & Hammond, K. (1985). Learning to read: A longitudinal study of word skill development in two curricula. In G. E. MacKinnon & T. G. Waller (Eds.), *Reading research: Advances in theory and practice* (Vol. 4, pp. 107-138). New York:

Academic Press.

Maclean, M., Bryant, P., & Bradley, L. (1987). Rhymes, nursery rhymes, and reading in early childhood. *Merrill-Palmer Quartely,33,* 255-281.

National Assessment of Educational Progress. (1985). The reading report card, progress toward excellence in our schools: Trends in reading over four national assessments, 1971-1984 (Report No. 15-R-01). Princeton, NJ: Educational Testing Service.

Nagy, W. E., & Anderson, R. C. (1984). How many words are there in printed school English? *Reading Research Quarterly, 19,* 304-330.

Nurse, J. & McGauvran, M. (1976). *Metropolitan Readiness Tests, Level II.* New York: Harcourt, Brace, Jovanovich.

Scardamalia, M. (1981). How children cope with the cognitive demands of writing. In C. H. Frederiksen & J. F. Dominic (Eds.), *Writing: The nature, development, and teaching of written communication (Volume 2, Writing: Process, development, and communication,* pp. 81-104). Hillsdale, NJ: Erlbaum.

Shanahan, T. (1984). Nature of the reading-writing relation: An exploratory multivariate analysis. *Journal of Educational Psychology, 76,* 466-477.

Singer, H. (1976). Substrata-factor theory of reading: Theoretical design for teaching reading. In H. Singer & R. Ruddell (Eds.), *Theoretical models and processes of reading* (2nd ed.). Newark, DE: International Reading Association.

Stanovich, K. E. (1986). Matthew effects in reading: Some consequences of individual differences in the acquisition of literacy. *Reading Research Quarterly, 21,* 360-406.

Wechsler, D. (1974). Manual for the Wechsler Intelligence Scale for Children-Revised. New York: Psychological Corporation.

Table 4.1. Writing samples of one good reader, Missy, and one poor reader, Shayna

Missy		**Shayna**	

Grade 1, February

Rabbit	posm	books	homes
maos	dore	mose	dore
hases	fowe	rrabt	tree
lefe	tree	petr	g
book	widor		
char	nut		

Grade 1, April

We go to school to read and lern oso to rats and rabbit to can read to and posom can read.	I see a books
	I see pesls
	I see a techr
	I see charls

I see mouse	I see a houe
I see boys	I see a wedl
I see grils	I see tadls
I see a tree	I see lags

Grade 2, November

There is a mole wearing a dress with glasses on! Giving a prize to a mouse. And it looks like she is paintting. There is class but I don'tnow what she teaching! She might not even be a teacher!	There is a Book.
	There is a Dorwe.
	There is a chrire.
	There is a shcool.
	There is a Boy.
	There is a Drees.
	There is a leves.
	There is a tree.
	There is a flowe.

Grade 2, April

The mouse gets a snack. For being good. The porcipine is eating his snack. There is pictures on the wall. And the students are playing around with their food. The techer looks very nice.	I see lost of books and pensolss. chears pichers Thery is a teacher Therisa door Thery is some boys and girls and the house The boys and girls are wearing dress. The teacher name is Ms Treadway.

Grade 3, January

Once opon at in animal veilige. The animals in 3-1 were being the nicest class you ever seen. they didn't arly talk. And there teacher was nice to. They drew nice pictures. They stayed in there seats and followed directions very good. One day the priceipal came to there door and then he opened it and the class was still quiet. The princeipal said to Miss Posom you got a good class and you are doing a good job. Then the princeipal said to the class I will give you doughnuts a lolly pops after school when you come to my ofes after shcool o.k. and the class said o.k. I will meet you after school. The teacher said you hear that were going to get doughnuts!

This is a picturea They is a teacher and books, children, pictureas, a door, pencls, a window, tables. chears, leavs, acorns, a pictureq of a with wall. and the techers name is Ms watts and. I know thee more names ther are Shayna, Elizabeth, Sherry. And They are two more nams That I now to. They are Sonya, Simone, They are nice to me Sometimes. And they are. some picturea of house to. I Love to make house and I Love to read about Move makers The teacher is nice.

Grade 4, January

The class is going on a fieldtrip tomorrow. They need to do extra work for tomorrow. Lenny mouse does not understand fractions. Larry porcupine is eating some of his lunch. Lisa feild mouse is drawing Mrs. Lee a picture. Laura squirrel is reading a story. Lucky bunny is throwing spitballs. The class is never going to get their work done! Lupie hamster is quietly doing his work. Lea ground squirrel is chattering to Lisa. Tomorrow they are going to have a lot of fun. Finaly they finish all of their work for today. But they have to finish tomorrow's work. But Larry porcupine did not finish his work so he had to stay to do it after shcool if he wanted to go onthe field trip. By the time lunch arrived Lucky ate so quickly he had a stomach-

There's is a teacher with Her class. One of the kids is asking her a quastion most of the kids are working, player and talking and there are. pitcher's on the wall there. is also a door. there is a window and they have desk and they have chairs. And Some are reading book's to.

ache. He went to the nurses office she said it would be allright for him to go on the field trip tomorrow, unless his tummy-ache got worse. Lenny mouse talked to his friend Lupie hamster. Lisa and Lea ground squirrel talked about the field trip the nextday. They went to the library that after noon. Everyone checked out books. The next day everyone was in their swimming suits. They went to the pond had a picnic and went swimming. Then they went hiking up a very, very long trail. They hiked for hours and hours. Then they got lost a sand storm came and covered up the trial. Everyone got very scared.
It was finnaly dawn then Lisa ground squirrel found a cave. The class stayed there overnight thank god they brought their lunches and had that for their dinner The next day Lenny saw a diffrent trail they droped big rocks on their way so the sandstorm could not cover up their trail. They walked for twenty five minutes. Then they came to a cabin knocked. then they opened the door then they discoverd it was a summer cabin. they found a map followed it back to their school. Every-one took turns calling their parents. They went home and never went to school again. they played all day had slumber parties every night Then Lisa and Mrs. Lee made arangments for a party and everyone spent the night at Lisa's house even Mrs. Lee.
The End

5

The Elementary Vocabulary Curriculum: What Should It Be?

Michael F. Graves

Shortly before or after they celebrate their first birthday, children are likely to utter their first word. Over the three months following the appearance of this first word, they may learn an additional fifty words. During this period, children are likely to speak exclusively in one word utterances. Then, after accumulating the fifty or so words, they begin stringing words together to form sentences, two-word sentences at first, then three-word sentences, and soon longer ones.

Things move rapidly after this. By the time children enter first grade, their phonological systems are largely or fully complete; they can recognize and produce all or nearly all the sounds in their language. Their syntactic systems, although not as advanced as their phonological systems, are well on their way to maturity; six-year-olds can understand and produce a large percentage of the indefinite number of sentence patterns in the language.

At this same time, as they enter first grade, children's vocabulary development is in one sense similarly impressive. Some first graders have learned upwards of 10,000 words (White, Graves, & Slater, 1990).

However, estimates of the average number of words known by high school seniors are in the 40,000-80,000 range. In contrast to the situation with phonology and syntax, then, first graders still have a long way to go in mastering the vocabulary of the language.

Of course, we cannot directly teach students anything like 30,000-70,000 words. This being the case, what sort of vocabulary program can best assist them in this learning process? To be sure, there is no single answer to this question of *best*. There are undoubtedly a number of viable plans and an even larger number of plans that are not viable. For more than 10 years, I have been working to develop and articulate what I consider to be **one reasonable plan** for a comprehensive vocabulary program for first through twelfth grade students (see Graves 1978, 1984, 1985, 1987; Graves & Duin, 1985; Graves & Prenn, 1986; Graves, Slater, & White, 1989). Such a plan should, in my judgement, include attention to both the vocabulary curriculum and vocabulary instruction–to what vocabulary is taught, to when during students' 12 years of public school the vocabulary and vocabulary skills we choose to teach are taught, and to how vocabulary is taught. Such a plan should also, in my judgement, be informed by theory, by research, and by a healthy dose of common sense. Finally, I believe that such a plan should indeed be comprehensive and should be fairly catholic in its outlook.

In this chapter, I concentrate on elementary vocabulary programs, paying particular attention to the vocabulary curriculum–what should be taught–as opposed to vocabulary instruction–how one should teach. I do so because, while there is a good deal of current information available on vocabulary instruction, there is much less on the vocabulary curriculum. Moreover, what considerations there are tend to recommend rather provincial curricula–stressing, for example, only the importance of teaching students to use context cues, or maintaining that certain methods or instruction are the most powerful and should be used exclusively or almost exclusively.

Here, I have attempted to take a broad view and describe a balanced and comprehensive curriculum. In what follows, I present a brief overview of the history of vocabulary research, note my assessment of our current knowledge about two critical issues relevant to vocabulary instruction, and then describe each of the two major parts of the curriculum.

A Brief History of Vocabulary Research

What is among the oldest if not the oldest archival study of English vocabulary, Kirkpatrick's "The Number of Words in an Ordinary English Vocabulary," was published in 1891, eight years before E. L Thorndike is reported to have begun his vocabulary studies (Clifford, 1978). Three decades later, in 1921, the first edition of *The Teacher's Word Book* was published. For about 30 years following this landmark publication, vocabulary was a central focus of educational research (Calfee & Drum, 1978).

Studies done between 1920 and about 1950 investigated vocabulary size, the vocabularies of different groups of students and various subject matters, vocabulary as it affected readability, and a number of other topics. Among the findings were that the set of most frequent words remains fairly stable, that the majority of frequent words are function words, that most words are polysemous, that frequent words have more meanings than less frequent ones, and that the English lexicon consists of a very small number of very frequent words, a small number of slightly less frequent words, and a huge number of relatively infrequent words, with the 100 most frequent words accounting for 50% of the running words in text and the 1,000 most frequent accounting for 90% of the words (Clifford, 1978).

In commenting on the significance of the vocabulary research of the period, the majority of which she attributes to Thorndike and his students, Clifford (1978) concludes that the work markedly influenced educational practice, with the greatest influence being that it brought control to the vocabulary used in school texts and tests.

Despite this influence, during the 1950s the frequency of vocabulary research declined sharply. In fact, in their review of reading research published in 1978, Calfee and Drum observed that "perusal of the current literature would suggest that the topic is a vanishing species" (p. 217). Further testimony to the lack of vocabulary research during the period is suggested by the fact that the first edition of *Handbook of Reading Research* (Pearson, Barr, Kamil, & Mosenthal,1984), which was published in 1984, contains 25 chapters, none of which are on vocabulary, and 899 pages, only eight of which include some mention of vocabulary.

Exactly why the research trailed off is a matter of speculation, but some reasonable inferences can be made. Both Clifford (1978) and

Calfee and Drum (1978) suggest that the lack of a coherent theory underlying vocabulary research was one important factor. Other possibilities include the shift from behaviorism to cognitivism (Neisser, 1967), the shift of linguistic interest to syntax following publications of *Syntactic Structures* (Chomsky, 1957), and the rise of psycholinguistics with its initial concentration on syntax (e.g., Miller, 1962; Slobin, 1966).

Whatever the exact cause of the demise of vocabulary study, it was relatively short lived, lasting something over 20 years. In the 1986 edition of the *Handbook of Research on Teaching,* Calfee and Drum devote nearly a third of their discussion to vocabulary and note that recent work offers a number of alternatives to the instruction currently seen in schools and for a research agenda in vocabulary. Further testifying to the resurgence of interest in vocabulary are the fact that the first AERA special interest group is fpr vocabulary and was established in 1985, that the first *Journal of Reading* (vol. 13, No. 7) devoted entirely to vocabulary was published in 1986, that the first scholarly collection devoted entirely to vocabulary (McKeown & Curtis) was published in 1987, and that the 1991 edition of the *Handbook of Reading Research* (Barr, Kamil, Mosenthal, & Pearson) contains two chapters devoted solely to vocabulary.

Just what caused this shift is again difficult to say, but the increasing willingness of psychologists and linguists to deal with semantics is certainly one reason (see Clark & Clark, 1978). Beyond that, a proposal to teach a basic vocabulary of 7,000 words to disadvantaged students (Becker, 1977) and a paper which seriously questioned that proposal (Anderson & Freebody, 1981) have undoubtedly precipitated some of the recent work.

Additionally, two extended lines of inquiry have promoted interest in vocabulary. In one of them, Anderson and Nagy and their colleagues have followed the Anderson and Freebody (1981) paper with a body of theory and research in which they generally argue against systematic vocabulary instruction and in favor of wide reading as a vehicle for vocabulary development (Anderson & Freebody, 1983; Freebody & Anderson, 1983a; Freebody & Anderson, 1983b; Nagy, 1985; Nagy & Anderson, 1982, 1984; Nagy, Anderson, & Herman, 1985; 1987, Nagy & Herman, 1987; Nagy, Herman, & Anderson, 1985). In the other, Beck and McKeown and their colleagues have pursued a line of theory and research in which they investigate a particularly rich sort of vocabulary instruction and in which they generally argue for systematic instruction (Beck, 1985; Beck, et al., 1980; Beck & McKeown, 1983; Beck, McKeown, McCaslin, & Burkes, 1979; Beck, McKeown, & Omanson, 1984, 1987; Beck, Perfetti, & McKeown, 1982; McKeown, 1985; McKeown, Beck, Omanson, & Perfetti, 1983; McKeown, Beck, Omanson, & Pople, 1985). Although the two lines of work began independently, they came be competing positions (see particularly Beck, 1985; Beck, McKeown, & Omanson, 1984, 1987; Nagy, 1985; Nagy & Herman, 1984, 1987), and this competition prompted further interest in the area.

This current interest is perhaps most recently attested to by two major reviews of research on vocabulary instruction published in 1991– Beck and McKeown's review in the *Handbook of Reading Research* and Baumann and Kameenui's review in the *Handbook of Research on Teaching the Language Arts.* Together, these two surveys and my 1986 review, which appeared in *Review of Educational Research,* make it clear that we know a good deal about vocabulary instruction, that there is still an enormous amount to be learned, and that there are both significant agreements and significant disagreements on the topic. Because these reviews are readily available and this chapter is not intended as a comprehensive review, I will not summarize the research here. However, in the next section, I do consider research on vocabulary size and research on what sort of instruction it takes to teach words well enough that word knowledge increases comprehension.

Current Knowledge On Vocabulary Size and In-depth Instruction

The renewed interest in vocabulary has made the past decade an interesting and exciting–yet sometimes difficult–time for developing a plan for a comprehensive vocabulary program. It has been particularly challenging for me because some of the major assumptions I made when I began formulating my plan turned out to be very wrong. Ten years ago I believed that direct instruction in a relatively small number of words stood at least a good chance of markedly improving students' reading comprehension, particularly the comprehension of young disadvantaged students. This–systematic, direct instruction for young disadvantaged students on several thousand specific words–was precisely what Becker recommended in his widely cited and debated *Harvard Educational Review* article that appeared in 1977. As a result of his experiences with the University of Oregon Follow-Through project, Becker had concluded that lack of adequate vocabularies was the single most important factor effecting the school failure of disadvantaged students. And he recommended systematic, direct instruction in vocabulary as a solution to this problem.

Unfortunately for Becker's argument, and for those like myself who were searching for a relatively easy approach to significantly building students' vocabularies, he had based this recommendation on Dupuy's (1974) estimate that the average high school senior had a basic vocabulary of about 7,000 words. The results of recent studies fail to support Dupuy's estimate, and consequently they also fail to support Becker's recommendation. Data collected by Nagy and Anderson (1982, 1984) indicate that the materials students read contain well over 100,000 different words. Data collected by Beck and McKeown (Beck, et al., 1982; McKeown et al., 1983) indicate that only deep and rich vocabulary instruction, instruction that may take 15 to 30 minutes per word, results in increases in reading comprehension. And data collected by White et al. (1990) on the size of students' reading vocabularies indicate that even first grade students have reading vocabularies ranging from 3,000-10,000 words and that their reading vocabularies indeed grow each year by the 3,000-4,000 words, figures consistent with those suggested by Miller and Gildea (1987) and Nagy and Herman (1987). Thus, the number of words that would need to be taught to substantially increase students' store of words is extremely large, and instruction that will directly result in increases in reading comprehension must be deep and rich.

These findings must, in my judgement, be taken into account in planning a comprehensive vocabulary curriculum. In the remainder of the chapter, I outline the plan I have thus far developed.

A Two-Part Vocabulary Curriculum

The plan divides a comprehensive program of vocabulary development into two parts–a Curriculum of Individual Words and a Curriculum of Strategies for Learning Words.

A Curriculum of Individual Words

Although providing instruction in individual words may appear to be a simple task for which a single instructional method or a small set of methods will suffice, such is not the case. Learning individual words constitutes a series of tasks that vary markedly depending on the word being taught, the learner's knowledge of the word and the concept it represents, and the depth and precision of meaning that we want the student to acquire. Importantly, the sort of instruction appropriate for accomplishing one of these tasks is often inappropriate for accomplishing others; we need to match the teaching method with the learning task and with the students who are doing the learning.

Here, I first describe six word-learning tasks and then discuss levels of word knowledge. Following that, I present guidelines for a curriculum of individual words that reflects these considerations.

Word-Learning Tasks

The six word-learning tasks I distinguish are learning to read known words, learning new words representing known concepts, learning new words representing new concepts, clarifying and enriching the meanings of known words, moving words into students' productive vocabularies, and learning new meanings for known words.

Learning To Read Known Words. Learning to read known words, words that are already in their oral vocabularies, is the task of beginning readers. Such words as *icicle, mansion,* and *schedule* are ones that students might be taught to read during their first three years of school. By the time they reach about the fourth grade, good readers will have learned to read the vast majority of words in their oral vocabularies (White et al., 1990). However, the task of learning to read many of the words in their oral vocabularies remains for a number of less able readers at all grade levels, and thus it is something that teachers who have less able readers in their classes need to be concerned with.

Learning New Words Representing Known Concepts. A second word-learning task students face is learning to read words which are in neither their oral nor their reading vocabularies but for which they have an available concept. For example, the word *elderly* would be unknown to many third graders, but third graders certainly have the concept of *older person.* All students continue to learn words of this sort throughout the elementary grades and beyond, and the largest number of words intermediate grade students learn is of this sort.

Learning New Words Representing New Concepts. A third word-learning task students face, and a very demanding one, is learning to read words which are in neither their oral nor their reading vocabularies and for which they do not have an available concept. Learning the full meanings of such words as *oligarchy, representative government,* and *saturated solution* is likely to require most intermediate grade students to develop new concepts. All students continue to learn words of this sort throughout their years in school.

Clarifying and Enriching the Meanings of Known Words. Still another word-learning task is that of clarifying and enriching the meanings of already known words. The meanings students originally attach to words are often imprecise and only become fully specified over time. Initially, for example, students might not recognize any difference between *happy* and *jolly,* or they might not realize what distinguishes a *city* from a *town,* or not realize that the term *virtuoso* is usually applied to those who play musical instruments. Students continue to refine their knowledge of words throughout their years in school.

Moving Words Into Students' Productive Vocabularies. The next to last word-learning task considered here is that of moving words from students' receptive vocabularies to their productive vocabularies, that is, moving words from students' listening and reading vocabularies to their speaking and writing vocabularies. Fourth graders, for example, might have a fairly thorough understanding of the word *delicate* when they hear it or read it, yet never use the word themselves. Even college students have much larger receptive vocabularies than productive ones.

Learning New Meanings for Known Words. The last word-learning task considered here, learning new meanings for words that students already know with one meaning, is not part of the continuum represented by the tasks listed thus far. The words of interest here are ones students can pronounce and know one meaning for but for which they will need to learn an additional meaning or meanings. These include words with a number of common meanings, such as *run*, and words with special meanings in particular subjects, such as *force* in physics. Such additional meanings may or may not represent new concepts.

Levels of Word Knowledge

In addition to there being different word-learning tasks, there are different levels of word knowledge, different degrees to which students can know words.

Beck, McKeown, McCaslin, and Burkes (1979) distinguish three levels of word knowledge: *unknown, acquainted,* and *established.* A word at the *unknown* level is just that, unknown. A word at the *acquainted* level is one whose meaning is recognized but only with some deliberate attention, and a word at the *established* level is one whose meaning is easily, rapidly, and automatically recognized. Beck, McKeown, and Omanson (1987) provide the following further illustration of these levels.

> A reader might meet the word *quaich* in a text, and have no knowledge of its meaning; one might have some general information about a word, such as understanding that *altruism* has a positive connotation, but knowing nothing about its specific nature; one might have a specific but narrow and context-bound knowledge of a word, such as knowing that a *"benevolent* dictator" is a ruler who does not mistreat people, but be unable to to understand how *benevolent* applies to other situations and types of behavior; one might hear the word *bucolic* used, and need to pause momentarily before remembering it describes something pastoral, or typical of rural life; finally, one might have full, rich decontextualized knowledge of a word, such as knowing not only that a *miser* is someone who saves money and lives as if poor, but being able to give examples of miserly behavior, consequences of acting like a miser and able to use the word beyond typical contents, for example by extending the concept to describe people who are stingy with other things besides money. (p. 148)

It is important to recognize that, while students need not learn all words thoroughly, they must learn most words they will encounter in reading well enough that their responses to them are automatic, that is, instantaneous and without attention (LaBerge & Samuels, 1974). Otherwise, the need to shift from attention to larger units of meaning–clauses and sentences–to individual words will overload memory limitations and thwart the meaning-getting process.

Obviously, we want any vocabulary instruction to move students' knowledge of the words taught beyond the unknown level. But learning a word thoroughly requires a number of exposures in a variety of contexts (Beck & McKeown, 1983) and thoroughly knowing a word involves a number of skills, including, perhaps, associating it with a range of experiences, readily accessing it, being able to articulate one's understanding of it, flexibly using it, and recognizing synonyms, metaphors, and analogies that employ the word (Calfee & Drum, 1986).

Certainly, no single encounter with a word is likely to achieve all of these goals. On the other hand–and this is a critical point underlying the vocabulary program outlined here–no single encounter with a word need accomplish all of these goals. Instead, any particular instructional encounter with a word can be considered as only one in a series of encounters that will eventually lead students to mastery of the word. Even a brief encounter with a word will leave some trace of its meaning and make students more likely to fully grasp its meaning when they again come across it (Jenkins, Stein, & Wysocki, 1984). Moreover, brief instruction provided immediately before students read a selection containing the word may be sufficient to prevent their stumbling over it as they read.

Thus, the curriculum described here includes a place for relatively brief vocabulary instruction methods that serve primarily to start students on the long road to full mastery of words, as well as a place for much more extensive and ambitious instruction that enables students to develop thorough understandings of words and perhaps use the words in their speech and writing.

Guidelines for a Curriculum of Individual Words

Here I outline a curriculum based on these considerations. I begin with some general guidelines and then presents some more specific suggestions for first and second grade, on the one hand, and for third grade through sixth grade, on the other. Although I strongly believe that the vocabulary curriculum ought to change over the elementary years, I should stress that these grade level designations are only approximations of when those changes should occur.

To begin, the curriculum would include a substantial amount of instruction in individual words. Although this statement may seem unnecessary, I include it because some authorities have suggested that there are so many words for students to learn that instruction in individual words cannot make a significant contribution to vocabulary development. In my judgment, the fact that we cannot teach all the words students need to learn simply does not mean that we should not teach some of them. Moreover, teaching individual words pays benefits beyond the learning of individual words. Teaching individual words focuses students' attention on words, lets them know that we value word knowledge, and leaves them with a richer store of words, which itself facilitates their learning additional words from context.

The curriculum would include a variety of different sorts of instruction. The existence of different word-learning tasks and different levels of word knowledge that we want to develop in students argues for including a variety of sorts of instruction. If this, too, appears to be an unnecessary statement, it is presented because some investigators have repeatedly argued for the superiority and seemingly exclusive use of certain types of vocabulary instruction.

The curriculum would include different words and different sorts of instruction for different students. Most notably, older students and more able readers would receive very little if any instruction in Learning to Read Known Words, while younger students and less able readers would receive a good deal of instruction in Learning to Read Known Words. Additionally, students nearing the end of the elementary grades and thus increasingly working with new and difficult topics would receive less instruction in Words Representing Known Concepts and more instruction in Learning Word Representing New Concepts.

Somewhat similarly, the curriculum might well include different words and different instruction for students for whom English is a second language. Exactly what this different instruction might consist of and these different words might be is, I believe, one of the most pressing matters for vocabulary research. Moreover, since different students for whom English is a second language have vastly different levels of proficiency in English, different students require different instruction. What can be said without further research is that the vocabulary curriculum for native speakers begins with the realization that kindergarten and first grade students begin school with large oral vocabularies and very rapidly acquire large reading vocabularies. What is appropriate for these students simply is not appropriate for students who have small or nonexistent oral English vocabularies or who do not acquire large reading vocabularies rapidly. For example, while the first word-learning task I have listed–Learning to Read Known Words–is the primary reading vocabulary task for first and second grade native speakers, this is a relatively minor task for children who come to school with very small oral vocabularies in English. The primary task for these students is likely to be that of incorporating new English words into both their receptive and productive vocabularies.

First and Second Grade. In first and second grade, much of the vocabulary curriculum should probably be devoted to further developing students' oral vocabularies. Much of this development could come informally and indirectly in student discussions of topics that necessarily require increasingly sophisticated vocabulary, in teacher talk that deliberately includes some new and interesting words, and in substantial amounts of reading to students from narrative and expository material which includes rich and skillfully used words. Additionally, teachers can take the opportunity to point out interesting and skillfully used words in children's speech, children's writing, their own speech, and the materials students read.

During these two years, for most students the primary task with reading vocabulary is Learning to Read Known Words. For the most part, these words should be drawn from upcoming selections. More often than not, reading selections should be preceded with instruction in a least a few words. Because students already know the meanings of these words, they can be taught using procedures that are simple and do not take a lot of time. Of course, during this same time, some more in-depth work with words is also called for–work with New Words Representing Known Concepts, Enriching the Meanings of Known Words, and Moving Words into Students' Productive Vocabularies. Moreover, there should probably be some instruction in Words Representing New Concepts, although this should probably be a small part of the curriculum and the new concepts taught should be common ones.

Of course, since the goal is automatic responses to words they encounter in reading, a substantial part of what students do to build and solidify their reading vocabularies should be practice, and the best practice is a lot of reading in materials students find interesting, enjoyable, understandable, relatively easy, and not packed with difficult vocabulary.

An additional possible activity for students whose reading vocabularies are small and do not appear to be growing at the rate of other students–and this group is likely to include students for whom English is not a first language–is the direct teaching of a specific set of words. The words to teach are of course the most frequent words, and a reasonable set of these is the 1,000 most frequent words in Carroll, Davies, and Richman (1971), a frequency count of the words used in materials read by 3rd-9th grade students. As noted earlier, the 1,000 most frequent words make up about 90% of running words students encounter in their reading. If students do not know the vast majority of them thoroughly–automatically–they are going to stumble a lot as they read, and reading is not going to yield much meaning or be much fun.

Two additional matters are crucial here. First, students certainly do not need to be taught words they already know. Thus, children who appear to lack these words in their reading vocabularies need to be tested to be sure that they do indeed lack them. Second, learning these words may represent different word-learning tasks and thus require different instruction for native speakers and non-native speakers. Virtually all native speakers will have their words in their oral vocabularies and know their meanings; for them, therefore, the word-learning task is Learning to Reading Known Words. Many non-native speakers, however, will not have these English words in their oral vocabularies; for these students, the word-learning task for at least some of these words will be Learning New Words Representing Known Concepts.

Third through Sixth Grades. Beginning in about third grade, for most students an increasing proportion of the curriculum would be devoted to developing reading vocabularies. This does not mean that attempts to develop students' oral vocabularies should cease. The emphasis with students for whom English is a second language and whose oral vocabularies are relative small would continue to be on oral vocabulary development, and some attention to the development of oral vocabulary would continue for all students. But for most students, most formal vocabulary work would be on reading vocabulary.

Beginning at this same time, the primary word-learning task would shift from that of Learning to Read Known Words to that of Learning

New Words Representing Known Concepts. These new words would be drawn exclusively or nearly exclusively from students' reading materials. With each succeeding year from third grade to sixth grade, New Words Representing New Concepts would receive increasing emphasis. These words, too, would be drawn exclusively or nearly exclusively form students' reading material. The assumption here is that at each increasing grade level, students' reading materials contain more and more new and difficult concepts and thus more and more time needs to be spent on instruction in such concepts.

Instruction in New Meanings for Known Words and instruction designed to Enrich the Meaning of Known Words would be given as the words in students' materials and the sorts of meanings they needed to understand the selections dictated.

Thus, the general rule throughout this period is that the words to be taught come out of students' reading materials, and the type of instruction used varies with the words and what students need to learn regarding them. There are, however, two exceptions to this general rule that I would recommend. One is that once or twice each year, the curriculum would include a one week unit in which full and rich meanings were established for a set of words. Beck and McKeown and their colleagues have provided several descriptions of such instruction (Beck & McKeown, 1983; Beck, McKeown, McCaslin, & Burkes, 1979; Beck, Perfetti, & McKeown, 1982). The other recommendation is that once or twice a year, the curriculum should include a similar unit designed to move words into students' productive vocabularies. Duin and I have described this sort of instruction (Duin & Graves, 1986, 1987, 1988).

There are several purposes here. One is simply to provide a change for students, a different sort of instruction to break up the normal routine. Another is to give students a real feeling and some appreciation for what it means to know a word well. Another is to provide students with a tangible demonstration of our interest in words and our belief that they are important and worthy of study. And still another, is the obvious one of getting students to actually use an increasingly sophisticated vocabulary.

I turn now to the other major part of the vocabulary curriculum, strategies for learning words independently.

A Curriculum in Strategies for Learning Words

As noted at the beginning of the chapter, students learn something like 3000-4000 words each year, many more words than can be taught directly. Thus, in addition to being taught specific words, students need to learn how to learn words on their own. Here, I consider five skills that students need to become independent word learners: using context, learning and using word parts, using the dictionary, developing an approach to dealing with unknown words in context, and developing a personal approach to learning words. Following that, I describe a curriculum of strategies for learning words.

Using Context. Even without instruction in using context, students learn a large proportion of the 3000-4000 words they learn each year from context. In fact, it seems likely that, as Sternberg (1987) has suggested, "most vocabulary is learned from context" (p. 89). However, gleaning a word's meaning from most contexts is no mean task. In fact, research suggests that students have only about a one-in-twenty chance of learning an unknown word they come across in their reading (Nagy, Anderson, & Herman, 1987). Fortunately, even a modest amount of reading exposes students to a huge number of unknown words; and given a typical amount of reading over a year's time, average students might acquire over 1000 words–or roughly one-third of the words learned during the year–from meeting them in the context of their reading (Nagy, Anderson, & Herman, 1987). Additionally, students learn a large number of words from oral contexts–day-to-day conversations, small group discussions, class discussions, lectures, films, and even television. If we can increase students' skills in learning from context, they can learn even more words from these sources.

Several schemes for classifying context cues and providing students' with instruction have been suggested, one of which, that proposed by Sternberg and his colleagues (Sternberg, 1987; Sternberg & Powell, 1983; Sternberg, Powell, & Kaye, 1983), seems particularly promising. The list below is a slightly modified version of Sternberg's system.

1. Temporal cues: cues regarding the duration or frequency of the _____ (unknown word), or when _____ can occur
2. Spatial cues: cues regarding the location or possible location of _____

3. Value cues: cues regarding the worth or desirability of _____ or the kinds of affects _____ arouses
4. Descriptive cues: cues regarding the properties of _____ (its size, shape, color, odor, feel, and so forth.)
5. Functional cues: cues regarding the possible purposes or uses of _____ or the actions _____ can perform
6. Causal/Enablement cues: cues regarding the possible causes or enabling conditions of _____
7. Class membership cues: cues about the class or classes to which _____ belongs
8. Definition or Synonym cues: cues to the meaning of _____
9. Contrasts or Antonym cues: cues that give contrasts to the meaning of _____

The following sentence shows how some of these cues operate and illustrates the important fact that context sometimes contains multiple cues to a word's meaning.

The portable *trekfer* has become a handy item to own in today's world because it makes it possible to place or receive calls wherever you happen to be.

In this rich context, *portable* is a descriptive cue, *item* a class membership cue, *handy* a value cue, *in today's world* a temporal cue, *makes it possible* an enablement cue, *to send and receive calls* a pair of functional cues, and *wherever you happen to be* a spatial cue. Admittedly, this is unusually rich context, and the unknown word is simply a nonsense syllable representing a word you already know. Still, the example does suggest the power of the system.

In addition to learning to use these cues to deduce word meanings as they are reading, there is some declarative knowledge about context that students need to know. Below are some of these facts, phrased as they might be presented to students.

*   Most words are learned from context. Therefore, it is really important to learn to use context well.
*   Sometimes, context clearly tells us a word's meaning. At other times, however, it only hints at a word's meaning.
*   Context cues include words, phrases, and sentences that tell us something about the unknown word.

- Cues can occur both before the unknown word and after it, and often there is more than one cue to a particular unknown word.
- The most useful cues are usually close to the unknown word, generally in the same sentence. However, we sometimes get cues in other sentences or even other paragraphs.

Learning to use these cues and learning some basic facts about context appear to constitute a reasonable complete context cue curriculum; however, the fact that the curriculum can be briefly described does not mean that it is quickly or easily mastered. Teaching students to use context cues is a major task.

Learning and Using Word Parts. Using word parts–suffixes, prefixes, and roots–is another approach that can aid students in learning the thousands of words they need to learn . In fact, recent evidence suggests that by the time they get to the seventh grade or so and are reading material that contains a large proportion of affixed words, students may learn as many new words from structural analysis of their word parts as they do from context (White, Power, & White, 1989). During the elementary years, the word-parts curriculum should consist primarily of instruction in suffixes and prefixes.

Suffixes. English contains a substantial number of suffixes. Fortunately, a small number of them are extremely frequent and consequently particularly worth teaching. The Table 5.1, based on the work of White, Sowell, and Yanagihara (1989), shows the 20 most frequently occurring suffixes and the number of suffixed words in the Carroll et al. (1971) word frequency count.

As can be seen, the Carroll et al. list, which contains the vast major of words appearing in materials read by third to ninth grade students, includes 2,100 suffixed words. The four most frequent suffixes account for about 1,500 of these words, and the 20 most frequent suffixes account for about 2,000 of them. These are the suffixes students need to know and be able to use.

Table 5.1. English Suffixes Ranked by Frequency of Occurrence

Suffix	Number of Different Words with the Suffix
-s, -es	673
-ed	435
-ing	303
-ly	144
-er, -or (agentive)	95
-ion, -tion, -ation, -ition	76
-ible, -able	33
-al;, -ial	30
-y	27
-ness	26
-ity, -ty	23
-ment	21
-ic	18
-ous, -eous, -ious	18
-en	15
-er (comparative)	15
-ive, -ative, -itive	15
-ful	14
-less	14
-est	12
All others	160 (estimated)
TOTAL	2,167

Most suffixes have grammatical meanings that are tacitly understood by students or abstract meanings that are very difficult to teach. For this reason, suffix knowledge is most useful as a decoding tool. The major goal in teaching suffix removal–teaching students to recognize suffixes and separate them from the root word so that they can recognize or decode the root. Listed below is the basic knowledge that students need to work effectively with suffixes. Here, and in the following lists of information for students, I have again phrased the information as it might be presented to students.

- Suffixes are word parts that are added on the end of root words.
- Identifying suffixes and mentally setting them aside while we look at the rest of the word can sometimes help us recognize the root word.
- Although adding a suffix to a root word sometimes changes the meaning of the word a lot, most of the time adding a suffix changes the meaning only slightly.

In addition to learning this basic knowledge about suffixes, students need to learn some of the pitfalls of working with suffixes. Here are the two major ones:

- Sometimes, when we set aside a suffix, we're left with something that looks like a root word but isn't.
- At other times, when we set aside a suffix, we're left with a root word that isn't spelled just right.

And here are the most important guidelines for spelling changes resulting from suffix removal.

- When a suffix is set aside, the remaining word sometimes needs to be changed in order to be spelled right.
- Sometimes, we need to subtract one of a doubled consonant after we remove a suffix in order to get the correct spelling of a root word.
- Sometimes we need to change an *i* to a *y* after removing a suffix.
- Sometimes we need to add an *e* after we remove a suffix.

Prefixes. As is the case with suffixes, English contains a substantial number of prefixes. Again, though, a small number of them are extremely frequent and thus particularly worth teaching. The Table 5.2, also based on the work of White et al. (1989), shows the 20 most frequently occurring prefixes and the number of prefixed words in the Carroll et al. (1971) list.

As can be seen, the material read by school-age children contains about 3,000 prefixed words; the four most frequent prefixes account for about 1,700 of these words; and the 20 most frequent prefixes account for about 2,800 of them.

Table 5.2. English Prefixes Ranked by Frequency of Occurrence

Prefix	Number of Different Words with the Prefix
un-	782
re-	401
in-,im-,ir-,il-,'not'	313
dis-	216
en-,em-	132
non-	126
in-,im-,'in or into'	105
over- 'too much'	98
mis-	83
sub-	80
pre-	79
inter-	77
fore-	76
de-	71
trans-	47
super-	43
semi-	39
anti-	33
mid-	33
under- 'too little'	25
All others	100 (estimated)
TOTAL	2,959

Unlike suffixes, prefixes usually have a clear lexical meaning which is attached to the base in a fairly straightforward way. Thus, students can use their knowledge of prefixes in unlocking the meanings of unknown words. Also, prefixes tend to be consistently spelled, and they occur at the beginning of words. Thus, they are relatively easy for students to recognize. For both of these reasons, knowing and being able to use a relatively small number of prefixes can be a powerful aid in learning vocabulary.

As is the case with learning to use context and learning to use suffixes, learning to use prefixes requires some basic knowledge.

- Prefixes are meaning-bearing units that are attached to the beginnings of words to change their meaning.
- Knowing the meanings of prefixes and how to use that knowledge in unlocking the meanings of new words is a powerful way of increasing our vocabularies.
- Although prefixes are very useful, they can present some problems: Some prefixes have more than one meaning. Also, some letter sequences that look like prefixes are not.

Non-English Roots. I have included this heading only to note that non-English roots are rare enough in elementary materials that I would not recommend any sort of formal curriculum in them during the elementary years.

Using Glossaries and the Dictionary

In the primary grades, glossaries are extremely useful tools–if students learn to use them. The first thing that students need to know about glossaries is that they exist and are there for their use. The second thing is what they are for; they provide meanings and pronunciations of difficult words in the book. The third thing is how to use them; the major task here is learning to use the pronunciation key. And the fourth thing is when to use them; students need to turn to the glossary when they encounter an unknown word they are unsure of and that word appears to be important to understanding the text.

Dictionaries are in some ways larger and more complex glossaries. Probably the most important thing students need to learn to do with a dictionary is to choose meanings appropriate for the context in which they have found the word. Another important thing students need to learn is which dictionaries are appropriate for them. Students also need to know the characteristics and features of the particular dictionary they use–what the entries for individual words contain and how they are arranged, what aids to its use the dictionary provides, and what features beyond the basic word list the dictionary includes. Much of the important information appears in the front matter of the dictionaries themselves, but it is very seldom read, and simply asking students to read it is not likely to be sufficient instruction. Thus direct instruction in how to use specific dictionaries is needed.

Developing an Approach to Dealing with Unknown Words

If students are going to effectively use what they learn about context cues, word parts, and the dictionary, they need some sort of plan for dealing with unknown words when they encounter them. The following list shows one plan.

- Recognize that an unknown word has occurred and decide whether you need to understand it to understand the passage.
- Attempt to infer the meaning of the unknown word from the context, word parts, and phonics.
- Turn to your glossary, the dictionary, or someone else to get the word's meaning.

This, of course, is only one approach; it obviously will not suit all students. But it does seem extremely important to give students something concrete such as this that they can try, consider, and then modify to fit their needs rather than assuming that they will develop a strategy on their own.

Adopting a Personal Approach to Building Vocabulary

As I noted at the beginning of this section, students will do much of their word learning independently. It therefore makes sense to encourage students to adopt personal plans to expand their vocabularies over time. Options include learning word parts, looking up novel words and keeping a file of them, making a commitment to learn a word a day and actually using those words, using vocabulary building books, doing crossword puzzles, and playing word games of various sorts.

Although one could certainly argue that some of these approaches are better than others, what probably matters most is that a student adopt some approach–some conscious and deliberate plan for improving his or her vocabulary–rather than no plan.

Guidelines for Curriculum of Strategies for Learning Words

As was the case with the overview of the curriculum on individual words, this section begins with some general guidelines and then presents some more specific suggestions for two age ranges. Here, the age ranges are first grade through third grade and fourth grade through sixth grade. Again, the grade level designations are only approximations.

To begin, each of these strategies would be directly taught.

The curriculum would be implemented deliberately and systematically rather than incidentally. For example, it would not be the case that prefixes were considered only if a prefixed word happened to come up in the context of normal reading. Instead, there would be a definite place in the curriculum for prefix instruction.

The strategies would be taught as procedural skills, with the recognition that declarative knowledge about the strategies is only one part of what needs to be learned and that what is really important is that students know how to use the strategies, when to use them, and where to use them.

The strategies would be taught using an active teaching model that included explicit explanation, cognitive modeling, scaffolding, the gradual release of responsibility, guided practice, and the development of true ownership of the procedure on the part of students (see, for example, Duffy & Roehler, 1989; Pearson, 1985).

Explicit explanation of the strategies would follow the suggestions of Winograd and Hare (1988) and include attention to what the strategy is, why it should be used, how to use it, when and where to use it, and how it could be evaluated. Additionally, in keeping with suggestions by Anderson (1989) and Brophy (1989), emphasis would be placed on students thoroughly understanding the strategies, on students' self-regulation of the strategies, on the teacher's role being both that of presenting information and responding to students' learning efforts, and on showing students that the strategies will be useful both in and out of school.

Finally, each of the strategies taught would be reviewed periodically. The reviews would begin with teacher-made, criterion-referenced tests, which would often be quite informal and take the form of teacher-led discussions. If these inquiries indicated that students already knew the material considered for review, the reviews would be greatly shortened or eliminated.

First through Third Grade. Although I just noted that instruction in the strategies would generally be deliberate and systematic, that does not mean that it would always start out that way. In particular, in the primary grades I would present information about context cues and word parts informally as opportunities presented themselves.

Work on an approach to dealing with unknown words would be somewhat more formal, and I would certainly plan times to discuss with children what they might do when they encounter words they do not know. Since, however, they will not yet have had much work with context or word parts, their options are limited.

Work on using glossaries and dictionaries would definitely be systematic, and would begin as soon as children's books contained glossaries and when dictionaries were first introduced.

Finally, students could begin adopting personal approaches to building vocabularies just as soon as they had internalized the concept of a word. Initially, something as simple as bringing in a favorite word each week would be appropriate. Later, other approaches could be suggested, and children could be asked to make a commitment to one of them over some specified period, and perhaps talk about what they thought of the approach once the period was over.

Fourth through Sixth Grade. Fourth grade seems a reasonable point at which to begin systematic instruction in both context cues and word parts. Given that there are nine types of context cues, three of them could be taught in grade four, three in grade five, and three in grade six. Graves and Buikema (1990) taught two of them in a one week unit with good results, and it seems reasonable to group the three for each year together in a single unit and to teaching them in about a week. Because context is such a powerful source for learning vocabulary, the initial unit should probably come early in the school year. This initial instruction could be followed by two two-day reviews, one perhaps in December and another in March. Additionally, when additional one-week units in the other cue types are taught in grades five and six, those taught in previous grades should probably be reviewed. Also, it is worth noting that instruction in any type of cue is likely to result in some general skill in learning from context that will be useful beyond that particular type of cue, and thus it is not the case that students will be unable to make any use of the cues to be taught in sixth grade until they are in sixth grade and have been specifically taught them.

In keeping with White et al. (1989), it seems appropriate to teach the nine most frequent prefixes–which together account for 76% of the prefixed words in Carroll et al. (1971)–in several lessons during the fourth and fifth grade. The remaining less frequent prefixes could be taught during the sixth grade or, since they are infrequent, be taught incidentally as they come up in students' reading. A two-three day unit should be sufficient for initially teaching three or so prefixes, and Graves and Hammond (1979) and White et al. (1989) have described and validated instructional procedures.

Also in keeping with White et al. (1989), I would teach suffixes beginning in grade four. As with prefixes, it makes sense to teach the most frequent suffixes first, and it makes sense to cover all 20 on the list by the end of grade six. Groups of three or four suffixes could be dealt with in two to three day units, and White et al. have validated a simple procedure for doing so.

Instruction in the other three strategies for learning words–Using Glossaries and the Dictionary, Developing an Approach to Dealing with Unknown Words, and Adopting a Personal Approach to Building Vocabulary–will have begun in the primary grades, so the task in the intermediate grades is largely one of review and extension. With glossaries, there is probably little left to do except to point out glossaries in new books, note any peculiarities they have, and generally advertise their use. With dictionaries, students need to be taught to deal with a wider array of dictionaries. Regarding the plan for developing an approach to dealing with unknown words in context, the possibilities need to be reviewed at the beginning of each year. Also, fourth or fifth grade would be a good time to discuss the merits of the plan presented and invite students to adopt individual approaches that are modifications of this plan. Finally, with adopting a personal approach to vocabulary building, the main thing might be to check with students at the beginning of each year on which personal approach they plan to use and get a commitment for the year.

Concluding Remarks

In discussing a vocabulary curriculum for the elementary grades, I have presented a brief history of vocabulary research, commented on current knowledge about vocabulary size and what constitutes in-depth instruction, and listed six sorts of tasks students face in learning specific words and five generative skills that students need if they are to become independent word learners. I have also discussed different levels of word knowledge that one can attain and some guidelines for selecting vocabulary, and I have discussed some principles that guide vocabulary instruction and some grade levels at which different aspects of the curriculum can logically be implemented

All in all, I have said a lot said about a topic that is often presented as being simple and straight forward. It is a legitimate question whether the approach suggested here is too complex. And it may be.

Even while admitting this, however, I want to argue that it is not. The thinking behind any curriculum that spans six years of schooling is bound to be complex. And it seems to me that it is up to those of us who are teachers, those who are administrators, and those who are teachers of teachers to grapple with and explicate this complexity. If we are going to be efficient–and given the dwindling resources schools have and are likely to get, efficiency is paramount–it is vital for individual teachers and those responsible for the vocabulary curriculum over the elementary years to know just what the curriculum is, what parts of the curriculum students have already mastered in the past, and what parts of it they will encounter as they continue in school. Only with such knowledge can we hope to effectively involve students in activities that lead to their mastering the knowledge and strategies that are important in vocabulary or any other area of study.

References

Anderson, L. M. (1989). Implementing instructional programs to promote meaningful, self-regulated learning. In J. Brophy (Ed.), *Advances in research on teaching,* Vol. 1 (pp. 311-344). Greenwich, CT: JAI Press.

Anderson, R. C., & Freebody, P. (1981). Vocabulary knowledge. In J. Guthrie (Ed.), *Comprehension and teaching: Research reviews.* (pp. 77-117). Newark, DE: International Reading Association.

Anderson, R. C., & Freebody, P. (1983). Reading comprehension and the assessment and acquisition of word knowledge. In B. Hutton (Ed.), *Advances in reading/language research, a research annual.* Greenwich, CT: JAI Press.

Barr, R., Kamil, M. L., Mosenthal, P., & Pearson, P. D. (Eds.). (1991). *Handbook of reading research* (Vol. II). New York: Longman.

Baumann, J. F., & Kameenui, E. J. (1991). Research on vocabulary instruction: Ode to Voltaire. In J. Flood, J.M. Jensen, D. Lapp, & J. Squire (Eds.), *Research on teaching the English language arts* (pp. 604-632). New York: Macmillan.

Beck, I. L. (1985, November). *Response to William Nagy's "Vocabulary instructions: Implications of the new research."* Paper presented at the meeting of the National Council of Teachers of English, Philadelphia.

Beck, I. L., McCaslin, E. S., & McKeown, M. G. (1980). *The rationale and design of a program to teach vocabulary to fourth-grade students.* Pittsburgh: University of Pittsburgh, Learning Research and Development Center.

Beck, I. L., & McKeown, M. G. (1990). Conditions of vocabulary acquisition. In P.D. Pearson (Ed.), *The handbook of reading research, Vol. 2.* New York: Longman.

Beck, I. L., & McKeown, M. G. (1983). Learning words well. A program to enhance vocabulary and comprehension. *The Reading Teacher, 36,* 622-625.

Beck, I. L., McKeown, M. G., McCaslin, E. S., & Burkes, A. M. (1979). *Instructional dimensions that may affect reading comprehension: Examples from two commercial reading programs.* Pittsburgh: University of Pittsburgh, Learning Research and Development Center.

Beck, I. L., McKeown, M. G., & Omanson, R. C. (1987). The effects and uses of diverse vocabulary instructional techniques. In McKeown, M.G., & Curtis, M.E. (1987). *The nature of vocabulary acquisition.* Hillsdale, NJ: Erlbaum.

Beck, I. L., McKeown, M. G., & Omanson, R. C. (1984, April). *The fertility of some types of vocabulary instruction.* Paper presented at the meeting of the American Educational Research Association, New Orleans.

Beck, I. L., Perfetti, C. A., & McKeown, M. G. (1982). The effects of long-term vocabulary instruction on lexical access and reading comprehension. *Journal of Educational Psychology, 74,* 506-521.

Becker, W. C. (1977). Teaching reading and language to the disadvantaged–What we have learned from field research. *Harvard Educational Review, 47,* 518-543.

Brophy, J. (1989). Conclusion: Toward a theory of teaching. In J. Brophy (Ed.), *Advances in research on teaching,* Vol. 1 (pp. 345-355). Greenwich, CT: JAI Press.

Calfee, R. C., & Drum, P. A. (1986). Research on teaching reading. In M.D. Wittrock (Ed.), *Handbook of research on teaching* (3rd ed., pp. 804-849). New York: Macmillan.

Calfee, R. C., & Drum, P. A. (1978). Learning to read: Theory, research, and practice. *Curriculum Inquire, 8,* 183-249.

Carroll, J. B, Davies, P., & Richman, B. (1971). *The American heritage word frequency book.* New York: Houghton Mifflin.

Chomsky, N. (1957). *Syntactic structures.* The Hague: Mouton.

Clifford, G. J. (1978). Words for schools: The applications in education of the vocabulary researches of Edward L. Thorndike. In P. Suppes (Ed.), *Impact of research on education: some case studies* (pp. 107-198). Washington, D.C.: National Academy of Education.

Clark, H. H., & Clark, E. V. (1978). *Psychology of language.* New York: Harcourt, Brace, Jovanovich.

Duin, A. H., & Graves, M. F. (1988). Teaching vocabulary as a writing prompt. *Journal of Reading, 22,* 204-212.

Duin, A. H., & Graves, M. F. (1987). The effects of intensive vocabulary instruction on expository writing. *Reading Research Quarterly, 22,* 311-330.

Duin, A. H., & Graves, M. F. (1986). Effects of vocabulary instruction as a prewriting task. *Journal of Research and Development in Education, 26,* 7-13.

Duffy, G. G., & Roehler, L. R. (1989). The tension between information-giving and mediation: Perspectives on instructional explanation and teacher change. In J. Brophy (Ed.), *Advances in research on teaching,* Vol. 1 (pp. 1-34). Greenwich, CT: JAI Press.

Dupuy, H. P. (1974). *The rationale, development and standardization of a basic word vocabulary test* (DHEW Publication No. HRA 74-1334). Washington, D.C.: U. S. Government Printing Office.

Freebody, P., & Anderson, R. C. (1983a). Effects of vocabulary difficulty, text cohesion, and schema availability on reading comprehension. *Reading Research Quarterly, 18,* 277-305.

Freebody, P., & Anderson, R.C. (1983b). Effects on text comprehension of differing proportions and locations of difficult vocabulary. *Journal of Reading Behavior, 15,* 19-40.

Graves, M. F. (1987). The role of instruction in vocabulary development. In M. G. McKeown & M. E. Curtis (Eds.), *The nature of vocabulary acquisition* (pp. 165-184). Hillsdale, NJ: Erlbaum.

Graves, M. F. (1986). Vocabulary learning and instruction. In E. Z. Rothkopf (Ed.), *Review of Research in Education* (Vol. 13, pp. 49-90). Washington, D.C.: American Educational Research Association.

Graves, M. F. (1985). *A word is a word... Or is it.* New York: Scholastic Book Services.

Graves, M. F. (1984). Selecting vocabulary to teach in the intermediate and secondary grades. In J. Flood (Ed.), *Promoting reading comprehension* (pp. 245-260). Newark, DE: International Reading Association.

Graves, M. F. (1978). Types of reading vocabulary to teach. *Minnesota English Journal, 19,* 2-17.

Graves, M. F., & Buikema, J. L. (1990, April). *Effects of teaching context cues on junior high school students' ability to infer meanings of unknown words.* Paper presented at the meeting of the American Educational Research Association, Boston.

Graves, M. F., & Duin, A. L. (1985). Building students' expressive vocabularies. *Educational Perspectives, 23* (1), 4-10.

Graves, M. F., & Hammond, H. K. (1979, December). A validated procedure for teaching prefixes and its effect on students' ability to assign meaning to novel words. In M.L. Kamil & A.J. Moe (Eds.), *Perspectives on reading research and instruction.* Washington, D.C.: National Reading Conference.

Graves, M. F., & Prenn, M. C. (1986). Costs and benefits of different methods of vocabulary instruction. *Journal of Reading, 29,* 596-602.

Graves, M. F., Slater, W. H., White, T. G. (1989). *Teaching content area vocabulary.* In D. Lapp. J. Flood, & N. Farnan (Eds.), (pp. 219-224). Englewood Cliffs, NJ: Prentice Hall.

Jenkins, J. R., Stein, M. L., & Wysocki, K. (1984). Learning vocabulary through reading. *American Educational Research Journal, 21,* 767-787.

Kirkpatrick, E. A. (1891). The number of words in an ordinary vocabulary. *Science, 18,* 107-108.

LaBerge, D., & Samuels, S. J. (1974). Toward a theory of automatic information processing in reading. *Cognitive Psychology, 6,* 293-323.

McKeown, M. G. (1985). The acquisition of word meaning from context by children of high and low ability. *Reading Research Quarterly, 20,* 482-496.

McKeown, M. G., Beck, I. L., Omanson, R. ., & Perfetti, C. A. (1983). The effects of long-term vocabulary instruction on reading comprehension: A replication. *Journal of Reading Behavior, 15,* 3-18.

McKeown, M. G., Beck, I. L., Omanson, R. C., & Pople, M. T. (1985). Some effects of the nature and frequency of vocabulary instruction on the knowledge and use of words. *Reading Research Quarterly, 20,* 522-535.

McKeown, M. G., & Curtis, M. E. (1987). *The nature of vocabulary acquisition.* Hillsdale, NJ: Erlbaum.

Miller, G. A. (1962). Some psychological studies of grammar. *American Psychologist, 17,* 748-762.

Miller, G. A., & Gildea, P. M. (1987). How children learn words. *Scientific American. 257* (3), 94-99.

Nagy, W. E. (1985, November). *Vocabulary instruction: Implications of the new research.* Paper presented at the meeting of the National Council of Teachers of English, Philadelphia.

Nagy, W. E., & Anderson, R. C. (1984). How many words are there in printed school English? *Reading Research Quarterly, 19,* 304-330.

Nagy, W. E., & Anderson, R. C. (1982). *The number of words in printed school English* (Tech. Rep. No. 253). Urbana, IL: University of Illinois, Center for the Study of Reading.

Nagy, W. E., Anderson, R. C., & Herman, P. A. (1987). Learning word meanings from context during normal reading. *American Educational Research Journal, 24,* 237-270.

Nagy, W. E., & Herman, P. A. (1987). Depth and breadth of vocabulary knowledge: Implications for acquisition and instruction. In M. G. McKeown & M. E. Curtis (Eds.), *The nature of vocabulary acquisition* (pp. 119-35). Hillsdale, NJ: Erlbaum.

Nagy, W. E., & Herman, P. A. (1984, April). *The futility of most types of vocabulary instruction.* Paper presented at the meeting of the American Educational Research Association, New Orleans.

Nagy, W. E., Herman, P. A., & Anderson, R. C. (1985). Learning words from context. *Reading Research Quarterly, 20,* 233-253.

Neisser, U. (1967). *Cognitive psychology.* New York: Appleton-Century-Crofts.

Pearson, P. D. (1985). Changing the face of reading comprehension instruction. *The Reading Teacher, 38,* 724-738.

Pearson, P. D., Barr, R., Kamil, M. L., & Mosenthal, P. (1984). *Handbook of reading research.* New York: Longman.

Slobin, D.I. (1966). Grammatical transformations and sentence comprehension in childhood and adulthood. *Journal of Verbal Learning and Verbal Behavior, 5,* 219-227.

Sternberg, R. J. (1987). Most vocabulary is learned from context. In M. G. McKeown & M. E. Curtis (Eds.), *The nature of vocabulary acquisition* (pp. 89-105). Hillsdale, NJ: Erlbaum.

Sternberg, R. J., & Powell, J. S. (1983). Comprehending verbal comprehension. *American Psychologist, 38,* 878-893.

Sternberg, R. J., Powell, J. S., & Kaye, D. B. (1983). Teaching vocabulary-building skills: A contextual approach. In A. C. Wilkinson, (Ed.), *Classroom computers and cognitive science* (pp. 121-143). New York: Academic Press.

Thorndike, E. L. (1921). *The teacher's word book.* New York: Teachers College.

White, T. G., Graves, M. F., & Slater, W. H. (1990). Development of recognition and reading vocabularies in diverse sociolinguistic and educational settings. *Journal of Educational Psychology, 82,* 281-290.

White, T. G., Power, M. A., & White, S. (1989). Morphological analysis: Implications for teaching and understanding vocabulary growth. *Reading Research Quarterly, 24,* 283-304.

White, T. G., Sowell, J., & Yanagihara, A. (1989). Teaching elementary students to use word-part clues. *The Reading Teacher, 42,* 302-308.

Winograd, P., & Hare, V. C. (1988). Direct instruction of reading comprehension strategies: The nature of teacher explanation. In C.E. Weinstein, E. T. Goetz, & P.A. Alexander, *Learning and study strategies: Issues in assessment, instruction, and evaluation.* New York: Academic Press.

6

Young Students' Social Studies Learning: Going for Depth

Isabel L. Beck and Margaret G. McKeown

In the middle of their elementary school years, students begin to make a transition from reading almost exclusively narrative texts to being expected to learn about new content areas from almost exclusively expository texts. Many students experience difficulty with this transition, and conventional wisdom suggests that the expository genre is at the heart of this difficulty.

In this chapter, we explore the characteristics of expository text that make it difficult for students by describing some recent research on social studies texts (Beck, McKeown, & Gromoll, 1989; Beck, McKeown, Sinatra, & Loxterman, in press; McKeown, & Beck, 1990; McKeown, Beck, Sinatra, & Loxterman, 1990). The aim of the research was first to analyze potential difficulties of the texts and then to investigate the effects of those difficulties on student learning. The investigation also examined ways to override the problems that expository texts present.

An issue often identified as the source of difficulty with expository text is its unfamiliarity. Young students are accustomed to reading narratives, which have a predictable structure that includes a goal or problem, attempts to solve the problem, and some form of resolution. This structure is familiar to young children even before their experiences with written language because narratives mirror human social interactions. So the notion is that because of its familiarity, narrative structure can serve as a framework for a reader's comprehension (Mandler & Johnson, 1977; Rumelhart, 1975; Stein & Glenn, 1979; Thorndyke, 1977). Expository prose, on the other hand, has no inherent structural elements. An expository text is structured to fit its communicative purpose, and thus its structure is derived from its purpose.

Research has been done to discover whether there is some basic set of expository patterns that writers employ. Several common structures have been identified, including cause/effect, comparison/contrast, problem/solution, description, and collection (Meyer, 1975). Although these structures describe the patterns of expository text to a great extent, they cannot serve as a framework for the reader in the same way that narrative structure can. One reason is that natural expository text can rarely be characterized by a single structure. Rather, most natural expository texts exhibit a mix of structures, and any structure may exist at the sentence, paragraph, or passage level (Hiebert, Englert, & Brennan, 1983; Meyer & Freedle, 1984). For example, a piece about air pollution in a city might begin with what appears to be a problem/ solution framework by presenting air pollution as a problem and exploring solutions to alleviate it. Yet, within the text there could be cause/effect structures that detail the sources of pollution and its consequences, descriptive passages that tell how buildings look because of the presence of pollutants, and comparison/contrast passages that sketch aspects of the polluted city in relation to a pristine environment.

Another reason that these structures do not have the power of narrative structure is that they are not unique to expository text; narrative contains these patterns as well (Stein, 1986). Indeed, children are typically introduced to these structures quite early in their school careers; for example, first grade workbook exercises ask students to contrast and compare objects or to mark a picture that identifies the cause of some effect. Thus the particular structures that characterize expository text are not new for students, rather the unfamiliar aspect is the content that these structures present within an exposition.

Even though the specific types of structures in expository texts are likely familiar, an important structural ingredient that makes narrative text easier for students is missing; that is, there is no overarching framework that a reader can use to organize and relate the information in the text. Thus, because students have no predictable structure which they can bring to an expository text, expectations about the text can only be based on knowledge of the content topic. However, because the purpose of expository text is to communicate new information (Black, 1985), the content topic is likely to be unfamiliar. Thus, two influences on comprehension take on increased importance when readers interact with expository text. One is the familiarity of the content or topic. The other is the extent to which the content of a specific text is organized in a logical way.

Problematic Features of Social Studies Textbooks

In consideration of the influence of these two issues in comprehending expository text, the Beck et al. (1989) analysis of social studies textbooks focused on whether the background knowledge assumed by the texts seemed realistic in terms of what target age students were likely to know, and the coherence of text, which is an aspect of organization or structure.

Background Knowledge

The purpose of expository text is to present new information. Yet, in order to learn information, a learner needs to be able to connect the information with what is already known. Thus, to be effective, an expository text must strike a balance between what a learner knows and does not yet know. If what a learner knows is not sufficient background for him or her to be able to understand the target ideas in the text, then the text is too difficult. Recent research has emphasized the role of background knowledge in comprehension. Because reading is a constructive process, readers need to integrate their knowledge with information from the text in order to understand the text. Research has indicated not only that a lack of knowledge about a topic impedes comprehension but also that the extent and depth of knowledge influence the quality of understanding derived from a text. Voss and his colleagues (Chiesi, Spilich, & Voss, 1979; Spilich, Vesonder, Chiesi, & Voss, 1979) showed how the quality of text recall differed between people with high and low knowledge of a topic. High-knowledge people were more likely to recall the sequence of events that developed the theme of the text and to integrate events to construct a representation of the text. Low-knowledge people were more likely to recall information peripheral to the main idea of the text. Similarly, Pearson, Hansen, and Gordon (1979) showed that children with high knowledge of a topic were better able to answer questions about a text that required them to draw inferences.

Our analysis of social studies textbooks led to the conclusion that many ideas and events portrayed in the books were beyond young students' grasp because the texts assumed unrealistic levels of knowledge. One example of the kind of knowledge assumed by the texts occurs in a section about Britain's taxation of the colonies that led to the rallying cry "No taxation without representation." The explanation of what led the colonists to that motto consists of the information that the colonists were not members of Parliament (which is described as "the British lawmaking body") and that their own colonial assemblies had not voted for the taxes that Britain wanted the colonists to pay. In order for this information to lead to an understanding of the motto about no taxation, a reader needs to know what it means to be members of–and therefore represented in–a government, and that the colonial assemblies were colonial governing bodies with members elected by the colonists. However, these two issues were not discussed in the text.

Another example occurred in the discussion of Britain's punishment of Boston after the Boston Tea Party. The text states that "The port of Boston was closed." But how this functioned as a punishment cannot be understood without knowing the role of a port as a supply line in the days before sophisticated road transportation.

Text Coherence

The coherence of a text, or a related construct, text considerateness, is also an important factor in determining a text's comprehensibility. Coherence refers to the extent to which the sequencing of ideas in a text makes sense and the extent to which the language used to present those ideas makes the nature of the ideas and their relationships apparent. A coherent text fits together in a logical way (Trabasso, Secco, & van den Broek, 1984). Similarly, *considerate* text is described as one that maximizes the possibility for a reader to gain information and establish relationships among concepts (Anderson & Armbruster, 1984). According to Anderson and Armbruster, a considerate text is characterized by a structure that conveys its purpose, logical relationships among connected ideas, unity of purpose, and audience appropriateness (i.e., the text fits the knowledge base of the target reader). Several studies have provided both further description of aspects that characterize considerate text and evidence for the facilitation provided by texts that display considerateness. Slater and Graves (1985) analyzed and revised text passages along four dimensions–structure, coherence, unity, and elaboration–and found that both skilled and less skilled learners had greater comprehension from the revised passages. Baumann (1986) made texts more considerate by revising them so that main ideas were stated explicitly at the beginning of discussion related to the ideas and were highlighted visually by italics and underlining. He found that students were better able to recall information about main ideas from the revised texts.

The influence on comprehension of several textual elements related to coherence has also been identified experimentally. Among those elements that affect comprehension negatively are the use of references that are ambiguous (Frederiksen, 1981), distant (Cirilo, 1981; Lesgold, Roth, & Curtis, 1979), or indirect (Haviland & Clark, 1974; Just & Carpenter, 1979), inclusion of concepts for which the reader lacks requisite background (Chiesi, et al., 1979; Pearson, et al., 1979) lack of clear relationships between events (Black & Bern, 1981; Kintsch, Mandel, & Kozminsky, 1977; Stein & Nezworski, 1978), and inclusion of events or ideas that are irrelevant to the rest of the text (Schank, 1975; Trabasso et al., 1984). Texts that have been revised in consideration of such elements of coherence have resulted in enhanced comprehension for young learners (Beck, McKeown, Omanson, & Pople, 1984; Beck et al., in press).

Our analysis suggested that social studies textbook presentations lacked coherence. Geography information, for example, often re-sembled a catalog of features rather than a sequence of related ideas. Consider, for example, a discussion of the tundra that characterizes the region as dark and gloomy for most of the year with winters that last from October until March, with no trees to break the strong winds, and with scraggly bushes and grasses as the only plant life able to grow there. The text then describes the nomadic existence of herders on the tundra. But the text fails to relate their lifestyle to the climatic conditions–that, for instance, because so little vegetation is available, these people must move about in order to find food for themselves and their animals.

Showing the Effects of Knowledge and Coherence on Comprehension

The analysis of textbooks provided strong suggestions about why young students might have problems with their content area reading. Further research then explored the issues of background knowledge and coherence with intermediate grade students. McKeown and Beck (1990) investigated the match between fifth graders' background knowledge and the information assumed by the text in a presentation about events leading to the Revolutionary War.

Fifth grade students were interviewed just before they studied the Revolutionary period. The interview was based on two broad notions that the analysis indicated were largely assumed by the textbooks: the role of England in the colonists' struggle for independence and ideas about representative government. The results showed that most students' knowledge about these issues and this period in history tended to be vague and contained many inaccuracies. For example, only 3 of the 35 students interviewed mentioned England when asked to talk about what the 13 original colonies were, and only 2 of the students were able to give any information about what representation in a government meant. Of course, such results were not surprising for students who had not yet studied this material formally; what may seem surprising, however, is that the textbooks do seem to assume that this information is under students' control already.

Two subsequent studies then investigated the impact of background knowledge and coherence on comprehension of expository text by comparing conditions in which students were given more or less coherent texts after having received more or less adequate background knowledge related to the topic (Beck et al., in press; McKeown et al., 1990). The less coherent texts were passages taken from a fifth grade textbook, and the more coherent texts were revised versions of those passages. The less adequate background knowledge was what was provided in the text and text-based lessons that students received in their regular classrooms. The more adequate background was a specially designed lesson based on concepts shown to be missing or difficult for students and needed for comprehension of the text to succeed.

Development of Text Revisions

The revisions made to the textbook passages were intended to establish coherence by clarifying, elaborating, explaining, and motivating important information and making relationships explicit. Our approach to revisions involved an attempt to simulate the process of the interaction between a reader–in this case a 10-year-old–and a text. Thus texts were evaluated by considering how each new piece of text information might be handled, the kind of knowledge that the reader would need to bring to bear, and how the developing text representation would be influenced.

Points where the process might break down, such as when the result of some action was not specific or when a new concept was not explained or elaborated, were hypothesized, and ways in which an ideal reader might repair such breaks were generated. These potential repairs were used as the basis for the revised version of the text. As we considered what might happen within this 10-year-old's comprehension process, we switched back and forth among a) hypothesizing what the student might be thinking, b) considering what seemed to be intended by the text, and c) constructing text statements that might bring about understanding of the intended notions for the target reader.

The goal of the revisions was to create a text based on a causal sequence of events with the information presented to explain the connections from a cause to an event and from an event to a consequence.

As an example of the kind of revisions made, consider how the original text portrayed one of the punishments imposed on Massachusetts after the Boston Tea Party. The text, after stating that the Intolerable Acts were "meant to punish the people of Boston," uses separate sentences to specify some of the actions taken, including "No self-government was allowed." The problem here is twofold. First, the punishment is not explicitly connected to the British actions, and second, what self-government is and, thus, what the lack of it means to the colonists is left for the readers to infer.

The revised text begins discussion on this aspect of the Intolerable Acts by explicitly labelling it as a British action: "Another thing that the British did was to stop self-government in Massachusetts." The revised version then continues, "This meant they no longer allowed the colonists to make any decisions about how their colony was run. The colonists used to be able to make some decisions on their own, but now Britain took those rights away."

Design of Instruction to Enhance Background Knowledge

In designing a background knowledge instruction module, we considered which concepts were prerequisite to the sequence of events presented in the text and evidence of what was missing from students' understanding based on the McKeown and Beck study (1990). The main focus of the content presented in the module was on distinguishing the major agents of the Revolutionary period, the colonists and Britain. To establish the purpose for the lesson, students were told that because they would soon be reading and learning about the American Revolution, which was described as "a war that the American colonists fought for their independence against Britain over two hundred years ago," they were going to talk about some things that might help them understand that time in history; specifically they were going to talk about some of the people and places that were involved in this period.

The module began by establishing five geographic and/or political entities, North America, Britain, France, Massachusetts, and Boston, that are referred to in the text, but about which, based on our data from previous studies, the students had confusions–and they had these confusions in spite of the fact that they had just finished several weeks of study about colonization which included many mentions of the entities. So the first component of the background knowledge module aimed at establishing these entities and relating them to what students might know about their existence today. To accomplish this purpose, some map work was done, and then the experimenter introduced two side by side charts. One was titled "Today, about 200 years after the Revolutionary War," the other was titled "Before the Revolutionary War, between about 1760 and 1775." Under each title, the five entities–North America, Britain, France, Massachusetts, and Boston– were printed down the side of the charts. The charts contained descriptors for each of the entities which were covered when the chart was first introduced.

Through a series of questions, the experimenter established the entities in terms of what they are today, and what they were before the Revolutionary War, uncovering each descriptor as it was discussed. For example, on the "Today" chart, Britain was described as, "A country

3,000 miles away from North America. Sometimes Britain is called England," and on the "Before the Revolutionary War " chart as "The country that owned the 13 original colonies." When all the descriptors were uncovered, students were encouraged to engage with the information by using it to answer questions such as, "Were the 13 original colonies near Britain?" (The relevant information on the charts was that the 13 original colonies were in North America and that Britain is 3,000 miles away from North America.)

Next students were asked to turn their thinking to "the people who lived in the 13 colonies, the people we call colonists." The intent of this section was to develop the notion that over the years the colonists were losing their British identity and developing an American identity.

To help students develop the notion of American identity, first the experimenter told the students that many of the people who came to the colonies in the 1600s were British, and even though they lived far away from Britain, they felt British. The script for the lesson used the term identity and explained that someone's *identity* is what they feel they are. Mention was made that the students had an American identity because they feel American. The experimenter explained that as years went by, a lot of the colonists began to lose their British identity, began to feel separate from the British, and they even began to call themselves Americans.

To encourage students to engage with the information, the experimenter asked the students, "Why do you think there was this change?" and provided prompts and questions toward developing the notion that the colonists had established a very different life style from that in Britain. For instance, she said, "Let's think of what the colonists had to do when they first came over here. Did they have houses to move into? Were there stores to go to?" Attention was also brought to the influence of the passage of time in changing the colonists' identity. That is, students were told "that a lot of time passed–about 100 years–between when people started coming to the colonies and the middle 1700s, the time we are talking about now." The students were then asked why the passage of time might bring about changes in how the colonists felt.

The final portion of the identity section involved the experimenter reading descriptions of people and the students deciding whether the individual would be more likely to have a British or American identity. For example:

> My name is Samantha Stevens. I spent many years of my life getting a school going in our town and helping to teach the children. I am very proud of the work I've done and how much our children learn. In Britain, only those who can afford it send their children to school. That used to seem fine to me. But here everyone goes to school–and I really think that is the way it should be! What is Samantha's identity?

The experimenter introduced the next topic to students by saying that having thought a little about the people who lived in the colonies, they were now going to be asked to think a little about how the 13 colonies were governed. To start this section the experimenter posed the question, "Who decided how things were run in the 13 colonies–was it the British, or was it the colonists, or was it both–the British and the colonists?" After the students made their choice, the experimenter established that both the British and the colonists were involved in running the colonies.

The experimenter explained that the 13 colonies "weren't united into one country. Each of the 13 colonies had their own little government" and that an important part of that government was something called a colonial assembly which made many of the rules and laws for the colony. It was also established that people became members of an assembly through elections.

Students were then told that, "in addition to the laws the assemblies made, the government over in Britain could make rules and laws that all the colonies had to follow...So the colonies had some self-government, but they did not have complete self-government." The final governmental information presented to the students was about Britain having a king and parliament, which was where the laws were made, "something like our Congress."

The last activity, intended to further reinforce the distinctions between the colonists and the British, involved "thinking a little more about the different ways that the British and the colonists acted and thought." Here the experimenter introduced a chart that had on one side an illustration of some British characters, including King George, and on the other side some colonial characters. She then read some "quotes" that were explained as, "something that someone in one of these groups might say" and the students were to decide whether it was probably said by someone in the British group or someone in the colonial group. For example, "I vote for people who go to the Massachusetts' Assembly." "I can make laws for all the colonies." "My grandparents sailed 3,000 miles across the Atlantic Ocean." "I vote for people in Parliament."

In summary, the content in the 35-minute knowledge module was based on information identified as important background information that had been assumed by the textbook presentation. It is important to emphasize that the material in the instructional module did not present the sequence of events described in the text, but introduced major agents and prerequisite concepts needed to construct a representation of that sequence from the text material.

Findings from the Studies
Across the two studies there were students who read either the original or the revised text with inadequate background knowledge and students who read one or the other version of the text after having background knowledge provided in the lesson we created. Comprehension was measured by recall of the text and by sets of open-ended questions that queried the sequence of events and the relationships among people and events described in the text.

The results showed that both coherence of text and background knowledge contributed to comprehension in separate ways. First, students who read the more coherent (revised) text, both those who were provided with adequate background knowledge and those who were not, had better comprehension than students who read the original text, either with or without the added knowledge lesson.

Second, students who received the background knowledge lesson showed a comprehension advantage over students who did not have that information available. Thus, having background knowledge did contribute to a more successful outcome, but background knowledge did not completely compensate for the problems of the text presentation–greater text coherence made for further enhancement to comprehension. Since the two groups had the identical background information available, it seems that the students who read the original text were unable to bring this information to bear as they read.

Of particular note was that the pattern of advantage found for students who received the background knowledge depended on which text they read. This pattern emerged when we examined students' responses to two types of questions asked as part of the study. The first type asked students about the roles of the agents in the Revolutionary conflict, such as "Who took part in the Boston Tea Party?" The other type of question involved understanding the principle that motivated the colonists' action in protesting British taxes, namely, that they refused to be taxed by a government in which they were not represented. We found that the knowledge module helped the readers of the revised text somewhat in responding to the agent questions and gave them a strong advantage in responding to the principle questions. For readers of the original text, their advantage was almost solely in response to the agent questions. Thus it seems that the advantage derived from the knowledge module was limited for readers of the original group to more basic issues–distinguishing the two sides in the upcoming conflict. Readers of the revised text, however, seemed to be able to combine the advantage of the knowledge module with the greater coherence of the revised text to build understanding of the more complex issues of the text.

Classroom Connections for Social Studies

The results of the work with upgrading text coherence and enhancing background knowledge clearly points out the inadequacies of textbook material in elementary social studies and suggest the need for rather extensive teacher intervention to compensate for what students do not get from the text. Of course, the assumption has always been that even with a textbook as the core of the curriculum, the teacher would add other aspects to social studies learning. Traditionally, this has been most likely to include preparing students to read the text by providing background information or a purpose for reading particular content, class discussion of text material, and activities such as having students do additional reading and prepare written or oral reports. Thus we realize that we are not contributing significantly to implications for practice merely by suggesting that teachers should intervene. Rather our concern in the rest of this chapter is with the extent to which things beyond the textbook enter the social studies curriculum and how those things are implemented: not *that* they are done, but *how* they are done warrants consideration.

The work we have done with elementary social studies texts and students and what students get from their texts has put us in a position to consider the kind of teacher intervention that will be most effective for learning elementary social studies. Our recommendations for classsroom practice can be capsulized as two bywords:–*Go for Depth* and–*Make Connections*! These are actually overlapping themes to a great extent, because the major reason to explore content in a deep way is to enable connections between ideas that make the content meaningful.

One thing that becomes clear from our research is that the level of intervention that is needed to make textbook content meaningful precludes attending to the breadth of material that is presented in the textbooks. For example, the fifth grade history texts cover early Native American civilization through the present day. There is no way that fifth graders can develop adequate understanding of all these topics in the course of a year.

Of course, the next issue along this line of thinking is, then what gets left out? But consider that, as the curriculum now stands, very little is getting in; that is, students leave their study of history with limited growth of knowledge, and often with misconceptions of past events and circumstances. So there is almost nothing to lose by cutting back on some of the attempted coverage. This view is stated, however, in full realization that coverage of a textbook in its entirety is often mandated for teachers. Thus, mindful of that framework, we recommend that several important topics be selected for indepth coverage, topics identified because of their influence across the curriculum.

Although we admit to a personal bias, one such topic for elementary American history might be the Revolutionary War. The Revolutionary period has special significance because of its influence in subsequent history topics and because its principles are strongly reflected in diverse aspects of American culture. Having selected a topic for indepth attention, we now move to considering sources from which to draw to develop content depth.

One obvious, available, and universally acknowledged resource for adding to the social studies curriculum is the use of tradebooks. It is a longstanding recommendation that literature be used in conjunction with social studies because it can serve to set the scene for periods in history or bring to life other cultures and other time periods. There are a variety of roles that tradebooks might play. A useful way of considering these roles might be to envision a continuum of how the books might be integrated into the curriculum. The continuum would begin with providing a list of resources for students to use independently, to having resources available in the classroom, to using recreational reading time to share a book that relates to a topic being studied, and finally to bringing tradebooks into the focus of instruction in direct ways.

Activities for each point on the continuum have instructional merit, although they have different goals and meet different learning needs. First, consider making a bibliography of books related to a topic available to students for them to pursue on their own. An abundance of titles in both literature and nonfiction are readily available on most of the topics covered in elementary social studies. One comprehensive source for such titles is new annotated bibliography from California's Department of Education, *Literature for History-Social Science K-8*. Additionally, current textbooks usually include bibliographies of readings on the topics they cover. Making a bibliography available has the advantage of introducing students to the greatest variety of material and alerts them to the range of writings on a topic; thus it has the greatest potential for containing "something for everyone." But it also demands individual motivation from students if any benefit is to accrue.

A second point along the continuum would be having a selection of the books available in the classroom for students to utilize in their independent reading. Having a selection of relevant books in the classroom increases their availability and therefore decreases the demands on student motivation, to some degree. A classroom library, of course, has numerous benefits beyond the potential for adding to students' understanding of topics being studied. Independent reading is encouraged as well as sharing of books and ideas from books within the classroom.

The third point would include the teacher's reading aloud one of the books to the class for recreational reading. Having the teacher read one particular book aloud to the class brings an even sharper focus to the sharing of literacy. It also gives the teacher an opportunity to introduce students to a piece of literature that may be beyond their independent reading level, and to initiate discussion of ideas from the book.

The primary reason for selecting a book that relates to a period of history being studied need not be to have students learn the historical content in the book. For example, imagine that a teacher whose fifth grade class is studying the American Revolutionary period decided to read *Johnny Tremain* to her students. We would not want to see the power and drama of that story subjugated to requiring the students learn the historical material that the novel contains. However, experiencing the story of Johnny Tremain may well help students understand the problems and motivations of the colonists in pre-Revolutionary America, even without making that an explicit goal of the shared piece of literature. Indeed, students may find themselves very involved in that past time and learning a great deal about it without intending to. This kind of learning can provide the context that can help students build connections to formally presented information. Indeed, we recall a 12-year-old who excelled in a social studies unit on westward expansion after having read *Old Yeller*.

Another way to use tradebooks to provide a context for the study of a period in history is to introduce students to significant players in the events of the period through biographies. Developing familiarity with some of the characters of a historical period can provide a basis for subsequent interest in and understanding of the chain of events underlying the period. In exploring how history was taught in earlier eras, we come across a sequence of study that initiated with the introduction of historic figures. In 1892, a historian named David Montgomery published a volume of biographical sketches that was intended to serve as an introduction to his history text for upper elementary students. As we leafed through the stories of Miles Standish, William Penn, Ben Franklin, Eli Whitney, Thomas Jefferson and the like, we could not help but feel a bit envious of those young learners. We were impressed with the quality of the sketches in terms of the way they captured both the humanity and special accomplishments of the individuals. As such, when young students subsequently encountered these people as agents in historical events they might well have had some sense of who they were and some identity with their efforts and goals.

Moving beyond implicitly establishing a context for learning brings us to the farthest end of the continuum. Here tradebooks would be brought into the focus of instruction by directly relating their content to what is being covered in the social studies textbooks. Information presented in tradebooks can help students make the connections that are required for the development of understanding a topic, whether it be the causes and consequences of events in history or the relationship of weather patterns to life in a region in geography. At this end of the continuum the focus would be on having students read selective portrayals of historical events being studied in order to discuss the key ideas and develop an understanding of how and why certain sequences of events occurred.

In our analysis of history content, our view was that a goal for fifth graders studying the period leading to the Revolution should be to develop an initial understanding of the sequence of events–*why* certain events led to subsequent events–that culminated in war between Britain and the colonies. Our research has demonstrated that the textbooks do not provide content that is sufficiently explicit to allow young students to develop understanding of events and phenomena, nor do the texts provide explanations adequate to promote drawing connections among sequences of ideas. Thus a teacher might draw from tradebooks the content that provides a basis from which students can construct understanding.

A demonstration of the benefits that students might get from tradebooks can be seen by comparing the treatment of the concept of "no taxation without representation" in a social studies textbook with a tradebook that focuses on the Revolutionary period. The textbook reads:

> **"No taxation without representation!"** The British lawmaking body was and still is called Parliament. The colonists were not members. The British started passing laws to tax the colonies. Britain thought the colonists should pay their share of the cost of the French and Indian War. The taxes would also help pay for keeping British soldiers in America. The soldiers would serve along the borders of the colonies to protect the settlers from Indian attacks. It seemed fair to the British that the colonists share these costs too. They put taxes on legal papers and everyday items such as glass, paint, and tea.
>
> The colonists got very upset about these taxes. Their own colonial assemblies had not voted for them. They did not welcome Parliament's tax laws. Their motto became, "No taxation without representation." (Silver Burdett, 1984, p. 106)

For students to understand the representation issue, they would have to interpret the first two sentences in this section to mean that Parliament was an elected body, but that the colonists could not take part in these elections. The next sentence tells that taxes were imposed, but note that before the colonists' reaction to the taxes is presented, five sentences intervene describing why Britain imposed the taxes.

In order for students to understand the colonists' reaction, that they are "very upset about these taxes," students would need to connect the initial sentences in the passage about Parliament's role, to the next two sentences about the colonial assemblies and about Parliament's tax laws not being "welcome." That is, students would need to interpret those two sentences to mean that the colonial assemblies, being the colonists' elected governmental bodies, had no say in determining British tax policy, and therefore the colonists did not feel that they had to follow British tax laws. They would then need to bring all this interpretation to bear to comprehend the final sentence about the colonists' motto. It was our judgment that this attempt to explain such a complex concept would fail because the text presentation is so brief and opaque.

Now consider the treatment of the "no taxation without representation" issue as discussed in the Landmark Series book on the American Revolution (Bliven, 1958, 1986). The Landmark Series is a series of tradebooks on American history published in the 1950s by Random House. The series was originated by Bennet Cerf who, as the father of a young boy, found a dearth of good history books for children. The books are individually authored by distinguished writers such as Shirley Jackson, Dorothy Canfield Fisher, and Quentin Reynolds. The Landmark Series book about the American Revolution was written by Bruce Bliven, the author of a number of books as well as many articles for such outlets as *Atlantic, Harpers, Saturday Review,* and *The New York Times.* Bliven presents the "no taxation without representation" issue in the Landmark Series as follows:

> To make matters worse, Lord Grenville had another money-raising idea: to tax a variety of papers–legal documents, newspapers, marriage licenses, college diplomas, ships' papers and a good many others. Starting in 1765, such papers had to carry a large blue paper seal called a stamp–a revenue stamp–as proof that a tax had been paid.
>
> The stamps were expensive. Furthermore, they denied a right that Americans treasured–the right to fix their own "internal" taxes. Matters like marriage licenses and college diplomas had nothing whatever to do with the British Empire's economics. They were purely Amercan affairs, and British interference–in the shape of that hated blue stamp–seemed obnoxious. In addition to a governor who was, in most cases, appointed by the King, each of the thirteen colonies had an Assembly, or legislature, elected by the people. These Assemblies, most Americans believed, had the right to decide on local taxes. In England, after a long fight, Parliament had won control of taxation. Americans, as British subjects living abroad, felt that their own legislatures should control American taxes. Or, as the popular rallying cry said it: "No taxation without representation!" (pp. 9-10)

Note that Bliven directly states that the taxes "denied a right that Americans treasured," and then goes on to explain what that right was, and how it was operationalized in the colonies in the form of the colonial assemblies. The choice of language also plays a role in communicating the message about the colonists' reaction to the taxes; Bliven writes that taxed items had "nothing whatever" to do with Britain's economy, and characterizes the taxes as British "interference" which the colonists found "obnoxious."

Another important aspect of bringing depth to learning in history is the inclusion of multiple perspectives. One of the most roundly criticized aspects of social studies textbooks is their single, "objective" perspective, and the general lack of acknowledgement that there even exists more than one lens through which to examine social and political events and phenomena. Even when attempts are made in textbooks to bring in multiple perspectives, they are often not very effective. Take for example the excerpt presented earlier on "no taxation without representation." The five sentences from "Britain thought the colonists should pay their share..." through the end of the paragraph are, indeed, an attempt to portray Britain's perspective on the issue. But the presentation is placed in the midst of the discussion of the rather complex issue of representation. Thus students receive half of one story–the colonists' view–followed by the other side of the story, and then the rest of the first story. Compounding the problem is that the two sides are not presented as contrasting views. The whole discussion is written as if it were all undisputed fact. Nowhere is there a hint that what the British thought about taxation was in strong conflict with what the colonists thought, and that neither side bought the other's argument. The result is that the text is unlikely to foster understanding of the two sides in the taxation debate.

Tradebooks provide an excellent vehicle for introducing and developing other perspectives. In some cases, both perspectives may be found in a single book. For example, the excerpt from Bliven presented earlier is followed by this paragraph that presents Britain's reaction to the colonists' objections:

> Neither the King, nor his ministers, nor even Parliament agreed.
> They all thought that the colonial Assemblies could not possibly be compared to the British Parliament, and they denied the American argument completely. (p. 10)

Another strategy is to use different books that emphasize various perspectives. Consider, for example, this discussion of the British position on taxation after the French and Indian War taken from Jean Fritz's *Can't You Make Them Behave, King George?* (1977).

> England had been fighting a long and expensive war, and when it was over, the question was how to pay the bills. Finally, a government official suggested that one way to raise money was to tax Americans.
>
> "What a good idea!" King George said. After all, the French and Indian part of the war had been fought on American soil for the benefit of Americans, so why shouldn't they help pay for it? The fact that Americans had also spent money and lost men in the war didn't seem important. Nor did the fact that Americans had always managed their own money up to now. They were English subjects, weren't they? Didn't English subjects have to obey the English government? So in 1765 a stamp tax was laid on certain printed items in America.
>
> King George was amazed that Americans objected. He was flabbergasted that they claimed he had no right to tax them. Just because they had no say in the matter. Just because they had no representatives in the English government. What was more, Americans refused to pay. If they agreed to one tax, they said, what would come next? A window tax? A tax on fireplaces? (pp. 30-31)

By juxtaposing the Bliven and the Fritz excerpts, there certainly is enough information to promote understanding of the two positions and how opposed they were, as well as to foster some lively discussion on the part of young learners. But why stop there? Fritz provides at least two other portrayals of this issue in other books. She writes in her story of John Hancock (1976):

> In 1765 the news was bad. England had enacted the Stamp Act, imposing taxes on Americans in 55 different ways. Americans, who had always managed their money in their own assemblies, considered the act unconstitutional. Naturally they were furious. John Hancock, too. He said there was nothing or no one on earth that could make him pay a penny of that "damned tax." He said it often and loudly. Once, at a dinner for members of Samuel Adams' Patriot Party, he said it so well that he was cheered. Huzza! Huzza! Huzza! John had never been huzzaed before and he was so pleased that he almost huzzaed himself. (p. 12)

And Fritz's book on Samuel Adams (1974) contains the following presentation:

> Meanwhile, England was imposing taxes on America. First a stamp tax on printed matter. No onecould obtain a marriage license now or a college diploma or even buy a newspaper without paying England a share of the money. This made the people of Boston so angry they tore down the governor's house, set fire to the tax office, and elected Samuel Adams a representative to the Massachusetts legislature. (p.15)

A teacher might introduce students to several descriptions of perspectives on an issue. Another tactic might be to establish the idea that a multiplicity of perspectives exists and then challenge students to find out how other groups or individuals reacted. There are a variety of further possibilities for promoting and enriching students' understanding of the perspectives on taxation vis à vis representation. And the variety of further possibilities is a major point. A goal in education that has currently taken on some urgency is that of developing critical thinking in students. Or, stated very basically, what can students *do* with the information they are acquiring? What seems clear to us is that students can not "do" much of anything unless they have a sufficient quantity and quality of information to allow critical consideration. Critical thinking does not happen in the abstract; one must think critically about something.

In terms of the potential engagement of critical thinking, consider an activity that is suggested in the teacher's manual of a fifth grade textbook, the same textbook from which the excerpt on taxation was taken. The text suggests that students debate the following resolution: "That colonists were right to disobey the laws imposed upon them by Great Britain." We submit that based on the information presented in the text, this will be a rather brief and shallow debate. There simply is not enough content to promote critical appraisal of the morality of the colonists' actions. Further we conjecture that, given the characteristics of the text's presentation, the arguments might indeed be weighted in favor of the British! Their position that the colonists should help pay the cost of a war jointly fought has face validity and is rather easy to grasp, while the perspective of the colonists, involving the notion of representation in a governmental body, is substantially more complex.

Development of indepth coverage is rooted in the notion of coming to understand something deeply, be it an idea, a concept, a topic, an attitude.

Given the materials in the kinds of elementary social studies text-books we analyzed, students encounter a breadth of information, but little that resembles depth of information. Yet, the point of teaching content area topics, in the case at hand a historical period, should not merely be to develop a catalog of events and characters. Rather it is to help students come to understand why events occurred and why one thing led to another and how the culmination of a sequence of events affected people's lives.

The message for instruction is that it is not sufficient to give students "just the facts" as the textbooks do. If facts are presented with inadequate explanatory material to tie the facts together and no framework into which the facts can be integrated, then the facts are unlikely to be memorable. And even if students do remember sets of discrete facts, that memory may appear in the form of stews of factoids. Examples of this phenomenon emerged in the background knowledge study (McKeown & Beck, 1990), in which we interviewed fifth graders both right before and right after they had studied the Revolutionary period and the subsequent founding of our government. Many students responded to a question about the Declaration of Independence by confusing it with the Constitution, the Mayflower Compact, or the Emancipation Proclamation, a response that we labeled "Document Stew." Because most such responses occurred in the interviews done at the end of fifth grade, it seemed that the more historical documents the students encountered, the thicker the stew got.

We have subsequently found further evidence of "factoid stews" in data from a longitudinal study that we are presently completing. For this study, we were able to re-interview 26 of the original population of fifth graders both before and after they had studied the same period in eighth grade. The data are not completely analyzed, but the stew notion seems quite prevalent. One eighth grader captured it when he said, "I have no idea about the American Revolution, you know, there are just too many wars... like the Civil War and the wars with different countries and I get them all mixed up. There have been just too many wars."

From our work with existing social studies materials, it is our conclusion that building an understanding of many of the complex concepts included in the social studies curriculum is unlikely to succeed unless the curriculum is based on richer and more varied material. Certainly, elementary textbooks could include such material, but presently they do not. But as we have demonstrated, such material is available from other sources. If depth is the goal–and we believe that understanding derives from depth–one task is to bring deeper and richer materials directly into the center of instruction.

References

Anderson, T. H., & Armbruster, B.B. (1984). Content area textbooks. In R.C. Anderson, J. Osborn, and R.J. Tierney (Eds.), *Learning to read in American schools* (pp. 193-224). Hillsdale, NJ: Lawrence-Erlbaum Associates.

Baumann, J. (1986). Effects of rewritten content text passages on middle grade students' comprehension of main idea: Making the inconsiderate considerate. *Journal of Reading Behavior, 18,* 1-22

Beck, I.L., McKeown, M.G., & Gromoll, E.W. (1989). Learning from social studies texts. *Cognition and Instruction, 6*(2), 99-158.

Beck, I.L., McKeown, M.G., Omanson, R.C., & Pople, M.T. (1984). Improving the comprehensibility of stories: The effects of revisions that improve coherence. *Reading Research Quarterly, 19,* 263-277.

Beck, I.L., McKeown, M.G., Sinatra, G.M., & Loxterman, J.A. (in press). Revising social studies text from a text-processing perspective: Evidence of improved comprehensibility. *Reading Research Quarterly.*

Black, J.B. (1985). An exposition on understanding expository text. In B. K. Britton and J.B. Black (Eds.), *Understanding expository text: A theoretical and practical handbook for analyzing expository text* (pp. 249-267). Hillsdale, NJ: Lawrence Erlbaum Associates.

Black, J.B., & Bern, H. (1981). Causal coherence and memory for events in narratives. *Journal of Verbal Learning and Verbal Behavior, 20,* 267-275.

Bliven, B., Jr. (1958, 1986). *The American Revolution.* New York: Random House.

Chiesi, H.L., Spilich, G.J., & Voss, J.F. (1979). Acquisition of domain-related information in relation to high and low domain knowledge. *Journal of Verbal Learning and Verbal Behavior, 18,* 275-290.

Cirilo, R.K. (1981). Referential coherence and text structure in story comprehension. *Journal of Verbal Learning and Verbal Behavior, 20,* 358-367.

Frederiksen, J.R. (1981). Understanding anaphora: Rules used by readers in assigning pronominal referents. *Discourse Processes, 4,* 323-348.

Fritz, J. (1974). *Why don't you get a horse, Sam Adams?* New York: Coward-McCann, Inc.

Fritz, J. (1976). *Will you sign here, John Hancock?* New York: Coward-McCann, Inc.

Fritz, J. (1977). *Can't you make them behave, King George?* New York: Coward-McCann, Inc.

Haviland, S. C., & Clark, H. H. (1974). What's new? Acquiring new information as aprocess in comprehension. *Journal of Verbal Learning and Verbal Behavior, 13,* 512-521.

Hiebert, E. H., Englert, C. S., & Brennan, S. (1983). Awareness of text structure in recognition and production of expository discourse. *Journal of Reading Behavior, 15,* 63-79.

Just, M. A., & Carpenter, P. A. (1978). Inference processes during reading: Reflections from eye fixations. In J. W. Senders, D. F. Fisher, & R. A. Monty (Eds.), *Eye movements and higher psychological functions* (pp. 157-174). Hillsdale, NJ: Lawrence Erlbaum Associates.

Kintsch, W., Mandel, T. S., & Kozminsky, E. (1977). Summarizing scrambled stories. *Memory and Cognition, 5,* 547-552.

Lesgold, A. M., Roth, S. F., & Curtis, M. E. (1979). Foregrounding effects in discourse comprehension. *Journal of Verbal Learning and Verbal Behavior, 18,* 291-308.

Mandler, J. M., & Johnson, N. S. (1977). Remembrance of things passed: Story structure and recall. *Cognitive Psychology, 9,* 111-151.

McKeown, M. G., & Beck, I. L. (1990). The assessment and characterization of young learners' knowledge of a topic in history. *American Educational Research Journal, 27,* 688-726.

McKeown, M. G., Beck, I. L. , Sinatra, G. M., & Loxterman, J. A. (1990). *The relative effects of prior knowledge and coherent text on comprehension.* (Submitted for publication.)

Meyer, B. J. F. (1975). *The organization of prose and its effect on memory.* Amsterdam: North Holland Publishing.

Meyer, B. J. F., & Freedle, R. O. (1984). Effects of discourse type on recall. American *Educational Research Journal, 21,* 121-143.

Pearson, P. D., Hansen, J., & Gordon, C. (1979). The effect of background knowledge on young children's comprehension of explicit and implicit information. *Journal of Reading Behavior, 11,* 201-209.

Rumelhart, D. E. (1975). Notes on a schema for stories. In D.G. Brown and A. Collins (Eds.), *Representation and understanding: Studies in cognitive science* (pp. 211-236). New York: Academic Press.

Schank, R. C. (1975). The structure of episodes in memory. In D. Bobrow & A. Collins (Eds.), *Representation and understanding: Studies in cognitive science* (pp. 237-272). New York: Academic Press.

Silver Burdett. (1984). *The world and its people.* Morristown, NJ: Author.

Slater, W., & Graves, M. (1985, December). *Revising inconsiderate secondary school expository text: Effects on comprehension and recall.* Paper presented at the National Reading Conference, San Diego.

Spilich, G. J., Vesonder, G. T., Chiesi, H. L., & Voss, J. F. (1979). Text processing of domain-related information for individuals with high and low domain knowledge. *Journal of Verbal Learning and Verbal Behavior, 18,* 275-290.

Stein, N. L. (1986). Knowledge and process in the acquisition of writing skills. In E.Z. Rothkopf (Ed.), *Review of research in education* (Vol. 13, pp. 225-258). Washington, DC: American Educational Research Association.

Stein, N. L., & Glenn, C. G. (1979). An analysis of story comprehension in elementary school children. In R.O. Freedle (Ed.), *Advances in discourse processing: Vol.2, New directions in discourse processing* (pp. 53-120). Norwood, NJ: Ablex, Inc.

Stein, N. L., & Nezworski, T. (1978). The effects of organization and instructional set on story memory. *Discourse Processes, 1,* 177-193.

Thorndyke, P. W. (1977). Cognitive structures in comprehension and memory of narrative discourse. *Cognitive Psychology, 9,* 77-110.

Trabasso, T., Secco, T., van den Broek, P. (1984). Causal cohesion and story coherence. In H. Mandl, N.L. Stein, & T. Trabasso (Eds.), *Learning and comprehension of text* (pp 83-111). Hillsdale, NJ: Lawrence Erlbaum Associates.

7

Reading Instruction and Learning Disabled Students

Joanna P. Williams

The chapters in this volume present a spectives about reading instruction. My perspective reflects my background; I was trained as an experimental psychologist. This chapter will discuss some recent studies that I have conducted, as well as some instructional applications suggested by my data.

The field of learning disabilities has had a short and honorable history, although it has been plagued by the problem of definition (Hammill, 1990). I am not going to step into that murky area in this chapter. In the early seventies, when I first began to work on reading instruction for learning-disabled children, I was very much perplexed by the question of what learning-disability really meant. I soon realized that many people had the same question. Only the clinicians, who trusted their intuitions, seemed to be able to tell who was learning-disabled and who was not; but they could not explain it to anyone else. And many researchers, though it was obvious that there was no clear, objective way to identify a child as learning-disabled, happily immersed themselves in investigations designed to identify a whole host of subtypes within the general learning-disability classification.

My own main interest was in reading and in instructional design, and so after considerable reflection, I decided that I could work with children whom someone else had labeled learning-disabled. My rationale was that what I was trying to do was develop materials and techniques for poor readers in general, a more inclusive category. If I was successful, than surely the learning-disabled subset would be helped.

I still hold that point of view, and I think that the evidence is bearing me out. In any event, it has let me stay out of the challenging but frustrating area of trying to identify the learning-disabled child and kept me focused instead on reading and reading instruction.

Before I turn to comprehension, my main topic in this chapter, I will offer a few observations about beginning reading, because at this point it is our big success story, and I think it provides a good model for comprehension research to emulate.

Beginning Reading

There has, of course, been some progress in the area of identifying learning-disabled children. We know that a large proportion of the children who have been identified as learning-disabled have difficulty with reading. Thus, there is a major overlap between these two labels, "learning-disability" and "reading disability" (Gough & Tunmer, 1986). I will focus my discussion on the learning-disabled children whose problem is reading. I will refer to these children as Generally Reading Disabled, or GRD, because they turn out to be deficient across a wide range of cognitive tasks: language skills of all types, listening comprehension, metacognitive and executive functioning–and often, though not necessarily, in general intelligence as well. It is not surprising to find that they exhibit problems across all stages of reading acquisition from word identification to comprehension, because their cognitive difficulties are reflected in all of the many components of the reading task.

Within this large population, the search for subtypes has, for the most part, not been very profitable. We have given up, fortunately, on visiles vs. audiles, and we are also losing interest in attempts to differentiate according to learning style–there does not seem to be much payoff there. However, over the last few years, we have been able to identify a relatively small proportion of children who can be character-ized as having a specific reading disability (Stanovich, 1988). Their difficulty seems to be located in their ability to deal with phonological skills. There is substantial support for the notion that phonological sensitivity is casually linked to reading, and moreover, that phonological processing ability is independent of intelligence and other cognitive tasks. Connie Juel (chapter 4) has presented some important data relevant to this point. Thus, children could have a specific difficulty in phonological ability that does not impinge on the rest of their cognitive processing. This is truly a *specific* reading disability; hence, I will call these children SRDs.

The difference between the GRD and the SRD groups is, presum-ably, that if we could get the SRD children successfully past the early stages of reading, in which phonological skills are so important, then they would have caught up with nondisabled children who had not demonstrated such phonological problems and they would not need further remediation. GRD children, on the other hand, would need remediation at every step of the way, focused not only on phonological skills but on other aspects of decoding and on higher-level comprehen-sion skills as well.

But what does this mean for instruction? Just because we have identified two groups as distinct does not mean that remediation should be qualitatively different for each group. Both groups need help on phonological skills. The SRDs theoretically need only that; the GRDs need that, plus work on other aspects of reading. One of these groups may need more remediation on phonological skills, perhaps on a more intensive basis or perhaps spread out over a longer time–or they may not. We do not know these details at this point. But in any event, this is a matter of modifying dosages, not changing the prescription. What the work on subtype identification has done for instruction so far is to isolate an important component of the reading task, one that is important for *all* reading-disabled students.

Indeed, it is difficult to conceive of any subtype research that could lead to a different kind of conclusion. Whatever specific difficulty is uncovered in a particular group of children (whose only problem is that specific difficulty), other children with more general difficulties will also benefit from well-designed instruction in that specific area.

Moreover, there is another group that should be considered– children who do not do very well in their first years of school but who are not considered disabled. The distinction between children who are candidates for special education and those who are simply poor at reading and need remediation has been made since the days of Gates and Dolch (Wixson & Lipson, 1991). What is different today is that with the recent explosion of the field of special education, the number of reading-disabled children has grown tremendously, and the number of remedial readers has become considerably smaller. This change over the years underscores the difficulty inherent in making a reliable identification of disability. It also makes it reasonable to assume that poor readers within mainstream education would also gain from the instruction in phono-logical skills that seems appropriate for both groups of special education students.

One additional point is worth noting. The remediation that we are talking about is focused on a component of the reading task itself– isolating and blending phonemes. Typically, when we have proposed theories of why children have trouble reading, we have with great excitement and expansiveness proposed very general remedies. For example, when the field latched on to visual-perceptual deficits, all sorts of training in visual-perceptual skills abounded; but they were found not to improve reading (Bateman, 1979; Williams, 1977). For children with these sorts of difficulties–and we now believe that they are relatively few– the appropriate remediation is to provide instruction on differentiating the actual alphabet letters and letter clusters.

More recently, reading has been conceptualized as a language process (Goodman & Goodman, 1979; Sulzby, 1988). This fits in with our current emphasis on the comprehension process and on instruction in reading comprehension. This focus has led to great enthusiasm for improving language in general and to expectations of seeing improve-ment in reading comprehension thereby.

But I am not convinced that we are going to get very far by stressing general language development and by making curriculum changes such as introducing lots of story-telling and diary-writing and class discussion. We are going to have to do some serious analytical work and be a good deal more precise about what is needed. We must remember that the big breakthrough in beginning reading was the discovery that we were neglecting one very specific aspect of decoding. With all the task analyses of the reading process that had been done over the years, no one had realized that there was a big problem in phoneme differentiation. Elkonin (1963), a Russian psychologist, drew our attention to this. Now, phonemic awareness is seen as a core element that is a challenge for many children and the *only* genuine difficulty for a smaller group (Gough & Tunmer, 1986; Liberman & Shankweiler, 1985; Williams, 1986).

In the area of reading comprehension, we are still searching for the counterpart of phonological skills in beginning reading.

Comprehension

Now I will turn to my main topic, comprehension. Comprehension is a general, all-encompassing term, and we have to somehow bring it down to size in order to deal with it. What must be involved in comprehension, as a minimum? I think that the heart of comprehension is the ability to get from a discourse–a text, since we are talking about reading comprehension–its gist or its point. Traditionally, this is called finding the main idea; Pearson and Johnson (1978) have described identifying main ideas as the "essence of reading comprehension." Indeed, without being able to understand the point of a text, one cannot draw appropriate inferences from it; nor can one compare texts without understanding the main points of each. This ability is fundamental to basic comprehension, to effective studying, and to critical thinking. Its importance is reflected in the fact that instruction in how to find main ideas has always been one of the most common elements of the elementary-school reading curriculum.

Children often have difficulty in identifying main ideas of even rather simple texts, in fact (Baumann, 1984; Williams, 1981); and available instructional materials have been evaluated and found wanting (Hare & Milligan, 1984). What is rather interesting about the complaints about the existing methods, however, is that they often deal with something that cannot really be improved. It is true that some basal reading programs as well as other forms of instruction provide examples that are anything but clear, so that even the teacher is hard-pressed to figure out what the main idea is supposed to be. That is just sloppy writing and can be corrected. But people also criticize the teachers' manuals for the explanations that they suggest that the teachers give to the children. These explanations go like this: "To find the main idea, pick out the most important point" or "If you have picked out the most important sentence, you have probably found the main idea." You can use such statements as explanations for the value of finding main ideas– i.e., as an explanation of how good such a strategy is, in reading; but that is just talking about getting main ideas; it is not telling or showing how to find one. The problem is that you cannot provide any better alternatives to such statements–try it! There is nothing you can tell a child directly that will tell him what to do. This is true of other comprehension skills besides main idea, and that is the real challenge of comprehension instruction.

Finding Main Ideas in Expository Text

The first set of studies I will describe deals with finding the main idea in expository text. We focused mainly on children in the fourth to sixth grades, both learning-disabled (GRD) and non-disabled. In a series of studies, we asked children to read short paragraphs, and to select an appropriate title from an array of choices and to write a summary sentence for the paragraph (Williams, Taylor & Ganger, 1981; Williams, Taylor & deCani, 1984). These are typical tasks that you might see in a classroom. All of our paragraphs were written on a very low readability level, so that difficulties with decoding would not confound our findings.

Consider the following paragraph:

> Cowboys had to protect the herd from cattle robbers. Cowboys had to brand cattle to show who owned them. They had to ride around the ranch to keep cattle from straying too far. Sometimes cowboys had to separate the cattle that were to be sent to market.

In this paragraph, each sentence instantiates a global topic, and the reader can construct a proposition that at a higher level subsumes the three sentences (van Dijk, 1980, p. 46): "Cowboys had jobs to do."

Various titles and topic sentences represent adequate expressions of the macrostructure of this paragraph. For example, the paragraph could be entitled "Cowboys," or it could be entitled "The Jobs of Cowboys." In van Dijk's terminology (1980), the first title contains the *general topic* of the paragraph and the second, the *specific topic of discourse*. Instead of titles, sentences might express either the general topic or the specific topic of discourse: "The paragraph is about cowboys," or "Cowboys had jobs to do." Sometimes our paragraphs included the sentence, "Cowboys had jobs to do" as a first, or topic sentence, and sometimes not.

As expected, we found that there was a clear developmental progression in ability across school grades, and that performance was better when readers had merely to select the main idea from an array than when they had to formulate it as a summary sentence; also, children performed better on paragraphs with topic sentences than on those without (although only when the topic sentence was highlighted).

We also worked with children with general reading disability who were 10 and 11 years old (Taylor & Williams, 1983). We compared these children with younger nondisabled children who were matched in terms of IQ and reading level. Across all our experimental tasks, the GRD students did just as well as the nondisabled children. This suggested to us that the two groups were not qualitatively different with respect to the ability to generate macrostructure, and that instruction that focuses on the development of main idea skills should not necessarily be different for GRD children than for ND children–a conclusion that is consonant with the general point of view that instructional development for the reading-disabled should focus on whatever strategies and techniques are effective for the general category of slow readers.

There was, however, one finding that differentiated the two groups. We included what we called parenthetical information in some of the paragraphs, information that was either unrelated to or else only tangentially related to the propositional hierarchy of the text. We did this on the grounds that natural text does not always consist of well-structured paragraphs, and so it is important for readers to be able to disregard anomalous information when reading for gist.

We asked the children to identify the inappropriate sentence in the paragraph. For example, in the cowboy paragraph, that sentence might read, "Cowboys often wear leather jackets and fancy boots." The position of the anomalous sentence was varied across paragraphs, appearing as either the second, third or fourth (last) sentence. Nondisabled children were better able to identify a sentence as anomalous, the closer it was to the end of the paragraph. The GRD children, however, showed no such effect; they were just as willing to accept the anomalous sentence even when it appeared late in the paragraph. This suggested that the

GRDs were not as good at building up a representation gradually as the information in each succeeding sentence was processed.

I do not believe that this finding can be explained by saying that GRDs do not monitor their comprehension. That is, in this study, I do not believe that when the students were faced with the task of saying whether a sentence belonged in the paragraph, they did not actually compare what the sentence said with their current representation of the paragraph. After all, such a comparison was explicitly set as the task. Rather, I interpret the results as showing that the GRDs' representation of the paragraph develops less completely or less adequately than that of the nondisbled child; so that when the GRD child *does* compare sentence and paragraph representation, the outcome of the comparison is not as likely to be on target.

From these findings, it looks as if perhaps GRDs do have specific problems with finding the main idea, though you have to look rather carefully before the difference between GRDs and NDs is seen.

Instruction in Main Idea

We went on, in this main idea work, to develop an instructional sequence, which was designed *for* GRD children but which as far as I am concerned would be just as useful for any poor reader who needed this sort of remediation (Williams, Taylor, Jarin, & Milligan, 1983). We used the same sort of simple, highly structured paragraphs as we had in our experimental studies and designed a program that emphasized clear definition of main idea and clear description of the task, and explanation of why it was important, something that has not always been done in instruction.

In addition, we incorporated general principles of instruction into the design: (1) the use of well structured examples of the prototypic task, (2) consistent modeling of the strategies being taught, (3) a sequence of tasks and also (4) a sequence of response demands that reflected a progression from easier to more difficult material, (5) the teacher gradually removing herself from the task, and (6) provision for extensive practice and feedback. We also chose to externalize some of the steps in the comprehension process that are, in actuality, implicit, that is, to externalize their thinking. We did this by having the students highlight some of the textual cues, that is, circle the most frequent word or idea, to help figure out the general topic of each activity. Note that there is nothing particularly innovative about this instruction–as Michael Graves (Chapter 5) has warned–it is wise to avoid the trendy.

One aspect of our training that was a bit different was our use of anomalous sentences and the systematic introduction of different types of anomaly, first sentences totally unrelated to the topic of the paragraph and then sentences that were tangentially related and therefore more of a challenge. Children were taught to identify the deviant sentence, to cross it out (as part of this "externalization" of the thought process), and then to formulate a main idea on the basis of the rest of the paragraph.

In evaluating the program, we worked with GRD children about 11 years old, about two grade levels below average reading level for their age. After ten lessons, children were better able to identify anomalous sentences and to write sentences both on (1) materials that had been used in training and (2) similar materials that had not.

One of our major concerns in this sort of work, of course, is to see that our instructional efforts lead to transfer, *i.e.*, that students will learn to work with new material: It is their ability to comprehend in general that we are concerned about. In this case, we can say that there was transfer, albeit only to similarly structured materials. We did not do any posttesting on other types of material. But although the texts used in this study were structurally simple, we are convinced that work with materials such as these is an appropriate beginning step in the development of a sophisticated understanding of main idea and in using this comprehension skill in a variety of more complex materials. What the student is getting is a basic model or a template; we cannot *tell* him directly how to find the main idea, but he is given a clear, simple pattern it provides him with something that he can use later as a standard for comparison, that is, on the model of pattern recognition.

Finding Themes in Narrative Texts

Now I want to move to some newer work I have been doing on a related topic. I started looking at narrative text and at a task that is somewhat analogous to finding main ideas in expository text, namely, finding themes.

What is a theme? Sometimes a theme is expressed in terms of a concept, such as "friendship" or "courage" (Lehr, 1988). Even kindergartners can recognize and match stories that have similar themes, although the ability to generate themes, i.e., to say, "That story is about friendship," does not appear until a later age.

Another way of defining theme is, in Lukens' words, "the idea that holds the story together, such as a comment about either society, human nature, or the human condition" (Lukens, 1982, p. 101). In children's literature, one common genre is the fable. Here, the theme, or point, is the didactic message or lesson embodied in the text, and it is often, though not always, explicitly stated in the form of a concluding generalization (Dorfman & Brewer, 1988; Dorfman, 1989). Children have to be older, typically, before they can tackle this task effectively.

While it is intuitively clear that the concepts of main idea and theme overlap, there are also real differences between the two concepts. Themes are more abstract and less tied to the text than are main ideas. "Courage," for example, involves a particular plot pattern but can be described outside of the context of any specific story (Seifert, Dyer, & Black, 1986). And "Slow but steady wins the race" or "Respect your elders" might each apply to many different stories. We would usually expect a successful reading of expository text to be more closely anchored to the text than the reading of a narrative text would be. It follows from this that, typically, the acceptable range of individual variation in readers' statements of a theme for a given text would be wider than that of a main idea.

There has not been much research that has dealt with the topic of theme. Instead, studies on narrative have addressed more straightforward elements of story structure such as setting, action, and goal. However, the question of "what does a story really mean?" is of interest now, for both theoretical and educational reasons. I will consider the educational reasons first.

Right now there is a great deal of interest in literature-based reading curricula. People have become very dissatisfied with existing reading programs (Hansen, 1987). Criticisms of the quality of texts and instructional methods commonly used have led to the rejection, in many quarters, of basal reading programs with their emphasis on abbreviated text selections and the development of isolated skills.

The new literature-based programs emphasize original, unadapted classics and contemporary multicultural literature (Atwell, 1984; Cullinan, 1987). There are other new elements in them: They rely on student-led, instead of teacher-dominated, group discussion and also use a lot of writing activities. At this point, as the development of these curricula proceeds, some of the programs are doing very well. But there is, according to Liebling (1989), a "potential for chaos" in the teaching of reading. She cites two serious problems: the lack of a specific curriculum and the lack of agreement as to which reading abilities should be taught and tested.

Ironically, reading-disabled children are probably likely to lose rather than gain from this reform. These students respond well to highly structured instruction and materials, the development of which runs counter to the philosophy of the new curricular movement. Thus, it behooves us to determine ways of successfully incorporating the very worthwhile goals of this new approach into instruction that is suitable for reading-disabled students.

Certain recent theoretical developments both serve to support this new curriculum thrust and to guide research. Two separate but congruent theories have been greatly influential. The first is from psychology: schema theory, which focuses on the way in which a person represents knowledge and the way in which one's representations affect the understanding of new information (Anderson & Pearson, 1984; Rumelhart, 1985). Skilled readers draw simultaneously on several different sources of knowledge as they read, both from information in the text and from their own prior knowledge. Reading is thus interactive. It is also constructive, in that meaning is not inherent in the words on the printed page but, rather, is constructed by the reader on the basis of the interacting sources of information (Rumelhart, 1977).

The second relevant theory is reader-response theory, a theory from the field of literature, that complements the current information-processing orientation of psychology (Cooper, 1985; Rosenblatt, 1938, 1978). The term "reader-response" indicates the importance of the reader's role, culture, reading experience, and preferences. This point of view represents a major revolution in literary theory, a revolution that rejects the idea that the objective text should be the focus of study. Rather, the reader should be the focus, for meaning is shaped by what each reader brings to the reading experience (Rosenblatt, 1938, 1978; Iser, 1974). Since any text contains gaps in the information provided, which readers fill in via inference-making, and since each reader is unique in ability, background and interest, each single reading of a text is different; there is no correct reading or understanding of a given text.

Given these ideas, it might be argued that it makes no sense to talk about "the" theme or "the" point of a story. But in my opinion, the intellectual attractiveness–and the genuine value–of reader-response theory along with schema theory can lead to dangerous overinterpretation. This may result in some unfortunate educational values, that is, the belief that since on theoretical grounds there is no main idea or theme in the text itself, instruction should allow and nurture the expression of any interpretation of a text, no matter how idiosyncratic. Taking this position to heart (actually unjustified in terms of theory), how would anyone ever communicate?

How, then in light of these theoretical stances, does one sensibly interpret and evaluate readers' comprehension responses? The literary critic Stanley Fish (1980) has developed the concept of "interpretive community," which emphasizes the notion that a person's perceptions and judgments–and readings–are interactive, are constructive, and are unique to the individual. But, he points out, they are obviously also shaped by the individual's environment. Personal meaning depends on the assumptions shared by the groups of which the individual is a member. The implication is that there is a text meaning on which a group of readers might agree, in addition to the infinite number of personal meanings that can be constructed for any given text. The sophisticated reader is able to derive both personal and consensual meaning from text. In this regard, it may be useful to think of theme as a family of related statements, rather than as a single statement (Golden, 1989). Individual responses may well differ, depending on previous experience, particular needs, and ability, but a successful reading is likely to contain core elements that are common across readers. And of course, complex stories may have multiple themes or theme families.

Much of the discussion of these theoretical issues resolves around a concern for teaching literature for its own sake. But people have also begun to use narrative extensively in a wide variety of other applications. In content area classroom learning, they are using biographies of notable figures in history and social studies, as Isabel Beck (Chapter 6) has pointed out; and in instructional programs teaching reasoning and interpersonal problem-solving, there is much discussion of case histories and problem instances (Shure & Spivack, 1978; Williams & Ellsworth, 1990). In addition, Richard Gardner(1986) has developed a technique of psychotherapy that involves an exchange of stories by child and therapist. The assumption is that it is easier to impart social knowledge when it is presented in the form of a concrete example, because the example immediately illustrates how that knowledge is related to real-life situations.

Reading-disabled children would seem to be prime candidates for interventions based on this sort of approach, given the problems that they have in the social arena as well as their academic difficulties. However, practically no work has been done on how reading-disabled students abstract and generalize from stories in such a way that the understandings gained can be brought to bear effectively on their own life experiences.

A Comparison of Disabled and Nondisabled Readers

In the study that I want to describe in this section (Williams, 1991b), we worked with children from private schools in New York City whose students came from similar, upper-middle-class backgrounds. The reading-disabled students attended an ungraded school specifically for students with learning disabilities. All had been classified by the school as reading-disabled, had test scores that fell within the normal range of intelligence, and had reading levels at least two years below what was expected for their age. The mean age of these students was about 13 1/2. Their grade-equivalent reading scores on the Comprehension subtest of the Gates-MacGinitie Reading Test ranged from 3-8 to 8-8–on the average, about the middle of the sixth grade.

A group of nondisabled students, drawn from the fourth, fifth, and sixth grades of a regular private school, was matched with the GRD group on reading level. Their mean age was 10 1/2. Another group of nondisabled students was drawn from the seventh and eighth grades. Their mean age (13 1/2) was matched with that of the GRD group. Their reading comprehension was at the 12th grade level.

We used a story taken from a collection by Jessamyn West, *Cress Delahanty* (1953). (West was the author of another story, *Reverdy*, that had been used by Golden and Guthrie, 1986, and also by Squire, 1964, in studies of nondisabled ninth graders.) The study portrayed the adolescent identity crisis by describing a teenage girl's attempts to be popular with her schoolmates. The girl goes through a series of antics, trying to show how witty and zany she is, but she is really acting very unlike her real self. She ends up losing what she really wanted, the editorship of the high-school yearbook, because her friends cannot take her seriously. They put her in charge of the joke page instead.

We met with students individually. The students listened to the story on tape, divided into three sections. They were asked to summarize each section and then make a prediction about what would happen in the next section. At the end of the story, we asked them to tell us the theme of the story and the basis on which they made their judgment. These focused questions were incorporated into a natural exchange between student and interviewer that lasted approximately 20 minutes. We taped and transcribed these discussions.

Design

First of all, let us look at the design. It includes a developmental comparison, i.e., the young nondisabled students (YND) and the older ones (ND). We expect that the latter group will perform better. Next, we can compare the reading-disabled subjects with their age-matched nondisabled peers (ND); this is the usual way to compare GRDs and NDs, and we expect that the GRDs will not perform as well: our tasks, after all, are clearly associated with the tests that are used to define reading disability.

The interesting comparison is between the reading-disabled students and the nondisabled students who are matched on reading level (YND). If the disabled students perform more poorly, then one could argue that *one* cause of their low reading level may be their lack of ability on the experimental tasks. That is, students who cannot perform well on these measures may, because of this difficulty, become disabled readers: the competencies that underlie performance on the experimental tasks are needed in the overall task of reading comprehension; those skills are weak; and this weakness has interfered with their acquisition of proficiency in reading comprehension (compared with children who are nondisabled and are acquiring proficiency at a normal rate). That is, if our reading-disabled students in this study turn out not to read as well as the NDs who are the same age, one reason might be because of their difficulties with the particular competencies we were looking at.

Measures and Findings

Our basic experimental tasks were quite straightforward, tasks that are similar to those seen on reading tests and to questions that teachers ask in classroom discussion: (a) summarize the story in your own words; (b) predict what will happen next; and (c) identify the theme. Remember that the students listened to the story and were interviewed. We were looking at comprehension here, and we did not want whatever difficulties the children might have with low-level reading skills to confound our determining how well they understood the story. Our tasks require higher-order comprehension at a level that is presumably the same whether the presentation mode is oral or written. Thus, we would expect that the GRD group and the YND group, matched on reading comprehension, would perform similarly on these measures.

And they did. On all of the basic measures–summaries, predictions, and theme statements, the older ND group was best, and the reading-disabled students were comparable to the reading level-matched younger nondisabled students. Because the latter two groups did not differ on these measures, it can be argued that whatever the reasons for the GRDs' low overall general reading comprehension level, their low level was not due to difficulties they had with respect to the specific comprehension tasks used in this study.

But we looked further. We did a very close analysis of the transcriptions of the interviews, to see if we could find some more subtle indications of how well the groups had comprehended the story. The protocols were quite rich, and we looked at several categories of potential difference. I will address only a few points here.

First, we wondered whether we had chosen too stringent a criterion for judging that a student's identification of the theme was acceptable. There is evidence in the literature that children have difficulty in articulating what they actually do comprehend; that is, there is a production deficiency. So we searched through the entire protocol for additional information as to whether students had any notion at all of the theme. Perhaps there was some incipient awareness that they were simply not able to formulate and articulate sufficiently well in response to a direct question.

Next, we also looked for indications of just what information the students were using to build their representations of the story. Were they possibly incorporating information into their representations that derived not from the text but from other sources, including their personal experiences? And might this modify the representation sufficiently to deflect them from comprehending the consensual theme? Let me explain why we asked this question.

A Relevant Finding from Another Study

In a previous study, we asked students to retell short problems that they had read and to predict the character's likely solutions (Williams, 1990; 1991a). We did a similar sort of structured interview here. There were four groups of students, two LD and two ND, which were ranked in terms of reading comprehension from lowest to highest as follows: LD-ND-LD-ND. In terms of most of our measures of problem representation (amount of information recalled, number of important components of the problem schema reported, error rate), there was nothing in the data to suggest that performance was not simply a function of reading ability.

However, a very different pattern emerged with respect to the students' tendency to incorporate information into their representations that did not derive from the text. The number of such idiosyncratic importations did not vary, as did the other measures, as a function of reading level. Rather, we found that the LD students made more importations than did the ND students. This was true even when an LD group with a higher readng level was compared to an ND group with a lower reading level. This suggested that the LDs' representations did not conform to the boundaries of the problem as presented in the text, and also that these students did not evaluate or edit as they read.

One might expect that such a pattern would lead to difficulties using the information gleaned from the text. And, in fact, the groups that made many importations–the LD groups–were the ones who did not do as well on solving the problem. We hypothesized that the LDs' representations were different, less adequate in some way, and that they had (necessarily) based their prediction of what the character would do on their faulty representation. Hence we wondered whether, in our study on theme, reading-disabled students would also show the same tendency to exhibit importations.

Further Findings

These additional measures showed quite different results from the measures based on our direct questions. On every one of them, the reading-disabled students performed less well than the nondisabled students matched on reading level. In our first comparison, we looked at the protocols for indications that the students had picked up some understanding of the theme, even if only at a very rudimentary level. It took some close reading to do this! Whereas on the actual theme statements the two groups performed equally poorly, the YNDs showed greater evidence that they had some incipient awareness of the theme. This finding suggests that they had in fact developed a more adequate representation of what the story was about.

Now for the hypothesis from the problem-solving study. We found that the GRD students were indeed more likely to bring into their discussion of the story idiosyncratic importations, i.e., information based on personal feelings or experiences rather than derived from the text. For example, one GRD student predicted that Cress would read the list of traits that she had written out loud to her class and then everyone would like her, "because I used to be like that–when I was a little kid–too shy." Another LD student said, "I think that they are going to try to stop her by sending her to another school. They will teach her a good lesson or a better way to behave–stop showing off."

As students develop effective comprehension skills, they must learn not only to bring in information from their world knowledge, but also how to evaluate and edit it. Our data suggest that GRDs are relatively poor in this ability. It seems quite reasonable to suggest that this difficulty may lead to a representation of the text, which, even if only subtly modified, can change one's focus and prevent one from getting the (consensual) "point."

We also found something we had not expected. The reading-disabled students made more pronunciation errors than either of the other groups. Many, but not all, of these errors occurred on proper nouns. The girl's name in the story was Cress; some of the GRD students called her Chess or Chris. They called her parents, Mr. and Mrs. Delahanty, Daly or Delly. The number of actual references that were made to the characters did not vary across the groups. Rather, the NDs and the YNDs seemed to be able either to master the pronunciation and so not make errors, or else to finesse the problem by substituting pronouns or phrases (like "the mother"). This indicates a flexibility of expression as well as an awareness of what is important and what is not, so that the relatively trivial matter of the characters' names could be dealt with and the central focus on the comprehension of the story could be maintained.

This finding is perhaps not very surprising; we are aware of the importance of basic skills. We talk about the "bottleneck" that results from a lack of these low-level skills and the subsequent slower advancement in reading proficiency because of this bottleneck (Perfetti, 1985). This problem is not limited to written language; it also appears in oral language.

It seems reasonable to conclude that on both counts, the important issue here concerns getting and maintaining a focus on the important information. If the student was challenged by the difficulty of pronouncing a character's name, the attention that had to be allocated to that task would not be available for the task of determining what the story was about. And if a student brought in extraneous information into his or her story representation, that representation would likely be a little off target, and comprehension would suffer.

This reminds me of one of Peter Winograd's findings. Winograd (1984) found that poor readers' summaries of expository text were more idiosyncratic, and more off the point, as judged by proficient adult readers, than were good readers' summaries; the poor readers selected especially colorful and salient information from the texts to include in their summaries, even though that information was not high in the propositional hierarchy. Ruth Garner made similar observations (Garner, Belcher, Winfield, & Smith, 1985); she used the nice phrase "seductive details." Consider how much more seductive are pieces of information that the student himself brings to bear on the text.

Comparison of the Main Idea Studies and the Theme Study

The two studies I have described are very different. The main idea work used expository text, a text that was contrived according to very clearly specified criteria for the experiment, it required reading, and the task was an artificial laboratory-like (or at least test-like) task. The theme study used narrative text, and a real story not developed for experimental purposes; no reading was required, and the data were collected in a situation involving more natural interchange. Yet both studies showed the same thing.

Difficulty in Determining Appropriate Text Boundaries

Reading-disabled students seem to have particular difficulty in focusing on the central point, and the data suggest that at least part of the reason for this difficulty is an inability to edit out associations that are irrelevant and off-target. Presumably this difficulty is part of what is holding them back from comprehending at the level at which their age-mates are comprehending (whether "reading comprehension" or "listening comprehension").

Now this is only a hypothesis. Is this truly a specific difficulty of some disabled children such that we could identify an SCD (Specific Comprehension Disability) group comparable to the SRD group that is deficient specifically in phonological skills? It may turn out simply that this is one component of the task of getting the point (call it main idea, theme, or whatever) that all poor readers, whether they are labeled general reading disabled, remedial readers, or whatever, find difficult.

I think it is an interesting question and worth more research. But let us consider it for a moment from the point of view of remediation. Getting the point is an important skill–perhaps the most important skill–in comprehension. We know that it is difficult for many children. We have evidence that one thing that contributes to poor performance is the importation of idiosyncratic content into a text representation. It seems to me that it is worth addressing instructional attention to the matter, whether or not it turns out that it is truly a *specific* disability.

Instruction

Can the difficulty be remediated? I would like to propose some implications for instruction that I think follow from our findings. Two are rather general. First, there should be opportunity for children to work, even on a strictly oral level, on low-level basic skills. The research evidence on this point goes far beyond what I have presented here, and is thoroughly convincing on that point.

Second, we should help students formulate and articulate ideas (to get instances of "incipient awareness" expressed effectively). This is a central challenge in language arts instruction. General strategies used in teaching writing should help here.

The third implication for instruction is more central to my own focus. We should try to help children develop story representations that demarcate story information as distinct from idiosyncratic information. That is, we should attempt to develop an awareness of the boundaries of a text. This is essential for effective comprehension and is the basis for even the most elementary critical reading. Given today's strong theoretical orientation focused on the constructive nature of reading, this is an area we are likely to neglect. Obviously, individuals who come up with atypical interpretations of a text are not "wrong," and teachers must be sensitive to the importance of encouraging a child's imagination and creativity, but they also must not let students get carried away—or get carried away themselves.

This is easier said than done, for we must beware of trying to modify too much and thereby eliminate or denigrate a student's own personal concerns. It is the particular issues that are salient to individual readers that determine their own readings of a text and the ultimate value of their reading experience. It is crucial that instruction honor individuality and, indeed, foster it.

We are now in the process of evaluating an instructional sequence that teaches what we call a "theme scheme." This is a series of questions that help students get the important information from a story–first, to determine the basic story grammar components, i.e., to understand the story on the plot level; to identify the theme of the story; to generalize the theme, from a statement, for example, like "King Midas should not have been greedy" to "We should not be greedy;" and to classify and to generate (tell) stories that involve similar themes.

We are working with GRD and ND children in the fifth and sixth grades. Results look promising: both the ND and the GRD children are developing the ability to understand the nature of a theme, to identify and formulate themes for specific stories, and to generalize them to "real-life."

We are trying to address the problems that arise from incorporating extraneous content into representations–the boundaries problem–without ignoring the importance of fostering the child's own ideas and concerns.

Summary

In summary, I am enthusiastic about the new reforms in reading comprehension instruction, and I welcome the emphasis on literature. But I would hate to see the new approach used badly and children shortchanged. And since it may in fact be a special challenge for reading-disabled children, perhaps we should be extra-vigilant about the effects of the new curriculum on them.

Our task is to develop instruction that is appropriate for those children who are having difficulties in reading. In my opinion, it matters less whether they are reading-disabled, specific-reading-disabled, learning-disabled, or simply remedial readers than it does to know what to teach and how to teach it. We must identify the particular aspects of the reading task that might be troublesome and develop effective ways of overcoming those difficulties. Such instruction is likely to be effective whatever label we give the child. So far, the evidence seems to suggest that the differences in optimal instruction for disabled learners and for nondisabled learners are quantitative, not qualitative. Whatever the level of their reading aptitude, all children can use a bit of instruction. Some children need considerably more than a bit. Many of us are convinced that this is the way to look at beginning reading instruction, and I think that it will turn out to be the way to look at reading comprehension instruction as well.

End Note

This work was supported by grants from the U.S. Department of Education (Office of Special Programs).

References

Anderson, R.C., & Pearson, P.D. (1984). A schema-theoretic view of basic processes in reading comprehension. In P.D. Pearson (Ed.), *Handbook of reading research*. New York: Longman, Inc.

Atwell, N. (1984). Writing and reading from the inside out. *Language Arts, 61*, 240-252.

Bateman, B. (1979). Teaching reading to LD and other hard-to-reach children. In L.B. Resnick & P.A. Weaver (Eds.), *Theory and practice of early reading,* vol. I (pp. 227-260). Hillsdale, NJ: Erlbaum.

Baumann, J.F. (1984). The effectiveness of a direct instruction paradigm for teaching main idea comprehension. *Reading Research Quarterly, 20*(1), 93-115.

Cooper, C.R. (1985). *Researching response to literature and the teaching of literature: Points of departure.* Norwood, NJ: Ablex.

Cullinan, B.E. (Ed.). (1987). *Children's literature in the reading program.* Newark, DE: International Reading Association.

Dorfman, M.H. (1989). *Understanding the points of fables: A developmental study.* Unpublished manuscript.

Dorfman, M.H., & Brewer, W.F. (1988). *Understanding the points of fables.* Unpublished manuscript.

Elkonin, D.B. (1963). The psychology of mastering the elements of reading. In B. Simon and J. Simon (Eds.), *Educational psychology in the USSR.* London: Routledge and Kegan Paul.

Fish, S. (1980). *Is there a text in this class?* Cambridge, MA: Harvard University Press.

Gardner, R. A. (1986). *Therapeutic communication with children: The mutual storytelling technique.* Northvale, NJ: Jason Aronson, Inc.

Garner, R., Belcher, V., Winfield, E., & Smith, T. (1985). Multiple measures of text summarization proficiency: What can fifth-grade students do? *Research in the Teaching of English, 9*(2), 140-153.

Golden, J. M. (1989). Reading in the classroom context: A semiotic event. *Semiotica, 73,* 67-84.

Golden, J. M., & Guthrie, J. T. (1986). Congruence and divergence in reader response to literature. *Reading Research Quarterly, 21,* 408-421.

Goodman, K.S., & Goodman, Y.M. (1979). Learning to read is natural. In L.B. Resnick & P.A. Weaver (Eds.), *Theory and practice of early reading,* vol. I (pp. 137-154). Hillsdale, NJ: Erlbaum.

Gough, P.B., & Tunmer, W.E. (1986). Decoding, reading, and reading disability. *Remedial and Special Education, 7,* 6-10.

Hammill, D.D. (1990). On defining learning disabilities: An emerging consensus. *Journal of Learning Disabilities, 23,* 120-124.

Hansen, J. (1987). When writers read. Portsmouth, NH: Heinemann.

Hare, V. C., & Milligan, B. (1984). Main idea identification: Instructional explanations in four basal reader series. *Journal of Reading Behavior, 16*(3), 189-204.

Iser, W. (1974). *The implied reader.* Baltimore, MD: Johns Hopkins University Press.

Lehr, S. (1988). The child's developing sense of theme as a response to literature. Reading *Research Quarterly, 23,* 337-357.

Liberman, I. Y., & Shankweiler, D. (1985). Phonology and the problems of learning to read and write. *Remedial and Special Education, 6,* 8-17.

Liebling, C. R. (1989). *Insight into literature: Learning to interpret inside view and character plans in fiction.* Unpublished paper. Cambridge, MA: BBN Systems and Technologies Corporation.

Lukens, R. (1982). *A critical handbook of children's literature.* Glenview, IL: Scott, Foresman.

Pearson, P.D., & Johnson, D.D. (1978). *Teaching reading comprehension.* New York: Holt, Rinehart, & Winston.

Perfetti, C.A. (1985). *Reading ability.* New York: Oxford University Press.

Rosenblatt, L.M. (1938). *Literature as exploration.* New York: Appleton-Century.

Rosenblatt, L. M. (1978). *The reader, the text, and the poem.* Carbondale, IL: Southern Illinois University Press.

Rumelhart, D.E. (1977). Understanding and summarizing brief stories. In D. LaBerge and S. J. Samuels (Eds.), *Basic processes in reading: Perception and comprehension* (pp. 265-303). Hillsdale, NJ: Lawrence Erlbaum Associates.

Seifert, C. M., Dyer, M. G., & Black, J. B. (1986). Thematic knowledge in story understanding. *Text,* 393-425.

Shure, M. B., & Spivack, H. (1978). *Problem solving techniques in childrearing.* San Francisco, CA: Jossey-Bass.

Squire, J. R. (1964). *The responses of adolescents while reading four short stories.* Champaign, IL: NCTE.

Stanovich, K. E. (1986). Cognitive processes and the reading problems of learning-disabled children: Evaluating the assumption of specificity. In J.K. Torgesen & B. Y. L. Wong (Eds.), *Psychological and educational perspectives on learning disability.* Orlando, FL: Academic Press.

Stanovich, K. E. (1988). The right and wrong places to look for the cognitive locus of reading disability. *Annals of Dyslexia, 38,* 154-177.

Sulzby, E. (1988). A study of children's early reading development. In A.D. Pellegrini (Ed.), *Psychological bases for early education* (pp. 39-75). Chichester, England: Wiley.

Taylor, M. B., & Williams, J. P. (1983). Comprehension of LD readers: Task and text variations. *Journal of Educational Psychology, 75,* 743-751.

van Dijk, T. A. (1980). *Macrostructures.* Hillsdale, NJ: Erlbaum.

Williams, J. P. (1977). Building perceptual and cognitive strategies into a reading curriculum. In A.S. Reber and D.L. Scarborough (Eds.), *Toward a psychology of reading* (pp. 257-288). Hillsdale, NJ: Erlbaum.

Williams, J. P. (1986). The role of phonemic analysis in reading. In J. Torgesen and B. Wong (Eds.), *Psychological and educational perspectives on learning disabilities* (pp. 399-416). New York: Academic Press.

Williams, J.P. (1990). Learning-disabled adolescents' difficulties in solving personal/social problems presented in text. In J. Baron and R.V. Brown (Eds.), *Teaching decision-making to adolescents* (pp. 237-270). Hillsdale, NJ: Erlbaum.

Williams, J.P. (1991a). Comprehension by learning-disabled and nondisabled adolescents of personal/social problems presented in text. *American Journal of Psychology, 104,* 563-586.

Williams, J. P. (1991b). Learning disabled readers' comprehension of theme in narrative. Final Report, Grant No. G008730078, U.S. Department of Education.

Williams, J. P., & Ellsworth, N. (1990). Teaching learning-disabled adolescents to think critically using a problem-solving schema. *Exceptionality, 1,* 135-146.

Williams, J. P., Taylor, M. B., & deCani, J. S. (1984). Constructing macrostructure for expository text. *Journal of Educational Psychology, 76,* 1065-1075.

Williams, J. P., Taylor, M. B., & Ganger, S. (1981). Text variations at the level of the individual sentence and the comprehension of simple expository paragraphs. *Journal of Educational Psychology, 73,* 851-865.

Williams, J.P., Taylor, M.B., Jarin, D.C., & Milligan, E.S. (1983). Determining the main idea of expository paragraphs: An instructional program for the learning-disabled and its evaluation. (Technical Report #25). Research Institute for the Study of Learning Disabilities, Teachers College, Columbia University.

Winograd, P. N. (1984). Strategic difficulties in summarizing texts. *Reading Research Quarterly, 19,* 404-425.

Wixson, K.K. & Lipson, M.Y. (1991). Perspectives on reading disability research. In R. Barr, M. L. Kamil, P. Mosenthal, & P. D. Pearson, *Handbook of Reading Research,* Vol. II (pp. 539-570). White Plains, NY: Longman.

8

Literacy in an Age of Integrated-Media

*Diana L. Miller Sharp, John D. Bransford, Nancy Vye,
Susan R. Goldman, Charles Kinzer,
& Salvatore Soraci, Jr.*

Over the past several decades, educators have viewed with dismay the proliferation of television and video technologies that seem to have relegated books to small, far corners in the world of choices for entertainment and information. Typical fifth graders now read only four minutes a day or less outside of school (Healy, 1990). This trend away from reading has given rise to the fear that television is leading to a cultural devaluing of print literacy skills.

The perceived clash between television and literacy has been accompanied by a spate of research aimed at determining whether print or video is the superior medium for conveying memorable information, particularly to children (e.g., Beagles-Roos & Gat, 1983; Meringoff, 1980). More recently, a few researchers have changed course, moving away from question of which is better toward more cognitively-oriented questions about how particular attributes of print or video might best be educationally suited for different types of learners or different types of learning goals (see Clark & Salomon, 1986, for review). Although this approach has promise, new advances in technology are demanding that new questions be asked even before all of the old ones are answered. Specifically, questions about the individual merits and demerits of print or video are being superseded by important questions about the effects of *combining* print and video in integrated media systems, where the two media are under computer control.

Our goal in this chapter is to explore from a cognitive perspective how print and video in controlled combination might complement each other in a synergistic fashion, leading towards enhanced learning and literacy, with a renewed emphasis on skills for reading and writing. We begin by describing a new look in books that has arisen from integrated media (IM) technology and is now available to the general public. At present, these "new look" books combine computers and print with still illustrations, rather than video, but we use them as a starting point for exploring the potential of IM systems from two perspectives. First, we explore IM as information-delivery systems. In this capacity, IM systems convey information and assist in developing background knowledge, a crucial component of literacy success. Our focus here is on how the elements of IM systems–still illustrations, video, and computers–can enhance print, so that children can most effectively comprehend and remember a given story or passage.

Of course, background knowledge is only one element of literacy, and so the information-delivery potential of IM systems is only of partial interest. The second section of our chapter explores IM systems as literacy-training systems. In this capacity, IM systems can address educators concerns that children develop skills for good reading and writing. We examine how the different components of IM systems can combine to form supportive environments where children can learn and practice traditional skills that are associated with reading and writing. The final section of our paper describes two IM programs that are currently in use as both literacy-training and knowledge-building environments.

Throughout the chapter, we stress that the propagation of IM technologies may demand that we reconsider what it will mean to be literate in the twenty-first century. We do not believe that print literacy will diminish in importance. However, conceptions of literacy may need to be expanded to include skills for effectively combining media in ways that are appropriate for particular curriculum goals. These new components of literacy have important implications for teachers, curriculum designers, and teacher educators in the coming years.

New Looks in Books

Discis Books (1990) is an excellent example of IM systems that combine computers, text, and still illustrations. In Discis books, the printed story and the illustrations are displayed on the computer screen and look like a book with pages. The reader can choose several ways of interacting with the book, including (a) listening to the book read aloud in its entirety (relevant text is highlighted as the reading progresses); (b) obtaining definitions for any of the words; (c) hearing any particular word or phrase pronounced on demand (with the reader relying on the printed text the rest of the time); and (d) listening to the names of key objects in the illustrations.

It is immediately apparent that this format has some potential advantages over traditional books, both in delivering information for comprehension and in encouraging the development of reading skills. First, as an information delivery system Discis books can provide vocabulary information and decoding help that might otherwise thwart comprehension of the story, especially when children want to read a book but do not have a teacher or other adult available to help them with unfamiliar words. When children effectively comprehend a story, they are likely to acquire new vocabulary words. Second, as a literacy-training system, Discis books can encourage children to practice decoding the print themselves and then to get feedback by listening to the text as it is read. Through this kind of practice, children may build up the automaticity with decoding that is characteristic of skilled readers (Adams, 1990; Perfetti, 1985).

It is also apparent to us that Discis books has some limitations, both in information delivery and in literacy training, but we believe these limitations can be overcome. In the following sections we describe how IM systems can be enhanced so that their potential is expanded.

Enhancing Information Delivery and Comprehension in IM Systems

In Discis books, the combination of visual illustrations and text takes much the same form as in traditional books, because Discis books only use the still, original illustrations found with the stories they computerize. One important question is whether this particular combination of illustrations and text is the most effective combination possible for supporting comprehension. Although many studies suggest that visual illustrations generally improve story comprehension, there is an extensive research literature on pictures and comprehension that shows quite clearly that different types of pictures vary in their effectiveness, and many pictures found in story books do not support comprehension and memory. For example, decorative pictures, which do not provide information about the actual situations in a story, do not help children remember stories (Levine & Lentz, 1982; Levin, 1981; Levin, Anglin, & Carney, 1987). A typical decorative illustration from the storybook *Thumbellina* shows Thumbellina surrounded by fanciful vines and creature from the story, but does not depict any particular scene in the story (Levin, 1981; Levin, Anglin, & Carney, 1987).

In order to take full advantage of the capabilities that new technology affords for information delivery, we need to know how to choose the best possible visuals for use in an integrated media system. To know that, we need to understand how pictures interact with text to promote story comprehension. The following subsections will, therefore, be primarily concerned with the marriage of print and illustrations, both static and dynamic, in IM systems. The final subsection will emphasize the added contributions to this marriage that are provided by computer control.

Picture Effectiveness: Support for Mental Models
One way to understand the differential effectiveness of pictures is to conceptualize pictures as tools for helping children build mental models.[2] Research has shown that effective readers and listeners construct mental models that contain information about the situations and scenes that a story describes (for more information on mental model theory, see Johnson-Laird, 1983 and McNamara, Miller, & Bransford, 1991). Recent research also suggests that mental models are in many ways like images, pictures, or movies. For example, when people read about objects arranged in a scene, they seem to use cognitive processes similar to those used for thinking about pictures of objects in scenes (Sharp & McNamara, 1991). In addition, readers seem to mentally switch scenes in their mental models when a main character moves from one building room or outdoor setting to another (Glenberg, Meyer, & Lindem,

1987; Morrow, Greenspan, & Bower, 1987). According to this view of mental models, pictures that help children imagine what scenes in a story might look like, and imagine how scenes change during the story, should help children to construct good mental models.[3]

As an illustration, imagine a group of children who are listening to a simple story about a thirsty bird who is unable to drink from a glass of water because its beak is not long enough to reach the water at the bottom of the glass. The bird suddenly get an insight and begins to put pebbles into the glass of water. When the water level is high enough, the bird is able to get the water that is in the glass. Children who are effective comprehenders will be able to listen to the sentences in the story and create a dynamic model of the situation in which the water level changes over time. Less effective comprehenders may not be able to understand this situation until they see pictures or movies that illustrate the water level rising with each pebble that the bird adds.

This mental model view of comprehension helps to explain why decorative pictures do not aid comprehension. In the bird story, an understanding of the spatial relationships between the bird, the pebbles, and the water level in the glass is critical for building an adequate mental model. A decorative picture that showed only a bird circling above a glass of water would not convey the spatial relationships related to the change in water level and would not aid mental model construction. In contrast, pictures that illustrated the actual events and state changes involving the bird, pebbles and water level would help children construct mental models. Research has found that pictures such as these are effective in improving comprehension and memory, especially when the pictures help organize complex scenes or parts of scenes that may be difficult to imagine (Bransford & Johnson, 1972; Levie & Lentz, 1982; Levin, 1981; Levin et. al., 1987).

Partial Pictorial Support
Other research suggests that certain pictures can act as frameworks for mental models, even if the pictures do not depict all of the information in the story. In a series of studies on partial pictures, first developed by Guttmann, Levin and Pressley (1977), children were given short stories or sentences that were sometimes accompanied by pictures illustrating only part of the story information. For example, some children were told "One evening Sue's family sat down to eat a big

turkey for dinner," and were shown a picture of the family seated at the table, with the mother's head occluding the center of the table where the turkey was supposed to be.

Across several studies, partial pictures significantly improved children's recall of the stories, including information that, like the turkey in the example above, was not actually shown in the picture. Apparently, children were able to use the pictures as mental model framework onto which other information from the story could be added and imagined. Importantly, this finding was qualified by several age-specific conditions. For example, partial pictures were helpful with multi-sentence stories for third graders but were only helpful with single sentence stories for kindergartners (Guttmann, et al., 1977). For first-graders, partial pictures were generally most helpful when they were presented both at study and during testing (Goldston & Richman, 1985; Ruch & Levin, 1979; Woolridge, Nall, Hughes, Rauch, Stewart, & Richman, 1982). Finally, preschoolers were helped only by the provision of two separate partial pictures; for example, the picture of the family combined with a separate partial picture of the turkey (Digdon, Pressley, & Levin, 1985).

Related research emphasizes that partial pictures need to be carefully constructed if they are to serve as mental model frameworks (Levie & Lentz, 1982). If a picture does not specify enough information about a scene, then children may be unable to imagine the rest of the scene that is described by the story. As an example, in one study children were given a story about a little girl who found a bird on some steps near her house. As a result, the picture helped children remember that the bird was on some steps, but did not help children remember that the little girl carried the bird in her pocket into the house (Willows, in Levie & Lentz, 1982). If the picture had contained more information, then, like the partial pictures described above, it may have been an effective framework, even if it did not actually show the girl carrying the bird.

Relationships Between Pictorial Support and Characteristics of Learners

Overall, the literature on visual pictorial support for comprehension suggests the importance of taking into account children's knowledge, skills and abilities when deciding how much pictorial support is necessary to facilitate mental model building. For example, older children in the partial picture studies seemed to be capable of both imagining a turkey and integrating this image with the partial picture of the family eating dinner; whereas the preschoolers needed to be shown both the turkey and the family, so that only the interaction of the two separate pictures had to be imagined. The finding that older children required less pictorial support to form mental models than younger children is consistent with the finding that imagery ability in a comprehension task increases with vocabulary and verbal skills (Pressley, Cariglia-Bull, Deane, & Schneider, 1987). These vocabulary and verbal skills appear to make additional working memory resources available for use by visual imagery processes (Pressley et al., 1987). With this in mind, the partial picture studies with younger children suggest that an increase in the support provided by partial pictures can offset memory resource problems that may be caused by a lack of adequate vocabulary or verbals skills, so that younger readers will be able to effectively use visual imagery for building mental models.

Differences in working memory resources during comprehension have also been proposed as a source of skill differences among readers of the same age (Baddeley, Logie, Nimmo-Smith, & Brereton, 1985; Daneman & Carpenter, 1980, 1983; Dixon, LeFevre, & Twilley, 1988; Goldman, Hogaboam, Bell & Perfetti, 1980; Masson & Miller, 1983; Perfetti & Goldman, 1976). According to one view, less-skilled readers expend more memory resources than skilled readers on decoding processes (Daneman, 1991; Perfetti, 1985). A greater expenditure of working memory resources on decoding means that fewer resources are available for mental model building. Providing pictures to less-skilled readers may create a larger facilitative effect than providing them to skilled readers because of these differences in available working memory resources. Levie and Lentz (1982) provide some support for this differential effect. Across several studies, less-skilled readers' text comprehension and memory performance reflected average improvements of 44% when the text included illustrations. For skilled readers, the average improvement due to illustrations was 23%.

Of course, even skilled readers can benefit from pictorial support when they encounter numerous pieces of unfamiliar information that threaten to overtax the limits of working memory. For example, consider the following description of a cap, from Flaubert's *Madame Bovary:*

His was one of those composite pieces of headgear in which you may trace features of bearskin, lancer-cap and bowler, night-cap and otterskin; one of those pathetic objects that are deeply expressing in their dumb ugliness, like an idiot's face. An oval splayed out with a whale-bone, it started off with three pompons; these were followed by lozenges of velvet and rabbit's fur alternatively, separated by a red band, and after that came a kind of bag ending in a polygon of cardboard with intricate braiding on it; and from this there hung down like a tassel, at the end of a long, too slender cord, a little sheaf of gold threads.

Lodge (1990) points out that a picture of the cap could help readers keep track of all the details and integrate them into a single image.

There is a plethora of research demonstrating that, in general, information that is generated by the learner is better remembered than information that is simply provided to the learner (Pressley, McDaniel, Turnure, & Wood, 1987; Slamecka & Graf, 1978; Wittrock, 1974). However the relationship between image generation and pictorial support is not so clear. Some researchers have reported that subjects who are provided with pictures for a text outperform subjects who are told to generate images for a text, even when the text seemed to be relatively easy to comprehend and imagine (Levin, 1981; Levin et al., 1987). Explanations for this finding include the notion that pictures provide concreteness for mental images that lead to mental models but that this concreteness produces overspecificity in the model. Another problem is that the quality of the images generated is difficult to determine from these studies (Levin, 1981; Levin et al., 1987). In order to maximize the amount generated, it may be that the ideal level of pictorial support may actually be the *least* amount necessary for a given reader to generate a mental model. One implication of this possibility is that the same pictures may have differential effects on skilled and less-skilled readers because they do not all need the same level of pictorial support (e.g., maximal or minimal support). Effective tailoring of pictorial support for learners of different skill levels may involve balancing the benefits of generation and the benefits of pictorial support.

Benefits of Dynamic Images
Breakthroughs in IM technologies make it much easier to create materials that go beyond still illustrations and include dynamic events. Perception theorists such as E. Gibson (1969) convincingly argue that dynamic events are readily perceived, even by infants, and that dynamic

event perception is not a process of first storing static images and then having to mentally transform them to create a perception of motion. Instead, events can be perceived directly (e.g., J. Gibson, 1966). Because of the ease of perceiving dynamic events, it seems clear that dynamic images can add a further dimension of pictorial support beyond static pictures, especially for information about state changes and actions. Story plot lines, for example, usually revolve around actions and changes that result from actions, and this kind of information is much easier to convey and comprehend if dynamic images rather than static illustrations are presented.

Data from a variety of media studies suggest that as an information-delivery system, dynamic video is superior to text or text plus static pictures. In particular, a number of studies that have compared story comprehension in different media suggest that children remember central story actions better for televised stories than for orally-presented stories, even when the orally presented stories are accompanied by static pictures (Gibbons, Anderson, Smith, Field, & Fischer, 1986; Hayes, Kelly, & Mandel, 1986; Meringoff, 1980), especially over longer periods of delay (Baggett, 1979). In addition, memory for details and vague characters is enhanced by television, (Beagles-Roos & Gat, 1983). Generally, the only time that memory for televised information is worse than memory for orally-presented information is when memory for dialogue and figurative language is tested, and this finding is not consistent across studies (Beagles-Roos & Gat, 1983; Gibbons et al., 1986; Meringoff, 1980; Hayes et al., 1986).

It is important to note that, just as in the static picture literature, one should not expect that every dynamic video will necessarily enhance comprehension. Kozma (in press) points out that videos can restrict the information that they provide in several ways. For example, "talking head" videos show only a character or group of characters on a screen, with all of the information provided through dialogue between characters. These sorts of video are analogous to the decorative pictures described earlier. In order for videos to support mental model building, they need to provide visual details about the setting, character actions, and changes in spatial relationships as the characters progress through the story. In reviewing or creating video for multi-media applications, the critical question is whether the video provides support for mental model building.

It is also important to stress that most of the studies we have reviewed used dynamic video that included a language-based audio track. The support for mental model building that comes from the marriage of dynamic images and linguistic information may actually be a product of a synergistic relationship between the two media. Just as dynamic images can support the comprehension of linguistic information, so can linguistic information aid noticing and understanding of events portrayed by the visual images. This type of synergy is illustrated in a study by Rolandelli, Wright, Huston and Eakins (1991). They studied children's comprehension of a video that was designed to be understood without narration. In some conditions, narration was added to the visual events. Results indicated that 5-year-olds benefitted from the combination of narration and video in two ways. First, they remembered more of the visually-presented material than did children who watched the non-narrated version, suggesting that language aided the interpretation of the pictures. Second, separate measures of children's attention to the visual information on the screen and their attention to information on the audio track showed that comprehension of the audio track was increased when children paid attention to the images on the television screen. In other words, children appeared to use the images on the screen to aid their comprehension of the narration on the audio track.

Computer Contributions to Pictures Plus Print

In describing the marriage of print and visual images, the preceding sections seem to lead to the conclusion that the most effective information delivery systems are movies that include visual support for mental model building along with linguistic information (audio or written text) that aids interpretation of the images. However, IM systems are an important step beyond movies, in part because computer control allows learners to selectively access and revisit particular scenes. Through digital technology, each frame of the dynamic visuals is given an address that can be instantly called up by a computer and replayed.

This capability is extremely important, because single viewings of complex topics usually result in learning that is quite superficial. In reading, learners often use look back strategies to help in the comprehension of unfamiliar material (Goldman & Saul, 1990). This kind of revisiting is not possible for television, where learners have no control over the presentation of shows and only revisit shows when programs are shown again in their entirety. Even with videotape, where the learner does have some control, it is extremely cumbersome to wind and rewind the tape in search of a particular scene. The ability to meaningfully search both text and video through the use of computer interfaces has been shown to enhance learning compared to merely re-reading a text or re-viewing a video (e.g., CTGV, in press (a); Dee-Lucas & Larkin, 1991). Videodiscs or other devices that permit random access to all frames can be controlled by computers; these types of systems enable the information delivery capability of IM systems to exceed what is possible through movies or videos alone.

Enhancing Literacy Training Through IM Systems

It is one thing to claim that IM systems can deliver information to children more effectively than text alone, and it is quite another to suggest that IM systems can be used to teach skills for reading and writing. Earlier, we described the way that Discis books could be used as an environment where children can practice decoding text, with support from computer feedback that can be provided when decoding difficulties are encountered. An important question to address, however, is whether IM systems can be used to teach literacy skills beyond the decoding processes needed for print. Several studies suggest that many reading difficulties are caused by poor comprehension strategies, rather than poor decoding performance (Healy, 1990). For example, listening comprehension, which does not require the decoding of print, is highly correlated with reading comprehension (e.g., Curtis, 1980; Juel, 1991; Pezdek, Lehrer, & Simon, 1984).

In the section below, we describe how video, when combined with text and computer control, can provide environments where children can learn and practice skills for comprehending and for communicating effectively–skills that form the basis of what it means to be literate.

IM and Traditional Literacy

Some educators may fear that children who learn comprehension and communication skills in IM systems will only be able to use these skills in other IM systems, thereby never becoming truly print literate. These fears tend to be fueled by arguments from researchers who suggest that video is not useful for building literacy skills, because reading and television-watching can involve very different kinds of cognitive skills. For example, Pezdek, et al. (1984) compared third and sixth graders' abilities to comprehend stories presented in a picture-book, as a radio program, and as a television program. Although there was a correlation between a child's comprehension and memory for a picture-book story and a radio story, there was no correlation between comprehension and memory for the televised story and either the picture-book story or the radio story. In addition, several researchers have shown that when children watch television, they tend to make more superficial inferences and access less background knowledge than they do when listening to a story (Beagles-Roos & Gat, 1983; Meringoff, 1980; Salomon, 1983a; Vibbert & Meringoff, 1981; but see Gibbons et al., 1986).

A closer look suggests that these findings do not seriously limit the potential for IM to act as a literacy training system. For example, the finding from Pezdek and colleagues (1984) may not mean that there are no common skills between reading and television watching; instead, it may mean that less-skilled readers who have trouble decoding sentences are able to be good television viewers. The memorable, dynamic images in television may help less-skilled readers and listeners overcome problems in comprehending the audio track so that these children can comprehend well the basic situations in a particular story. The lack of a correlation between television watching and reading could therefore be turned to an advantage in an IM system. The level of basic comprehension afforded by video could pave the way for learning about advanced comprehension skills that normally would be out of reach for less-skilled readers faced with a story all in print. We will elaborate on this point in subsequent sections.

Of course, the success of IM systems for teaching literacy skills will still depend on the transferability of skills from video to reading and listening. This transfer could only take place if these higher order comprehension skills are similar across television watching and reading. Salomon (1983b) argues that the same general cognitive processes are used for many aspects of comprehending both print and television, and recent research with college students provides evidence that there are general comprehension skills that are shared across verbal and pictorial modalities (Gernsbacher, Varner, & Faust, 1990).

Similarly, research suggests that one reason children often only make superficial inferences for televised stories is that children believe television watching is less demanding than reading. Consequently, children invest less effort in making inferences when watching television than they do when reading (Salomon, 1983). However, research has also found that special instructions can change children's perception of television-viewing and increase their inferential learning from television (Salomon, 1983a). Our "Young Sherlock" project, discussed later in the chapter, also found that students presented with video tend to view it as entertainment unless other ways and purposes for viewing are provided. In short, available evidence suggests that although video alone cannot serve effectively as the sole medium for a literacy-training program, it can serve as a valuable component of an IM system for teaching literacy skills.

Defining Targeted Skills: Higher Order Comprehension and Representational Literacy

One way that IM systems can move beyond teaching decoding skills is by creating environments where all learners, including less-skilled readers, can practice higher order comprehension skills that take place after an initial mental model has been formed. Many important literacy lessons are based on the premise that readers have constructed an adequate mental model of the story situation. For example, lessons that focus on the analysis and discussion of plot structures, character development, and comparisons across different stories all require that children have comprehended the basic story actions that different characters have performed. If initial comprehension has failed, then lessons on these elements within a given story are also doomed to failure. One of the strengths of IM systems is that less-skilled readers are not excluded from learning these higher order skills simply because they have often failed to effectively encode basic story information. IM systems offer less-skilled readers an alternative route to the kind of mental model that is necessary for learning higher-order aspects of comprehension.

The second way that IM systems can move beyond decoding instruction is by focusing on mental model building skills per se, so that children can learn to create mental models. When children are faced with information that is presented in a single medium, e.g. print, they need to provide their own support for mental models through *mental translations* from text to pictorial representations. The set of skills necessary for conversions from one modality to another belong to a group of skills we call representational literacy. Our developing notion of representational literacy highlights the importance of teaching children to be fluent with (a) translating from language to pictures, so that children can create mental images for what they hear or read about, and (b) translating from pictures to language, so that children can talk and write about what they see and experience.

IM systems are ideal for developing representational literacy. Students can first attempt to mentally translate information and then use the IM system to check the sensibility of their representations. For example, children reading the thirsty bird story described earlier might periodically switch from text to video, in order to ensure that they were correctly imagining the interrelated actions of the bird, the stones, and the change of water level in the glass. Of course, children will not need to match all elements of their images to the video; in fact, unless the text specifically states a rich description of the bird, the type of glass, and so on, then we would expect the imagination of these elements to vary from child to child. Children can, however, use the video to correct misconceptions or fill in gaps in their mental images. By teaching children to fluently manipulate their own internal representation, we can prepare them to be literate in a variety of contexts, including contexts of reading, listening, writing, and oral communication.

Two Projects that Utilize IM

We have been working on two projects that were designed to capitalize on the advantages of using IM for conveying background knowledge and for developing a variety of literacy skills. The first project is aimed at teaching historical information and higher order comprehension skills to older elementary children; the second is targeted at teaching basic skills of representational literacy to young, nonreaders. Both projects are concerned with teaching literacy skills necessary for dealing with oral language and print, but they are also capable of extending literacy skills into media beyond print.

The Young Sherlock Project

The Young Sherlock project uses video-based stories as focal contexts for teaching both general literacy skills involved in good writing and reading, and background knowledge, including vocabulary, elements of story grammars, and historical information. We refer to the video contexts as macrocontexts because they are intended to stimulate learning over an extended period of time (i.e., several months), and can be used to integrate learning across content areas that are separate in most school curricula. This particular program is called Young Sherlock because the initial focal context used was the movie, *The Young Sherlock Holmes.* As secondary video, *Oliver Twist* was also used.

As noted elsewhere (Bransford, Kinzer, Risko, Rowe, & Vye, 1989), the notion of using video rather that books to begin a language arts class that emphasizes reading and writing seems at first glance to be counterintuitive. Nevertheless, there are a number of advantages of using the video–advantages similar to those discussed earlier in this chapter. For example:

(1) The video provides more support for individual differences than the text because even less-skilled readers can enter into class discussions;

(2) There are many more cues for mental-model building (e.g., setting, what the characters look and sound like) in the video than in the book;

(3) It is possible to communicate richer plots and subplots in the video than is possible in a book designed for fifth grade reading levels;

(4) There is much more information to notice in the video than the book, and this stimulates research by students in order to explore points in more detail.

It is important to note that the *Sherlock* and *Oliver* videos were not simply shown once or twice in a linear format. Students were allowed to revisit scenes as needed so that they could study various points in detail. As we discussed earlier in this chapter, the opportunity to revisit scenes represents a powerful advantage of videodisc presentation as compared to videotape or television.

The opportunity to revisit scenes and notice new details provided one of the key features of the curriculum. The video macrocontexts served as anchors to which teachers and students could relate curricular content that otherwise would often be presented in an arbitrary, disconnected fashion. Both the extended time spent on the macrocontext and the video format of the macrocontext allowed children to develop rich understandings (i.e., mental models) of the story and its setting. These mental models were then used to stimulate children to explore related information in texts and to improve the way that children constructed their own stories in writing exercises. In particular, children learned about the Victorian era in depth by studying the elements of setting in the movie and then conducting research (using texts) to determine the historical accuracy of the film (CTGV, 1990). Data collected at the end of the project confirmed that students in the project had developed elaborate mental models of what it was like to live in particular historical periods such as the Victorian era. Of particular note is the fact that this knowledge provided support for a greater range of inferences when students read texts set in the Victorian time period (Bransford et al., 1989; Bransford, Bye, Kinzer, & Risko, 1990).

Students also extensively studied the plot sequence, character development, and the relationship between character motives and events in the movie. Data indicated that students in this curriculum were able to use knowledge about these elements in the film to improve their own writing and to use new, targeted vocabulary in their own stories (CTGV, 1990). In short, the video-based macrocontexts were effective in enhancing, rather than hurting, traditional literacy skills.

Later extensions of the program allowed children to practice the kind of new communication skills that recent technology has made possible. Some classes were able to publish their ideas and research findings in an IM format that allowed them to add text, sounds, and pictures to their products plus use the computer to control relevant video. Children need to have experience with integrating different media if they are to be literate adults in the twenty-first century, fluent with multiple forms of communication. Venezky, Wagner and Ciliberti (1991) point out that expectations for functionally literate adults increase exponentially over time. It seems clear that new societal demands and expectations will arise as literacy-related technology continues to change; functional literacy requirements will increasingly encompass the ability to process increased amounts of information, from diverse sources, while including the necessity of merging print, static, and dynamic pictures (including charts, maps, and so on). Current curricula for teaching IM communication skills are virtually nonexistent, and little research exists on ways to teach children how and when to combine different media for the most effective transmission of their ideas. If education is to keep pace with developments in modern communication, literacy programs will have to be adapted to include skills in both traditional language and print mediums and newer, IM that include computers and video.

The Young Children's Literacy Project

The Young Children's Literacy Project uses computers and video to move beyond the static illustration and partial picture studies described earlier (e.g., Guttmann et al., 1977) to create learning environments that not only provide mental model frameworks for comprehension but also teach mental model building skills to young children who are at-risk for school failure. The project is new and still in its first stages of research but is based on previous work showing that at-risk kindergartners are far behind their peers in their ability to comprehend stories that are told to them (Johnson, 1987). Our present project confirms these findings: many inner-city kindergartners in our pilot work could not answer simple questions from a short ten-sentence story that was told to them just seconds earlier, and some children were unable to recall even a single piece of information from the story.

In pilot work, we have tried to improve these children's comprehension skills by using video to teach them what it means to translate sentences from stories into pictures. For example, we read them sentences from stories such as "Jimmy got on his bike, and then the front wheel fell off." We then showed them two different video clips; one clip matched the sentence, and the other showed the handlebars (rather than the wheel) falling off the bike. Children were asked to determine whether each video matched the sentence. Initially, many children were confused by this task. However, after we provided the children with feedback on the correct and incorrect video matches, they quickly learned to pick out relatively subtle errors in the translation from language to pictures. In short, this type of video training seemed to be an effective way to model and communicate to children what we mean when we say "Try to imagine what this sentence would look like."

Dynamic video also allows us to present a host of video images that a child can use to build a framework for a mental model. After we presented the kindergartners with video training, as described above, we read them short stories, accompanied by video. Unlike current IM programs, where a single static picture usually serves for a whole page or more of text, we accompanied each sentence of the story with its own video clip, so that children could experience the dynamic translation of a single sentence into visual form. The video clips were either faithful representations of the sentences, or clips analogous to the decorative pictures described earlier, in that they provided little information about the situation of the story. For example, in one story, a little mouse finds himself being chased by large bugs in a tunnel. The helpful video showed the mouse as he walked down the tunnel, turned around, saw the bugs, and began to run down the tunnel away from the bugs. The non-helpful video showed only a head shot of the mouse against a grey background, with the dynamic turning of the mouse's head as he looked behind him. After we read this initial portion of the story, we asked the children to imagine that the bugs all fell into a large hole in the ground, so that the mouse was able to get away safely. After children had heard a series of three stories, we asked them to remember each of the stories. In addition to verbal questioning, we also asked children to discern whether or not another video clip matched the portion of the story that we asked them to imagine, and to explain why the clip did or didn't match.

Our pilot work strongly indicates that children who saw helpful video accompanying the initial portion of the story were better than children who had seen non-helpful video or no video at remembering both the initial information in the story *and* at remembering the part that we told them to imagine. In fact, several children showed a dramatic improvement in verbal fluency after they had participated in the video training and after they had seen the initial portion of a story on video.

As an illustration, Table 8.1 shows the protocols from two children who were told the mouse-bugs story after they had participated in the video training procedure. Child 1 saw helpful video with the beginning of the story, and Child 2 saw non-helpful video. As shown, Child 1 remembered information from the story, including the to-be-imagined information about the bugs falling into a hole, but Child 2 did not remember any information. Providing the helpful video after the story did not seem to help Child 2. Table 8.1 also shows protocols from these same children after they heard a story about a mouse and a cat. The helpful video accompanying the beginning of the story showed the mouse on a piano being surprised by the appearance of a cat. The to-be-imagined sentences described the mouse jumping down from the piano and hiding under it. This time Child 2 saw helpful video with the story, and Child 1 saw no video at all. As the protocols show, only the child who saw the helpful video accompanying the beginning of the story remembered the beginning and the to-be-imagined events. Once again, helpful video shown after the story did not seem beneficial.

Table 8.1 Sample Protocols from At-Risk Kindergartners

Mouse-Bugs Story

Helpful video:

E: (pointing to helpful video on the screen) Can you tell me that story?

Child 1: Yes. He running, then all the spiders came and chased him.

E: And then what happened?

Child 1: And then, and then, and then they falling in the hole.

E: Who fell in the hole?

Child 1:All of the spiders.

E: Ok, did the mouse fall too?

Child 1: No.

Non-helpful video:

E: (pointing to non-helpful video on screen) - Do you remember a story about that?

Mouse-Cat Story

Helpful video:

E: (pointing to helpful video on the screen) Tell me that story.

Child 2: He saw a big cat.

E: He saw a big cat.

Child 2: And then he jumped down on the ground underneath the piano to hide from the big cat.

No video:

E: Can you tell me that story (the one you heard with the tv off?)

Child 1: Um. What story?

E: Remember the story I told you about the little mouse? What happened to the little mouse?

Child 1: What? Where?

Child 2: No

E: Look at this part here and see if this helps you to tell some of it. (points to helpful video on the screen). Now can you tell me a story about that on the screen?

Child 2: No

E: What's happening there?... Do you remember anything about this story?

Child 2: (shakes head no).

E: What are those things chasing him? What's going on?

Child 2: (no response).

E: Do you remember he went to a piano?

Child 1: I don't know that.

E: He went to a piano, and remember he saw a cat?

Child 1: (shakes head no)

E: Why don't you turn the tv on. (shows helpful video). That was part of the story I told you. I didn't show it to you before, but I told you about it. Do you remember what happened next?

Child 1: (shakes head no).

Our pilot works suggests that video can serve as an effective mental model framework for stories by providing children with the background information about a story situation as well as video images that help children keep track of what the characters and the scenes look like and how the particular spatial relationships in a story are organized. The kind of video tasks we have so far described have been aimed at teaching comprehension and production at a simple level, using single sentences or very short stories, and we are currently in the process of extending our comprehension tasks into a program that can be used teach comprehension skills at multiple levels of complexity. Because the video medium is highly memorable, as long as children realize that they need to carefully attend to the information, video should also be capable of providing mental model frameworks for more complex stories and higher-order comprehension skills. For example, we are developing longer video stories that will allow us to reach children to help a character decide what the best course of action is at a particular point in the story, to predict what the consequences of a particular action will be, and to use information from previous scenes to make decisions for a later scene. With the initial portion of the story presented on video, even young children with limited language skills should be equipped with a powerful framework that will allow them to participate in and practice these complex, higher order comprehension skills.

In addition to providing means for teaching visualization and comprehension skills, video tasks can also provide new ways for teachers to assess comprehension skills of children who are not verbally fluent. Most teachers know that simply asking children if they understand part of a story is an ineffective measure of whether or not they really understand. Similarly, asking a child to repeat or explain part of a story may also be an unreliable measure if the child is shy or has language deficiencies. In contrast, asking a child whether or not a video clip matches part of a story can be a good, nonverbal test for comprehension, as long as the video clips are carefully constructed to match or not match particular elements in the story. Moreover, video clips can provide opportunities for the child to engage in meaningful language production. For example, children can practice expressing, in language, what a video shows and how it may be different from what was told in the story.

The ability of video to facilitate mental model building should also lend itself well to teaching important, basic knowledge, as well as story content. For example, we are creating video stories that can be used to teach and enhance mental model building while also introducing students to important content relevant to inquiry involving science, mathematics, reading, and writing. By using the video to help children understand this kind of information, we hope to help them develop useful schemas that they can use in math and science tasks. The power of having a video story as an anchor for math and science instruction has already been shown with older children (CTGV, in press (a); CTGV, in press (b)).

Finally, we envision our program on representational literacy not only teaching children to fluently translate between language and pictures, but also recognizing when language is particularly suited for expressing an idea, and when pictures are a more effective means of expression. Both language and pictures have their own strengths and limitations. As we have noted previously, it is our belief that in this age of IM, it will become increasingly important for children to know how to choose the most effective medium or combination of media for communicating their ideas.

Summary and Conclusions

We began this chapter by noting that many people who love books are concerned about the influence of video on children's development. We argued that when video is combined with oral and written language in IM systems, a new environment emerges with properties that have the potential to dramatically enhance learning and literacy. In our discussion, we attempted to show how new IM technologies make it possible to design learning environments that are superior to either text alone, text with pictures, or video alone as in television or in videotapes.

We discussed the advantages of IM systems from two perspectives—the advantages for information delivery, and the advantages for literacy training. From the perspective of information delivery, we noted that currently available talking books may be under-utilizing the support that IM systems can provide through pictorial images, especially dynamic images on video. An examination of cognitive and educational research revealed that certain types of pictures can help readers form mental models, and that the amount of support that is necessary will likely depend on the age and abilities of the reader. We also noted that the ability to combine text with video is especially powerful when computers provide interface to revisit specific video scenes.

From the perspective of literacy training, we suggested that IM systems like talking books could be expanded into environments that support a variety of skills associated with reading and writing, particularly higher order comprehension skills. We also suggested that conceptions of literacy may need to be broadened to include skills of representational literacy. According to our developing notions, a child who is representationally literate should be able to (a) fluently translate from information represented in language to information represented in mental images (as in comprehension), (b) translate from information seen in the world or in pictures to language (as in production), and (c) recognize the strengths and weaknesses of language and pictures for expressing particular kinds of ideas (as in effective communication). Ideally, video and text in an IM system will act synergistically to promote these skills:

  * As a framework for language comprehension, video can provide background knowledge and spatial images of characters and setting that can be used for imagining subsequent story events. Dynamic video can also model the translation from sentence to

image, making it an effective means for helping children learn to translate story information that they hear into mental models.

* As a framework for oral discussion, video can serve a shared context for exploration and verbal communication between children and teachers. The oral discussion can then serve to highlight information that might otherwise be overlooked in the video.

* As an environment for teaching effective communication, IM can provide experiences with language and pictures that highlight their respective strengths and weaknesses. A continuing challenge for teachers and curriculum designers will be to structure these experiences so that children learn to intelligently select and blend media in order to best achieve communication goals.

We end this chapter by concluding that IM environments may provide learners with an appreciation for and a fluency with language that is beyond what they might achieve in traditional, language-based environments. In particular, the combination of language (oral and print) and dynamic images seems to have the potential to teach and assess the kind of skills that will allow children to be highly effective language users who can also combine media as needed in an advanced technological age.

End Notes

1. Preparation of this paper was made possible by a grant from the National Institute of Child Health and Development, #2 PO1 HD15051-11.
2. For similar and independently formulated views, see Glenberg and Langston (in press) and Kozma (in press).
3. We take the view that mental models can involve more information than a mental image, but mental images are still extremely useful tools that can lead to well-structured mental models.

References

Adams, M. J. (1990) *Beginning to read: Thinking and learning about print.* Cambridge, MA: The MIT Press.

Baddeley, A. D., Logie, R., Nimmo-Smith, I., & Brereton, N. (1985). Components of fluent reading. *Journal of Memory and Language, 24,* 119-131.

Baggett, P. (1979). Structurally equivalent stories in move and text and the effect of the medium on recall. *Journal of Verbal Learning and Verbal Behavior, 18,* 333-356

Beagles-Roos, J., & Gat, I. (1983). Specific impact of radio and television on children's story comprehension. *Journal of Educational Psychology, 75,* 128-137.

Bransford, J. D., & Johnson, M. K. (1972). Contextual prerequisities for understanding: some investigations of comprehension and recall. *Journal of Verbal Learning and Verbal Behavior, 11,* 717-726.

Bransford, J. D., Kinzer, C., Risko, V., Rowe, D., & Vye, N. (1989). Designing invitations to thinking: Some initial thoughts. In S. McCormick, J. Zutrell, P. Scharer & P. O'Keefe (Eds.), *Cognitive and social perspectives for literacy research and instruction* (pp. 35-54). Chicago, IL: National Reading Conference.

Bransford, J. D., Vye, N., Kinzer, C. & Risko, V. (1990). Teaching thinking and content knowledge: Toward an integrated approach. In B. F. Jones & L. Idol (Eds.), *Dimensions of thinking and cognitive instruction.* Hillsdale, NJ: Erlbaum.

Clark, R. E., & Salomon, G. (1986). Media in teaching. In M.C. Wittrock, (Ed.) *Handbook of research on teaching.* (3rd ed.) (pp. 565-478). New York: Macmillan.

CTGV Cognition and Technology Group at Vanderbilt. (1990) Anchored instruction and its relationship to situated cognition. *Educational Researcher, 19*(3), 2010.

CTGVCognition and Technology Group at Vanderbilt. (in press, b). The Jasper series: A generative approach to improving mathematical thinking. In *This Year in School Science.* Washington, D.C.: American Association for the Advancement of Science.

CTGVCognition and Technology Group at Vanderbilt. (in press, a). The Jasper experiment: An exploration of issues in learning and instructional design. In M. Hannfin & S. Hooper (Eds.), a special issue of *Educational Technology Research and Development.*

Curtis, M. E. (1980). Development of components of reading skill. *Journal of Educational Psychology, 72,* 656-669

Daneman, M., & Carpenter, P. (1983). Individual differences in integrating information between and within sentences. *Journal of Experimental Psychology: Learning, Memory, and Cognition, 9,* 561-583.

Daneman, M., & Carpenter, P. (1980). Individual differences in working memory and reading. *Journal of Verbal Learning and Verbal Behavior, 19,* 450-466.

Daneman, M. (1991). Individual differences in reading skills. In R. Barr, M. Kamil, P. Mosenthal, and P.D. Pearson (Eds.), *Handbook of reading research:* Vol. II (pp. 512-538). New York: Longman.

Dee-Lucas, D., & Larkin, J.H. (1991). *Review strategies and content integration with traditional text and hypertext.* Prepublication manuscript, Carnegie Mellon University, Department of Psychology, Pittsburgh.

Digdon, N. L., Pressley, M., & Levin, J. R. (1985). Preschooler's learning when pictures do not tell the whole story. *Educational Communication and Technology Journal, 33,* 139-145.

Discis (1990). Discis books, Vol 1. Toronto, ONT: Discis Knowledge Research, Inc.

Dixon, P., LeFevre, J., & Twilley, L. C. (1988). Word knowledge and working memory as predictors of reading skill. *Journal of Educational Psychology, 80,* 465-472.

Gernsbacher, M. A., Varner, K.R., & Faust, M. E. (1990). Investigating differences in general comprehension skill. *Journal of Experimental Psychology: Learning, Memory, & Cognition, 16,* 430-445.

Gibbons, J., Anderson, D. R., Smith, R., Field, D. E., & Fischer, C. (1986). Young children's recall and reconstruction of audio and audiovisual narratives. *Child Development, 57,* 1014-1023.

Gibson, E. J. (1969). *Principles of perceptual learning and development.* New York: Appleton-Century-Crofts.

Gibson, J. J. (1966). *The senses considered as perceptual systems.* Boston: Houghton Mifflin.

Glenberg, A.M. & Langston, W.E. (in press). Comprehension of illustrated text: Pictures help to build mental models. *Journal of Memory and Language.*

Glenberg, A. M., Meyer, M., & Lindem, K. (1987). Mental models contribute to foregrounding during text comprehension. *Journal of Memory and Language, 26,* 69-83.

Goldman, S. R., Hogaboam, T., Bell, L. C., & Perfetti, C. A. (1980). Short term retention of discourse during reading. *Journal of Educational Psychology, 72,* 647-655.

Goldman, S. R., & Saul, E. U. (1990). Flexibility in text processing: A strategy competition model. *Learning and Individual Differences, 2,* 181-219.

Goldston, D. B., & Richman, C. L. (1985). Imagery, encoding specificity, and prose recall in 6-year-old children. *Journal of Experimental Child Psychology, 40,* 395-405.

Guttmann, J., Levin, J. R., & Pressley, M. (1977). Pictures, partial pictures, and young children's oral prose learning. *Journal of Educational Psychology, 69,* 473-480.

Hayes, D. S., Kelly, S. B., & Mandel, M. (1986). Media differences in children's story synopses: Radio and television contrasted. *Journal of Educational Psychology, 78,* 341-346.

Healy, J. M. (1990). *Endangered minds: Why our children don't think.* New York: Simon and Schuster.

Johnson, R. (1987). *Uses of video technology to facilitate children's learning.* Doctoral dissertation, Vanderbilt University.

Johnson-Laird, P. N. (1983). *Mental models.* Cambridge, MA: Harvard University Press.

Juel, C. (1991). *Longitudinal research on learning to read and write with regular and at-risk students.* Paper presented March 14-15, 1991, at The Maryland Conference on Literacy for the 90s: Perspectives on Theory, Research and Practice, College Park, MD.

Kozma, R. B. (in press). Learning with media. *Review of Educational Research.*

Levie, W. H., & Lentz, R. (1982). Effects of text illustrations: A review of research. *Educational Communication and Technology Journal, 30,* 195-232.

Levin, J. R., Anglin, G.J ., & Carney, R. N. (1987). On empirically validating functions of pictures in prose. In D.M. Willows and H.A. Houghton (Eds.), *The psychology of illustration (Volume 1: Basic research)* (pp. 51-85). New York: Springer-Verlag.

Levin, J. R. (1981) On the functions of pictures in prose. In F. J.

Priozzolo and M. C. Wittrock (Eds.), *Neuropsychological and cognitive processes in reading* (pp. 203-228). New York: Academic Press.

Lodge, D. (1990). Narration with words. In H. Barlow, C. Blakemore, &. M. Weston-Masson, M. E.J ., & Miller, J. A. (1983). Working memory and individual differences in comprehension and memory of text. *Journal of Educational Psychology, 75,* 314-318.

Masson, M.E.J. & Miller, J.A. (1988). Working memory and individual differences in comprehesion and memory of text. *Journal of Educational Psychology, 75,* 314-318.

McNamara, T. P., Miller, D. L., & Bransford, J. D. (1991). Mental models and reading a. In R. Barr, M. Kamil, P. Mosenthal, and P. D. Pearson (Eds.), *Handbook of reading research: Vol. II* (pp. 490-511). New York: Longman.

Meringoff, L. K. (1980). Influence of the medium on children's story apprehension. *Journal of Educational Psychology, 72,* 240-249.

Morrow, D. G., Greenspan, S. L., & Bower, G. H. (1987). Accessibility and situation models in narrative å. *Journal of Memory and Language, 26,* 165-187.

Perfetti, C. A., & Goldman, S. R. (1976). Discourse memory and reading comprehension skill. *Journal of Verbal Learning and Verbal Behavior, 15,* 33-42.

Perfetti, C. A., (1985). *Reading ability.* New York: Oxford University Press.

Pezdek, K., Lehrer, A., & Simon, S. (1984). The relationship between reading and cognitive processing of television and radio. *Child Development, 55,* 2072-2082.

Pressley, M., Cariglia-Bull, T., Deane, S., & Schneider, W. (1987). Short-term memory, verbal competence, and age as predictors of imagery instructional effectiveness. *Journal of Experimental Child Psychology, 43,* 194-211.

Pressley, M., McDaniel, M. A., Turnure, J.E. & Wood, E. (1987). Generation and precision of elaboration: Effects on intentional and incidental learning. *Journal of Experimental Psychology: Learning, Memory, and Cognition, 13,* 291-300.

Rolandelli, D. R., Wright, J. C., Huston, A. C., & Eakins, D. (1991). Children's auditory and visual processing of narrated and nonnarrated television programming. *Journal of Experimental Child Psychology,*

51, 90-122.

Ruch, M., D., & Levin, J. R. (1979). Partial pictures as imagery-retrieval cues in young children's prose recall. *Journal of Experimental Child Psychology, 28,* 268-279.

Salomon, G. (1983a). The differential investment of mental effort in learning from different sources. *Educational Psychologist, 18,* 4250.

Salomon, G. (1983b). Television literacy and television vs. literacy. In R. W. Bailey and R. M. Fosheim, (Eds.,) *Literacy for life: The demand for reading and writing* (pp. 67-78). New York: The Modern Language Association of America.

Sharp, D. L. M., & McNamara, T. P. (1991). *Mental models in narrative comprehension: Now you see them, now you don't.* Prepublication manuscript, Vanderbilt University.

Slamecka, N. J., & Graf, P. (1978). The generation effect: Delineation of a phenomenon. *Journal of Experimental Psychology: Human Learning and Memory, 4,* 592-604.

Smith (Eds.), Images and understanding: *Thoughts about images, ideas about understanding* (pp. 141-153). New York: Cambridge University Press.

Venezky, R. L., Wagner, D. A., & Ciliberti, B. S. (1990). *Toward defining literacy.* Newark, DE: International Reading Association.

Vibbert, M. M., & Meringoff, L. K. (1981). Children's production and application of story imagery: A cross-medium investigation. Harvard Project Zero, Harvard University, [ERIC Document Reproduction Service No. ED 210682]

Wittrock, M. C. (1974). Learning as a generative process. *Educational Psychologist, 11,* 87-95.

Woolridge, P., Nall, L., Hughes, L., Rauch, T., Stewart, G., & Richman, C. (1982). Prose recall in first-grade children using imagery, pictures, and questions. *Bulletin of the Psychonomic Society, 20,* 249-252.

9

Authentic Assessment of Reading and Writing In the Elementary Classroom[1]

Robert Calfee

Paradigm shifts resemble earthquakes–you know that they will happen, but it's difficult to predict when. Paradigm shifts also differ from earthquakes–they are more subtle. You sense an earthquake immediately, but it may take decades or centuries to appreciate the impact of a paradigm shift.

Authentic assessment may represent a fundamental shift in the way that educators think about the outcomes of schooling. It is too early to be certain, and we can only reflect on the import of present rumblings. Several features distinguish the new movements:

- *Production* is more important than *recognition;* students must demonstrate that they can actually do something, rather than simply picking the "right" answer.
- *Projects* are more important than *items*, a choice of depth over breadth. A related contrast is the emphasis on validity over conventional definitions of reliability.

- *Informed judgment* is more important than *mechanized scoring*. The teacher replaces the Scantron as the central character in the assessment process.

Practice has moved ahead of theory , it appears. Teachers are "doing portfolios;" they are reviewing student projects; they are encouraging exhibitions. Psychometricians seem puzzled by this activity, at a loss to know how to standardize the events, uncertain about how to speak of reliability and validity (e.g., Hambleton & Murphy, in press).

My goal in this chapter is to review the concept of alternative assessment in a specific situation: *teacher assessment of student achievement in the literate use of language in the elementary grades.* This domain is especially interesting for present purposes. On the one hand, elementary reading achievement is a centerpiece of the psychometric enterprise; standardized tests are more common in elementary reading and language than any other area of school achievement. Writing achievement in the elementary grades has been less important; standardized writing tests do not usually appear until eighth grade. On the other hand, portfolios and writing journals have found their most welcome reception in the elementary grades, building perhaps on a long tradition of informal assessment (Pikulski & Shanahan, 1982). The situation has the makings for a battle royal!

This review comprises two intermingled parts. My primary effort will be the development of a conceptual framework for classroom-based assessment of reading and writing. To provide a concrete context for the framework (an important feature, given an audience of both practitioners and theoreticians), I will present a specific situation from recent experiences with elementary schools on portfolio development, to exemplify the more abstract concepts.

What Is the Problem?

On my desk is a stack of recent articles and books, all proposing various alternatives to present testing practices: *authentic assessment, portfolios* and *exhibits,* and *performance testing* are popular terms. The stack reflects dissatisfaction with current approaches. Scarcely news– since Walter Lippman, voices have attacked the "tyranny of testing." Few of us want to be assessed. Remember when last you renewed your driver's licence.

What seems novel in today's discourse is that it is not simply an attack, but involves a concerted effort to find alternatives and complements to standardized tests. It directly addresses the *internal-external* conflict in educational assessment (Calfee & Drum, 1979; Calfee & Hiebert, 1989; Cole, 1989; Haertel & Calfee, 1983). Tests mandated by powers outside the classroom versus ongoing assignments and observations by teachers. Tests are designed to provide policy-level accountability, whereas classroom work serves to guide instruction. The gap between the two areas is enormous in both purpose and method. Externally-mandated assessment has displaced teacher-based activity in recent years, with detrimental effects on curriculum, instruction, and the validity of assessment itself

The new alternatives provide an opportunity to achieve a better balance between internal and external assessment. Unfortunately, many proposals have an "anything goes" air (e.g., Tierney, Carter, & Desai, 1991; Harp, 1991; but also see Belanoff & Dickson, 1991), and can easily become occasions for reinventing and rebuilding the wheel. To be sure, teachers gain a sense of professional control over assessment only as they engage personally in the process of formulating and implementing an assessment design, a process that in many ways parallels the work of an applied researcher (Hiebert & Calfee, 1992). But schools and teachers, given limited time and resources, cannot expend energy pursuing new projects unless these have a clear purpose and audience.

Alternative assessments provide an unusual opportunity to reform practices in curriculum and instruction, and to support the emerging calls for professionalization. The key to realizing this potential, in my judgment, is the creation of a solidly grounded conceptual framework for classroom assessment, and the development of working models that demonstrate the value of alternative approaches. Certainly no area of schooling is better suited to this challenge than the acquisition of literacy in the early grades.

The Assessment Task

What needs to be assessed in elementary reading and writing? What does the teacher need to know, and why? What about the students? Parents? Other teachers? The principal? We have all passed through elementary school, and familiarity makes it hard to appreciate the issues. The perils of unauthentic practice are vividly portrayed by Cohen

(1980) in *First Grade Takes a Test,* a delightful work that describes the "meta-thoughts" of young children on their first encounter with a standardized test (also cf. Calfee, Chapman, & Venezky, 1972). The children are isolated, the task makes little sense, the activity does not connect with other classroom routines, and the outcome has little obvious consequence.

This perception contrasts sharply, of course, with the designers' intentions. The test incorporates specific reading objectives (decoding, vocabulary, and so on), the items are refined to insure internal consistency, the total score correlates with subsequent test scores, and the aim is to "measure" student achievement as a guide for instruction as well as an index of accountability. Some standardized tests (e.g., *Degrees of Reading Power*) guide the teacher in selecting reading materials for individual students; many provide profiles of student strengths and weaknesses. Basal end-of-unit tests direct teachers to assign remedial worksheets and supplemental activities. The underlying machinery may not be obvious to student or teacher, but obviousness is not intended.

What might an alternative look like? What would you experience in a classroom that captured the spirit of current proposals? Let me sketch a slightly elaborated scenario from recent personal experience. Ms. K's thirty students are a blend of third and fourth graders of widely ranging backgrounds, interests, and achievement levels. Several youngsters have been labeled as learning disabled, others are from disadvantaged families, and the eight fourth graders were candidates for retention.

In September and early October, Ms. K organized each week around a series of little lessons, each entailing a short text or a familiar topic. Students were organized in small working groups to read, analyze, and prepare a short presentation. By mid-October, the teacher's journal contained brief entries about each student: proficiencies, predilections, and problems in reading and writing. Students had also begun to compile their own personal journals, which combined free writing (a Monday task) and assigned topics (usually on Wednesday or Thursday). Samples of student work (individual and group) appeared on the walls, and each student had begun to accumulate a folder of selected reading-writing papers.

For the post-Halloween parent conferences, Ms. K prepared a one-page summary for each student, reviewing areas of particular competence and particular need. The summary drew on both her journal entries and student materials. The causal observer might puzzle over the summary headings: literature, science, social studies, group participation, citizenship, art/music, and physical education. Where are reading and writing? Ms. K's response is quick and simple: "We work on reading and writing all day long, and we don't need to study them separately."

Let us move past the winter months to late April. The teacher gathers the class:

> There's only one more real month of school! It's time to start our "big" project. This spring you're going to do your *"roots,"* your family history. When you've finished the project, you will have your own *book* to keep.

The *Roots* project is Ms. K's culminating assignment for the school year. From one perspective, the project yields a genuine product. On the other hand, it also provides the context for the teacher's summative assessment of individual student achievement.

The project proceeds in several phases. First is a viewing of excerpts from the *Roots* television series. Students discuss the story, and prepare what might appear to others as a book report, but which students see as the prologue to their own text. For Ms. K, the exercise provides an opportunity to assess student proficiency in the narrative concepts of character, plot, setting, and theme.

The second phase entails the analysis of several biographical pieces, ranging from *Little House on the Prairie* to a newspaper article about Norman Schwarzkopf. The aim of this task is to develop a "shopping list" of information categories and sources to guide the students' research into their family's past, an excursion into exposition. Interviews, Bibles and genealogies, letters, and photo albums appear on a wall chart as potential sources of background information. Much of the design work is collaborative; the teacher notes the contributions of individual students, as well as their effectiveness as group participants. The students then spend a week on data collection, primarily an individual job, although the results are regularly reviewed in collaborative groups.

The third and final phase is the preparation of the report, and presentation of the product to various audiences. The student books are quite extensive, a 100 pages or more. Each includes a title page, table of contents, dedication ("To my parents, without whom this report would not be possible"), thematic overview (the *Roots* story), research on *My Family*, and a "back to the future" piece in which the youngsters describe themselves in the year 2000, the year after high school graduation. The material includes considerable text, along with art work, graphics, and artifacts. The preparation phase entails extensive redrafting of the various segments, peer review, final polishing, and presentation of the project during a back-to-school night in late May.

So much for the project—where does assessment fit into the picture? The linkages among student learning, curriculum, and instruction may appear seamless and difficult to analyze. A conversation with Ms. K, however, gives insight into the underlying process. The assessment hinges on information in the teacher journal as much as the final student product.

The assessment is *integrative*. The project yields a wealth of information about reading and writing, as well as research skills. The portrait extends over a broad reach of the elementary curriculum, formal (literacy, literature, social studies, art) and informal (initiative, cooperation, persistence). The casual observer may see a collage, but the teacher has prepared a design with explicit coverage of each element.

The assessment emphasizes *top-level* competence. From the teacher's perspective, the most critical achievements are top-down: the capacity to wrestle with the overall structure of a discourse, an awareness of audience, a sense of thematic coherence. Her observations also note the micro-skills of spelling, grammar, neatness, and "nice touches." Final products are all polished, but students differ in the amount of guidance needed to complete the job, and in the fluency with which they approach revision, important information for the student, and for next year's teacher.

The assessment emphasizes *meta-language*, the capacity to articulate performance. When I was in elementary school, we had to "show our work" in math problems; the right answer with the wrong reasoning did not count. Ms. K adheres to the same principle. In the scenario, reliance on group activities in planning, reviewing, and presenting all has the purpose of encouraging genuine meta-discourse among students. Ms. K focuses most of her direct instruction on *technical language,* on labels and concepts that help students communicate with one another about reading and writing.

The assessment is *situated*. Every student produces a final product of exceptional quality, and so it is virtually impossible to grade on the basis of differential performance. But students vary in the amount of support and encouragement they need during the project, in their approach to the task, in their ability to sustain the effort, in their willingness to assist and to seek out assistance. The social dimension is especially important to Ms. K. She encourages students to serve as peer reviewers for tasks from the initial draft to the mechanics of spelling and grammar. They become competent in monitoring and criticizing their own work.

Finally, the assessment is guided by *developmental standards*. The teacher's notes are synoptic, readable only by other professionals. But her guideposts are as clearly articulated as a scope-and-sequence chart. Her assessments are not numeric, but they refer to growth, and to relative strengths and weaknesses, as illustrated in Ms. K's summary comments for one student:

> Sam is immature for a fourth grader, and he will need support if he is to do well in fifth grade. His oral language skills are exceptional, and he works hard on topics that interest him: science, computers, and games. He has made great progress in his writing and spelling, but lacks fluency in mechanics. He is better with exposition than narrative; he lacks the empathetic ability that I expect in an eleven year old, which also shows up in his group participation. He enjoys cooperative tasks, but tends to be overbearing and strong willed. He does not listen well, and is impatient with what he sees as mundane tasks like documenting or summarizing.

The teacher prepares a similar paragraph for each student that she adds to the district's standard report card. She finds that parents value these comments as highly as the official grades. They are also pleased about the *Roots* project, which they view as the best indicator of their student's achievement. The fifth grade teachers find Ms. K's comments interesting, but are not quite sure how to use the information. They have grown accustomed to her idiosyncracies, but prefer more conventional indicators (e.g., the student's achievement level in the basal series,) and more grade differentiation (Ms. K gives every student an A in reading and writing on the final report card).

Understanding the Example:

A Conceptual Framework

What does the preceding illustration *mean?* The portrait includes elements of Dewey and whole language, of process writing and Hilda Taba. But the example also incorporates the elements of a design for achieving the terms of the title:

- *assessment:* to estimate value for taxation; to determine the amount of a payment, tax or fine; to evaluate or appraise [from Old French *assesser*, to sit beside as an "assistant judge"]. The key element in this definition is the *rendering of an evaluation for a set purpose.* Assessment requires a "bottom line."
- *authentic:* worthy of trust, reliance, or belief; having an undisputed origin; genuine; real [from Greek *authentikos, authoritative*]. At root, the issue is validity; how adequately does the evidence support the interpretation.
- *reading and writing in the elementary classroom:* the key business of schooling for young children is to support development of the literate use of language. Authentic curriculum is essential to authentic assessment.

To guide your analysis of the preceding scenario, let me suggest several questions that serve as a lens, a *design framework*, for viewing assessment in general and authentic assessment in particular (also cf. Murphy & Smith, 1990):

- What will be assessed?
- How and when will it be assessed?
- Why; for what purposes and audiences?
- Who will design and conduct the assessment?
- How will the assessment be interpreted and reported?

While a complete answer to these questions is beyond the scope of this chapter, the scenario informs each of these issues, and provides the foundation for examining the relation of the illustration to externally-mandated standardized tests.

What should be assessed?

This question is at root a curriculum matter. As Murphy and Smith (1990) put it, "Coming up with a portfolio . . . is choosing what to teach (p. 1). The politics of literacy has a history of divisiveness. Basic skills versus reading for meaning, phonics versus whole language, basal readers versus integrated reading-writing–the catalog of battlegrounds is extensive.

The definition of literacy depends on social and cultural decisions. Given the aspiration toward a fully educated citizenry, the national commitment to equal educational opportunity, and the emergence of an information society, it seems clear that *functional literacy* is an inadequate goal for any student in today's schools. Rather, the goal should be *critical literacy*, the capacity to use language in all forms to think, to solve problems, and to communicate. My own efforts in that direction (Calfee, 1991) emphasize an integrated language arts curriculum, a balance between purposeful engagement in holistic projects and the acquisition of explicitly defined skills. I assume that such a curriculum demands the collaboration of a professional teaching staff who operate as a *community of inquiry* (Schaefer, 1967), who exemplify the curriculum aspiration in their daily lives.

A basic-skills curriculum is relatively easy to define. The task is divided into subtasks, each of which is presented for study, repeated for practice, and tested for mastery. The process is mechanistic, and can be easily computerized. A critical-literacy curriculum is more subtle, more interactive, more holistic. In this curriculum, the first grader's reading of Lionni's *Swimmy* cannot be judged by rate and errors, but requires an ear attuned to stress and style, to the child's sense of audience reaction and engagement. The interplay between parts and wholes is ongoing; analysis and synthesis are part of every lesson. The basic-skills curriculum, in contrast, builds from parts to wholes, from phonics toward comprehension, from words to sentences to texts, from "learning to read" toward "reading to learn" (Chall, 1983), from reading to writing. Basic skills are obviously performance-based: "The student applies the *final-e* rule for vowels" is measured by a 10-item multiple-choice test. Critical literacy requires the analysis of contextualized performance. The teacher needs X-ray vision (and audition) to detect skills and strategies that are embedded in complex activities.

My purpose here is not to present the arguments for and against these positions–my bias is probably evident, but the issues are complex both conceptually and pragmatically. Rather, my point is that decisions about curriculum goals are an essential requisite for the design of assessment systems. The school that adheres strictly to a prescribed basal reading-writing format is probably well served by existing standardized testing methods, for both external and internal assessment. The school that eschews analytic review of student achievement may want to rely on "portraiture" (Eisner, 1991, on a narrative of student accomplishments, or on simply exhibiting student projects. The school that attempts a curriculum balancing analysis and synthesis, skill and purpose, individual and group work, takes on the challenge of seeing constants in the midst of diversity. This task is difficult, but the scenario shows that it is possible.

How, When, and Who?

While the answers to these questions are not self-evident, certain guidelines suggest themselves. First and foremost, the answers depend on the curriculum. For a curriculum of critical literacy, for instance, genuine evaluation must meet the criteria listed earlier: integrative, top-level, reflective, situated, and developmentally normed.

Given these criteria, assessment should be embedded in regular classroom activities, ongoing throughout the school year, with the teacher acting as the designer, manager, and interpreter. This approach to assessment places the teacher in the role of an applied researcher, whose experiments are a vital part of ongoing professional responsibility and growth (Calfee & Hiebert, 1991).

The current proliferation of articles, volumes, and newsletters on alternative assessment gives a rich array of practical approaches, many of which appear promising and engaging. The advice generally assumes that the teacher is free to select activities, and that assessment is ongoing. To be sure, some states and districts are beginning to mandate alternative assessments, and textbook and test publishers are beginning to turn out pre-prepared portfolio systems (e.g., the Psychological Corporation's *Integrated Assessment System*).

By and large, however, the movement springs from genuine engagement by classroom teachers in finding more appropriate approaches to assessment of student achievement. These aspirations generally rest on a thin conceptual base; a file cabinet filled with student folders for display to interested parties, but lacking commentary, context, or evaluation. Individual teachers quickly gain notoriety as "portfolio persons." Several states are encouraging or mandating alternative assessment, as an activity valuable in its own right, as a complement to state-level testing, or as a replacement for standardized test (Pelavin, 1991). While teachers may be typically involved in these latter activities, the response to external mandates is often "anxiety, fear, and resentment" (response to a survey by the Center for the Study of Writing).

Why and for Whom?

An analysis of *why* suggests several distinctive possibilities, which vary in the degree of authenticity. One "why" is to *guide instruction,* both for individual students as well as for the whole class. If September's activities suggest a general lack of writing capabilities, and a disinterest in writing, the teacher may decide to emphasize small-scale writing activities during the holidays. If three students enter in mid-year, all recently arrived from Cambodia and with limited English capacity, no need to administer a diagnostic test to determine the need. Direct observation provides valid data. More generally, classroom-based assessment is the most authentic source of information when the purpose is to guide instruction.

A second "why" is *feedback* to students, to parents, and to other teachers. Students are accustomed to assessment: worksheets with smiley faces, spelling tests marked 15/20, paragraphs with red checks marking spelling and punctuation errors. They are less aware of the larger scope of the assessment process, although they may be wise enough to inquire, "Will this be on the test?" They may know who is the "teacher's pet," but not why. They may sense who is smart and who is not. They generally expect standardized tests in the spring, and have interesting opinions about this machinery (Paris, Turner, & Lawton, 1990). But their meta-knowledge of assessment is scanty, except for youngsters who move to the upper tracks in the later elementary grades, for whom testing becomes the touchstone for schooling. As for parents and colleagues, assessment has the potential to serve as the primary means of communication. The routines of grades, conferences, and casual remarks presently fulfill this purpose, but with lots of "slippage." The authenticity of current approaches is questionable.

A third "why" is for *accountability* to the principal and to district officials. This purpose/audience category marks the shift from internal to external. To be sure, the principal in a small school or district may serve as a head teacher, and the superintendent may be a frequent classroom visitor. In most situations, however, administrators' responsibilities do not connect directly with curriculum and instruction. They may support the practice of writing portfolios, and a student play may be a delightful digression, but the bottom line must be standardized, numerical, and aggregable.

Accountability becomes even more complex and remote when the stage shifts to large urban districts, or to the state and national levels. In the early days of the National Assessment of Education Progress, the "nation's report card," discussion included genuine tasks, much like the current rhetoric. Efficiency, standardization, objectivity, and aggregability, along with concern about technical reliability and validity, led to implementation of a system not dissimilar from prevailing standardized tests. My hunch is that today's calls for performance-based state and national tests will succumb to the same administrative pressures, unless we find a way to connect classroom-based assessment to accountability in an efficient and persuasive manner.

Achieving this connection will have two benefits. On the one hand, it has the potential to enhance the data base for policy decisions. In addition, it will provide the motivation that is now lacking to support a move toward authentic classroom-based assessment. The scenario painted at the beginning of this chapter may appeal to many educators, but I doubt that it will become prevailing practice until the model connects with broader purposes and audiences, including the need for accountability.

Achieving this connection will not be easy. While one can imagine methods for complementing current indicators (mostly standardized multiple-choice tests) by measures springing from classroom-based teacher assessments (Valencia & Calfee, in press), the trust of policy makers in such measures is undermined by several factors: the language of outcomes, the reliance on teacher judgment, the wide-ranging diversity in contexts, and the difficulty of establishing clearcut standards.

Suppose that, as in Olympic exercises, the classroom teacher is required at the end of each year to present his or her achievement rating for various facets of reading and writing for each student. This simple technique yields judgments that can be aggregated for comparison with other indicators, the task is even cheaper than standardized testing, and teachers already perform a similar job when assigning grades.

Grades are not standardized, to be sure, but teachers also perform as raters in state and district writing tests. for which they receive short-term intensive training, and are checked by other raters. Teacher ratings from classroom activities like Ms. K are less easily checked, and do not conform to a "training" paradigm. The distrust of teacher judgment does have a foundation in reality; the inadequate pre-service preparation of teachers and the mindless scripts in teacher manuals do not generate confidence about teachers' capacities to render informed judgments—opportunities for further professional development would be essential if teacher judgement is to play a more significant role in the access of student achievement.

Even with an agreed-upon agenda of outcomes and given adequate professional preparation, policy makers may feel uncomfortable with a system where variability in assessment conditions is the norm, where they must rely on teachers to render normative judgments in the midst of diversity. This fear is partly a concern with grade inflation, with overestimation of student achievement. It is also important to look at the other side of the issue. One can easily arrange conditions so that children fail a task; authentic assessment calls upon the teacher to arrange conditions that are optimal for student success, as well as investigating situations that are less supportive and more challenging.

The bottom line, in any event, is that connections between teacher-based assessments and policy-level measures are possible, and have the potential to enhance current indicators. The barriers are partly technical but largely psychological—on the one hand, can teacher judgments be trusted; on the other hand, can policy makers understand these judgments?

Making the Image Real

Alternative approaches to authentic assessment, especially those that engage the classroom teacher in the development, implementation, and interpretation of achievement outcomes, are likely either to die a quiet death or be shaped to fit a standardized Protean bed. A few teachers will persist in taking charge, no matter what happens on the surface. Today's headlines may be little more than recognition of these idiosyncrats. But the pressure toward authentic assessment also carries promise–for redefining curriculum and instruction, for more valid indicators of achievement outcomes, and for enhancing the professional development of teachers.

The barriers are substantial: time, money, motivation, and institutional support. The counter currents are also substantial: the impetus for a national test and curriculum, the continuing claims of teacher incompetence and institutional inadequacy. Conceptual and technical support for alternative assessment approaches is weak, and researchers only see lean years ahead.

Nonetheless, several forces may converge to support the vision of authentic, classroom-based assessment. The assembly-line curriculum is being severely criticized in several quarters, including the industrialists who provided the model for mechanized schooling. Sole reliance on multiple-choice tests is now questioned by "hardheaded" policy makers for practical reasons: the instruments are easily foiled, and teaching students to recognize the right answer is poor preparation for genuine responsibility. A "no cheating," competitive mentality does not fit a world where cooperative skills matter as much as individual accomplishment.

Time will tell, of course, but we may not have a great deal of that precious commodity. My sense is that we should expend our scarce resources in a careful examination of good working models of authentic assessment, informing both research and practice. In particular, we should seek out elementary schools serving significant proportions of students at risk for school failure, schools with an institutional commitment to authentic assessment integrated into an overall program for enhancing curriculum and instruction. These models will be more informative, in my judgment, than large state-wide efforts (except as the latter promote the former), or the activities of isolated teachers "doing their thing." Understanding the potential of the new movements will most likely spring from an appreciation that teachers are not only capable of authentic assessment, but that this concept is essential for improved schooling, a genuine shift in paradigmatic thinking (Calfee, 1987; Newmann, 1991).

End Note

1. The work reported herein was supported under the Educational Research and Development Center Program (R117G10036) as administered by the Office of Educational Research and Improvement, U.S. Department of Education. The findings and opinions expressed in this report do not reflect the position or policies of the Office of Educational Research and Improvement or the U.S. Department of Education.

References

Belanoff, P. & Dickson, M. (Eds.). (1991). *Portfolios: Process and product.* Portsmouth NH: Boynton/Cook Publishers.

Calfee, R. C. (1987). The school as a context for assessment of literacy. *The Reading Teacher, 40,* 738-743.

Calfee, R. C. (1991). The inquiring school: Literacy for the year 2000. In C. Collins & J. N. Mangieri (Ed.), *Reading and writing in the twenty-first century.* Hillsdale NJ: Erlbaum.

Calfee, R. C., Chapman, R., & Venezky, R. L. (1972). How a child needs to think to learn to read. In L. Gregg (Ed.), *Cognition in learning and memory.* New York: John Wiley & Sons.

Calfee, R. C., & Drum, P. A. (1979). How the researcher can help the reading teacher with classroom assessment. In L. B. Resnick & P. A. Weaver (Eds.), *Theory and practice of early reading.* (Vol 2). Hillsdale, NJ: Erlbaum.

Calfee, R. C., & Hiebert, E. H. (1991). Teacher assessment of student achievement. In R. Stake (Ed.), *Advances in Program Evaluation,* Vol. 1. JAI Press.

Calfee, R. C., & Hiebert, E. (1988). The teacher's role in using assessment to improve learning. In C. V. Bunderson (Ed.), *Assessment in the service of learning.* Princeton, NJ: Educational Testing Service.

Chall, J. S. (1983). *Stages of reading development.* New York: McGraw-Hill.

Cohen (1980) *First grade takes a test.* New York: Greenwillow.

Cole, N. (1988). A realist's appraisal of the prospects for unifying instruction and assessment. In C. V. Bunderson (Ed.), *Assessment in the service of learning*. Princeton, NJ: Educational Testing Service.

Eisner, E. W. (1991). *The enlightened eye*. New York: Macmillan.

Haertel, E., & Calfee, R. C. (1983). School achievement: Thinking about what to test. *Journal of Educational Measurement, 20,* 119-132.

Hambleton, R. K., & Murphy, E. (in press). A psychometric perspective on authentic measurement. *Applied Measurement in Education.*

Harp, B. (1991). *Assessment and evaluation in whole language programs*. Norwood MA: Christopher-Gordon Publishers.

Hiebert, F., & Calfee, R. C. (1992). Assessment of literacy: From standardized tests to performances and portfolios. In A. E. Farstrup and S. J. Samuels (Eds), *What research says about reading instruction*. (pp. 70-100) Newark, DE: IRA

Murphy, S., & Smith, M.A. (1990). Talking abut portfolios. *The Quarterly of the National Writing Project and the Center for the Study of Writing, 12* (1), 1-3, 24-27.

Newmann, F. M. (1991) Linking restructuring to authentic student achievement. *Phi Delta Kappan, 72,* 458-463.

Paris, S. G., Turner, J. C., & Lawton, T. A. (1990). Students' views of standardized achievement tests. Paper presented at the American Educational Research Association, Boston MA.

Pelavin, S., (1991). *Performance assessments in the states*. Washington, DC: Pelavin Associates.

Pikulski, J. J., & Shanahan, T. (Eds.) (1982). *Approaches to the informal evaluation of reading*. Newark, DE: International Reading Association.

Schaefer, R. J. (1967). *The school as a center of inquiry*. New York: Harper & Row.

Tierney R. J., Carter, M. A., & Desai, L. E. (1991). *Portfolio assessment in the reading-writing classroom*. Norwood MA: Christopher-Gordon Publishers.

Valencia, S. W., & Calfee, R. C. (in press). The development and use of literacy portfolios for students, classes, and teachers. *Applied Measurement in Education.*

10

Elementary School   Literacy Instruction: Changes and Challenges

Linda B. Gambrell

This volume contains a range of chapters on current literacy issues which are both provocative and insightful. Each of the chapters reflects a commitment to the important goal of achieving higher levels of literacy for all our students. In this chapter, I focus on three predominant themes that run across the chapters in this book: a) the changing face of reading instruction, b) teacher as decision maker, and c) literacy learning for at-risk readers. In the first section of this chapter, which focuses on the changing face of reading instruction, I present a series of studies that some of my colleagues and I conducted from 1980 to 1990 which suggest that, indeed, there are signs that reading instruction is changing, particularly with respect to the kinds of materials being used. Next, I discuss a recently completed study of young children's metacognitive awareness about literacy learning in literature-based and conventional classrooms. Then, I discuss work presented by several of the authors in this volume which addresses or raises questions about the current trend toward literature-based reading instruction.

The second section of this chapter deals with the teacher as decision maker—a theme that emerges in each chapter of this book. It is clear that teacher decision-making is critical to effective literacy development. In this section, I address some of the issues raised here by the authors with respect to the call for greater teacher involvement in curriculum decisions related to literacy learning and assessment.

A third predominant theme is that of literacy learning for at-risk readers. This is a theme interwoven throughout the book. Many of these chapters hit at the very heart of this major issue—how do we most effectively help those students who are at risk of reading failure?

The Changing Face of Reading Instruction

More than ever before, we are seeing reading instruction based on the use of children's literature and the integration of reading-writing processes. The research of the l980s has led us to an active-constructive model of reading that emphasizes the interaction between the reader and the text in the meaning-getting process. The research of the l980s also provided important insights about the relationships between reading and writing. Most importantly, this reseach has led us to rethink the reading curriculum. As Barr (Chapter 2) notes, "more and more teachers are beginning to experiment with alternative forms of literacy instruction."

Over the last several years I have been engaged in exploring changes in reading instruction, particularly with regard to the use of instructional materials and how the instructional context affects children's metacognitive knowledge about reading and writing processes. In this chapter I will draw primarily on a series of three studies that focused on reading programs. The first study, conducted in l980, was designed to ascertain the reading programs teachers used in elementary school classrooms. This study was replicated in l990 in an attempt to determine current reading program practices. The third study investigated the effects of literature-based and basal programs on children's literacy learning.

Elementary School Reading Programs in 1980

In l980, 93 teachers, kindergarten through sixth grade, from 3 Eastern states and the District of Columbia, responded to a survey about classroom reading instruction. The teachers were asked to read the following list of program descriptors:

___ basal program
___ basal program supplemented by _____
___ children's literature
___ children's literature supplemented by _____
___ language experience
___ language experience supplemented by _____
___ other

The teachers were then asked to check the program descriptor that best describes their classroom reading program. If their basic program was supplemented by any other approach or material, they were instructed to fill in the blank with a brief description. In response to this survey, *all* teachers reported using a basal program as the primary basis for reading instruction. Only five percent of the teachers reported that they supplemented basal instruction and these were primarily kindergarten teachers. The supplemental programs were fairly evenly distributed among children's literature, language experience, and phonics programs. These results which indicate almost sole reliance on the use of basal programs were not entirely unexpected. However, it was somewhat surprising that teachers reported so little use of supplementary materials or approaches.

Elementary School Reading Programs in 1990

In 1990, 84 teachers from 7 Eastern states and the District of Columbia responded to the same survey question about their reading program. The survey question and directions were identical to those of the 1980 survey with the exception of the addition of the program descriptors "whole language program" and "whole language program supplemented by _____."

Eighty percent of the teachers in the 1990 survey reported that "basal program" best described their reading program. One significant difference from the 1980 survey, however, was that 52% of these teachers indicated they supplemented the basal program with children's literature. A small percentage of teachers (3%), reported that they supplemented the basal program with both children's literature and language experience.

Only 4% of the teachers identified their program as whole language. Another 10%, however, reported using whole language supplemented by basals. Only 1% reported a children's literature-based program. Another 5%, however, reported using children's literature suppplemented by basals. None of the teachers reported using language experience as the basis for their reading program.

Elementary School Reading Programs 1980 - 1990

It should be noted that the survey results described here are based on teachers' reports of reading programs rather than observations of actual practice. But the findings of the 1980 survey are consistent with observational research in the literature which revealed the heavy reliance on basal programs (Durkin, 1978-79; Barr, 1989). Furthermore, these teacher reports are consistent with a series of studies on reading comprehension instruction that I conducted in the early 80s. In these studies (Gambrell, 1986; Gambrell, 1987), teachers were invited to volunteer to participate in an investigation of reading comprehension instruction. I then requested permission to observe and tape record one of their "best" reading comprehension lessons. In the course of these studies I observed over 50 reading comprehension lessons across all reading group levels in grades 1, 2, and 3. The one constant throughout the investigation was that teachers chose basals as the reading material for every "best" reading comprehension lesson I observed. These observations confirm and lend credence to the findings of the extensive use of basal materials reported in the 1980 survey which relied on teacher report.

The results of the 1990 teacher survey suggest that there have been significant changes in reading programs since 1980. It is especially interesting that there appears to be a shift away from sole reliance on basal programs for elementary school reading instruction. While most teachers still reported that basals are the primary basis for instruction, an impressive number of teachers in 1990 reported that they supplement basal programs with children's literature. Twenty percent of the teachers reported using something other than basal programs as the primary basis of their reading program—children's literature (6%) and whole language programs (14%). While the percentage of teachers reporting the use of alternative programs was small, it is still a noteworthy change from reported practice in 1980 of almost total reliance on basal programs. In general, the results of the 1990 survey suggest that today's teachers are increasingly making use of children's literature in their reading programs.

Literature-Based and Basal Programs: Differences in Young Children's Literacy Awareness

While there is still heavy reliance on basal materials, it appears that more teachers are moving toward literature-based reading programs. This finding in my own research led me to question whether instructional context would affect young children's metacognitive knowledge about reading and writing. My observations and experiences in classrooms using literature-based programs and basals programs suggested that the literacy experiences were indeed quite different.

Previous studies on young children's metacognitive knowledge have focused primarily on reading, and particularly on word knowledge, the relationship between spoken and written words, concepts of what reading is, what it involves, and how one learns how to do it (Hiebert, l983; Myers & Paris, 1978; Papandropoulou & Sinclair, 1974; Ryan, McNamara, & Kenney, 1977). A smaller number of studies have examined children's metacognitive knowledge about writing (Boljonis & Hinchman, 1988; Rowe, 1989). But a review of the research revealed that young children's metacognitive knowledge about reading and writing with respect to instructional context had not been investigated. Yet it seems probable that instructional context (literature-based vs. basal programs) influences literacy development and, in particular, young children's metacognitive knowledge about reading and writing.

Hence, we (Gambrell & Palmer, 1991) developed two questionnaires (one for reading and one for writing) to determine if there were differences between young children's metacognitive knowledge about reading and writing with respect to literature-based and basal programs at the end of grades one and two. Fifteen questions were designed to probe variables related to reading and writing processes (cf. Myers & Paris, 1978). The questions were parallel in nature (e.g., What is reading (writing)? How could you become a better reader (writer)? Tell me about the best thing you have read (written) this year?)

We used the questionnaires to interview 152 first and second graders from two schools in a rural school system in an Eastern state. For this program-comparison study, the school system identified two schools, one using a literature-based program and one using a conventional basal program. For two years prior to the study, one school had implemented an integrated, literature-based language arts curriculum. The teachers in this school had participated in staff development programs that emphasized whole language learning, and in particular, literature-based instruction and the integration of reading and writing. The second school used a conventional program that consisted of a basal series, workbooks, and the use of children's literature during voluntary reading time. For two years prior to the study, the teachers in this school had particpated in staff development programs primarily associated with the basal program used in the school.

We found that children in literature-based programs reported greater metacognitive knowledge about reading and writing than those in basal programs. The differences were more pronounced for writing than for reading at both grade levels, suggesting that literature-based programs may be especially effective in developing metacognitive awareness related to writing.

First grade. At the first grade level, differences in metacognitive awareness between children in the literature-based and the basal programs were stronger for writing than for reading. Somewhat surprisingly, the children in the literature-based program reported a greater awareness of independent strategies for figuring out how to read and spell unfamiliar words than their basal program counterparts. With respect to writing, the children in the literature-based program were more aware of task variables than children in the basal program. Fifty-eight percent of the children in the literature-based program reported that good writers think about the meaning of what they are writing, while their basal program counterparts focused more on non-meaning aspects of writing such as knowing how to spell words. In response to the question, "Tell me about some of the things you write at school," the children in the literature-based program gave meaning-oriented responses such as "stories," "poems," and "thank-you letters," (77%) more often than the children in the basal program (37%). Finally, when asked to tell about "the best thing you have written this year," children in the literature-based program responded more often with elaborated story/topic information (97%) than children in the basal program (67%).

Second grade. By second grade, children in the literature-based program were more aware of reading/writing strategies, task demands, and learner traits for both reading and writing than were children in the basal program. Children in the literature-based program reported greater awareness of strategies for identifying unfamiliar words (decoding and context strategies = 74%), than did children in the basal program (30%). In response to the question, "Why do people read?", children in the literature-based program reported reasons associated with pleasure (41%), knowledge (37%), and utility (19%), while children in the basal program reported overwhelmingly that the reason people read is to obtain knowledge (77%). This result suggests that children in the literature-based program were more aware of a range of functions for reading than their basal program counterparts. Furthermore, in response to the question, "What kind of reader are you?," 74% of the children in the literature-based program reported that they were "good" readers as compared to only 48% in the basal program. When asked, "What you think good writers think about when they write?," children in the literature-based program reported more meaning-oriented strategies than children in the basal program (literature-based = 63%; basal = 26%). When asked, "Why do people write?," 37% of the children in the literature-based program responded with reasons primarily related to pleasure, as compared to only 13% in the basal program. Also, more children in the literature-based program gave reading/writing related reasons such as "you write about what you like about stories" (19%) than those in the basal program (4%). Children in the literature-based program also reported that they wrote more stories both in school and at home (school = 89%; home = 85%) than those in the basal program (school =43%; home 35%).

When asked, "What makes something hard to write?," more children in the literature-based program were aware of reasons why something might be difficult to write than children in the basal program. Fifty-seven percent of the children in the literature-based program responded with word level concerns ("when you have a long word," "when I don't know how to spell a word"), as compared to only 26% of the children in the basal program. More children in the literature-based program also identified topic related-concerns (37%) than children in the basal program (17%). Some of the topic related reasons for difficulty in writing were, "when I don't know what to write about," and "sometimes its hard to explain something." Reasons related to mechanics were reported by only 7% of the children in the literature-based program as compared to 35% in the basal program. Some of the reported reasons related to mechanics were "cursive writing" and "copying from the board."

In response to the question, "What kind of writer are you?," 67% of the children in the literature-based program reported they were "good writers" while only 35% of the children in the basal program did so. Interestingly, 61% of the children in the basal program gave no response or an inappropriate response to this question.

For both reading and writing, metacognitive differences between the literature-based and the basal programs were more pronounced at the second grade level. This finding supports the notion that program effects may be cumulative in nature. It must be noted, however, that the results could have been affected by initial differences between the two schools since it was not possible to randomly assign students to literature-based and basal programs. There is also the possiblity of a novelty effect whenever a new program is being compared to a some-what more traditional one. However, the findings of this study are consistent with those of other recent studies (Beljonis & Hinchman, 1988; Mervar & Hiebert, 1989) that suggest that literature-based programs promote greater metacognitive awareness about reading and writing than do conventional basal programs.

Changes: Issues and Implications

From the research my colleagues and I have conducted, it seems clear that classroom practice, with respect to materials used for reading instruction, is in a period of change, moving toward greater inclusion of children's literature. It also appears that there are substantial differences in the metacognitive awareness about reading and writing for children in literature-based and conventional basal-program classrooms. Several of the authors in this volume emphasize the trend toward literature-based instruction in the reading program as well as in the content areas. In particular, Barr notes that teachers are beginning to move toward more literature-based forms of instruction. She notes that this trend will ultimately influence time allocation decisions and grouping decisions with regard to reading instruction. Barr believes that literature-based instruction holds promise in that it can provide more supported forms of literacy learning which will enable a more diverse group of children to actively participate. This concept is in line with the social cognitive model of emergent literacy proposed by Mason et al. (Chapter 3). The social cognitive model of reading emphasizes the importance of effective literacy-related social interactions, which is a primary focus of literature-based instruction.

Beck and McKeown (Chapter 6) advocate the use of literature in conjunction with social studies texts. They suggest that literature related to social studies topics be available in the classroom for teacher read-aloud sessions, for recreational reading, independent study, and as the focus of direct instruction. Literature, used in these ways, provides context for the social studies curriculum. This inclusion of literature, according to Beck and McKeown, brings depth to learning by providing multiple perspectives. Literature provides an excellent way for introducing and developing an appreciation of different perspectives on social studies issues. Beck and McKeown go so far as to state that in-depth understanding of social studies is unlikely to succeed unless the curriculum extends beyond the textbook and is based on richer and more varied reading materials.

Teacher as Decision-Maker

Several of the authors in this volume address issues that are particularly important in light of the changing face of reading instruction. Barr's rich descriptions of classroom grouping practices and materials selection emphasize the importance of the teacher as decision maker, particularly in view of emerging literature-based programs. Barr notes that as we move to literature-based instruction, decisions once addressed by basal authors will need to be addressed by teachers. Literature-based instruction requires that the teacher make many decisions about literacy learning with regard to materials, pacing, instruction, and assessment. Barr also notes that teachers who develop literature-based programs must possess considerably more knowledge about children's literature and teaching strategies than those who use basal materials.

Juel (Chapter 4) raises critical issues about the reading and writing development of young children that have implications for teacher decision-making. Juel's research suggests that children who have a relatively smooth transition into reading will like to read, read more, and have more opportunities for literacy growth. These increased opportunities will in turn help them become even better readers and more acomplished writers. What kinds of teacher decisions are needed with regard to materials, time, and grouping in order to facilitate this smooth transition into reading?

Graves' chapter 5 provides interesting insights about the need for high quality vocabulary instruction, while at the same time raising may issues related to teacher decision-making. According to Graves, an adequate time allocation is needed for indepth vocabulary instruction. He presents a strong rationale for indepth vocabulary instruction on both individual words and strategies for learning words. However, in light of Barr's findings that some teachers average as low as 7-11 minutes a day for reading instruction, the importance of teachers' decisions about time use is apparent. In particular, teachers not only need to make appropriate decisions about how time is allocated for vocabulary instruction, they need to make decisions about how to provide meaningful vocabulary instruction in the context of literacy learning so that vocabulary instruction is not viewed as a "tack-on".

The teacher also plays an important decision-making role with respect to assessment. As Calfee (Chapter 9) states, ". . . teachers gain a sense of professional control over assessment only as they engage personally in the process of formulating and implementing an assessment design." Alternative assessments which are more closely linked to instructional methods are consistent with Calfee's conceptual framework for classroom assessment. He proposes that classroom assessment should be integrative, emphasize top-level competence, focus on metalanguage, should be situated, and should be guided by developmental standards. All of the elements of classroom assessment, as described by Calfee, depend on the teacher as decision-maker. In particular, Calfee concludes that the movement toward authentic assessment carries promise for enhancing the professional development of teachers *because* they are directly involved as decision-makers.

Literacy Learning for the At-risk Reader

Another issue that emerges in this volume is the relevance of literature-based reading instruction for at-risk readers. Williams (Chapter 7) acknowledges the current interest in literature-based reading curricula and is enthusiastic about such reforms in reading instruction. She notes that reading disabled students learn well with highly structured instruction and materials. In contrast, literature-based programs typically lack a specific curriculum. Thus, the needs of reading disabled students and the philosophy of literature-based programs may easily find themselves in conflict. Hence, we need to give particular attention to how at-risk readers respond to literature-based instruction and, as Williams suggests, we may need to provide more structure within such programs for at-risk readers.

One of the most current issues in literacy is how can technology be used to enhance learning, particularly for the at-risk student. Sharp et al. (Chapter 8), describe a "new look" in books that arises from integrated media technology under computer control. The Discis Books which combine computers, text, and still illustrations, have great potential for developing vocabulary and decoding skills. Perhaps of most importance is the fact that the Discis books encourage children to practice word recognition and decoding skills in context and offer immediate feedback since children can listen to the text as it is read. This kind of practice may be of particular importance to at-risk readers who, as Juel (Chapter 4) notes, lag behind good readers in word recogntion skills. Another important point is that the newer integrated-media, such as Discis Books and The Young Children's Literacy Project, may provide motivation for at-risk readers who have experienced early frustration with traditional books. As Juel notes, poor readers hate reading, and as such, they avoid reading—even to the point of choosing to clean the mold around the bathtub! Motivation is a critical component in the learning process. Therefore, we must be particularly mindful of the motivational aspects of technology for developing the literacy skills of at-risk readers. This new medium of integrated-media has vast potential for both teaching and assessing the kinds of skills that children need in order to be highly effective language users.

In conclusion, the chapters in this volume emphasize three themes which I think will be of primary importance in the decade of the 1990's as we strive toward achieving higher levels of literacy for all our students. These themes—the changing face of reading instruction, teacher as decision-maker, and literacy learning for at-risk readers—focus on moving toward the goal of achieving high literacy for all students through improving instructional delivery, involving teachers in in-structional decision-making, and by paying particular attention to those students who need the most support in their literacy development—at-risk readers. The "big" message in this volume is clear—all students deserve a chance for achieving high literacy. The chapters in this volume provide insights and raise many relevant questions that help move us toward reaching this worthwhile goal.

References

Barr, R. (1989). The social organization of literacy instruction. In S. McCormick & J. Zutell (Eds.), *Cognitive and social perspectives for literacy research and instruction* (pp. 19-33). Thirty-eighth Yearbook of the National Reading Conference. Chicago, IL: National Reading Conference.

Boljonis, A., & Hinchman, K. (1988). First graders' perceptions of reading and writing. In J. E. Readence & R. S. Baldwin (Eds.), *Dialogues in literacy research* (pp. l97-ll4). Chicago, IL: National Reading Conference.

Durkin, D. (l978-79). What classroom observations reveal about reading comprehension instruction. *Reading Research Quarterly, 14,* 48l-533.

Gambrell, L. B. (1986). Reading in the primary grades. In M. R. Sampson (Ed.), *The pursuit of literacy* (pp 102-107). Dubuque, Iowa: Kendall/Hunt.

Gambrell, L. B. (l987). Children's oral language during teacher-directed reading instruction. In J. E. Readence & R. S. Baldwin (Eds.), *Research in literacy: Merging perspectives,*(pp. 195-200). Rochester, NY: National Reading Conference.

Gambrell, L. B., & Palmer, B. M. (1991). *Children's metacognitive knowledge about reading and writing in literature-based and conventional classrooms.* Paper presented at the National Reading Conference, Palm Springs, CA.

Hiebert, E. H. (1983). Knowing about reading before reading: Preschool children's concepts of reading. *Reading Psychology, 4,* 252-260.

Mervar, K., & Hiebert, E. H. (1989). Literature selection strategies and amount of reading in tow literacy approaches. In S. McCormick &

J. Zutell (Eds.), *Cognitive and social perspectives for literacy research and instruction* (pp. 529-535). Thirty-eighth Yearbook of the National Reading Conference. Chicago, IL: National Reading Conference.

Myers, M., & Paris, S. (1978). Children's metacognitive knowledge about reading. *Journal of Educational Psychology, 70,* 680-690.

Papandropoulou, I., & Sinclair, H. (1974). What is a word? Experimental study of children's ideas on grammar. *Human Development, 17,* 241-258.

Rowe, D. W. (1989). Preschoolers' use of metacognitive knowledge and strategies in self-selected literacy events. In S. McCormick & J. Zutell (Eds.), *Cognitive and social perspectives for literacy research and instruction* (pp. 65-76). Chicago, IL: National Reading Conference.

Ryan, E., McNamara, S., & Kenney, M. (1977). Linguistic awareness and reading performance among beginning readers. *Journal of Reading Behavior, 9,* 399-400.

11

Reading as Cognition and the Mediation of Experience

John. T. Guthrie and Michael Pressley

Reading is an activity of mind that extends the reader's experience. On the one hand, the cognitive requirements of reading have been studied extensively by psychologists, cognitive scientists, and reading researchers. On the other hand, the experiential functions of reading have been underscored by psychologists, anthropologists, reading researchers, and literary critics. This volume reflects these two streams of inquiry. One set of papers emphasizes the mental operations required by reading. The second set describes the connection of reading to experience, including the social contexts of language, the narrative understandings of children, and the acquisition of knowledge about the world. Thus, we divided the chapters of this volume into those addressing cognitive bases of reading and those relating reading to particular types of experience. Although the papers can be grouped into these two sets, we emphasize the unity of the volume, in that all the chapters pertain to reading instruction. The instructional emphasis in the chapters is timely since rapid acceleration in the improvement of reading among all students is increasingly important for at least three reasons:

(1) Reading achievement in the United States is low, although lower level, literal reading skills are nearly universal among high school graduates. From reports of the National Assessment of Educational Progress, we know that many students of all ages are inadequate in higher-order processes of reading. For example, although 17-year-olds can successfully identify the main character in a sports article of a newspaper, these 17-year-olds cannot identify the argument in an

editorial in the same newspaper (Kirsch & Jungeblut, 1986). Although 95 percent of students leaving our high schools can read the title of a bus schedule, only 5 percent can read the bus schedule to plan a trip across a city.

2) We have not yet created a nation of readers. With few exceptions, children do not read frequently enough to expand their minds, their friendships, their knowledge, or their reading achievement. Intermediate grade children read less than 15 minutes a day on average outside of school (Winfield, et al., 1986). This is disturbing because students who choose to read widely and frequently have substantial cultural advantages over those who do not read (Guthrie, Schafer, & Hutchinson, 1991). They enter the work force at a higher level, and they participate more frequently in community activities such as local organizations, clubs, religious groups, and business agencies. Becoming an active reader is vital to economic and cultural development of youth.

(3) There is a need to increase the knowledge base of students. Our children know less than they should (Ravitch & Finn, 1987). Only 32 percent of our 17-year-olds can place the time of the Civil War in the correct half century, between 1850 and 1900. Only 70 percent of 17-year-olds can locate Great Britain on a map. The knowledge crisis is evident in preschoolers and lasts a lifetime.

In summary, the challenges for instruction are to increase higher forms of reading comprehension, increase the amount of reading that children do, and prepare students to extend their knowledge more continuously and effectively through reading.

Cognitive Bases of Reading

One set of chapters from this volume pertains to the fundamental findings of the cognitive processes in reading. Many of the most critical issues in decoding, lexical development, and comprehension are covered, with the contributions as a whole providing a window about how basic research can increase understanding of the important social problem of improving reading achievement.

Decoding

Juel portrays the cognitive learning of early readers. Her view is that children go through three cognitive phases from kindergarten to grade 4. The phases are matters of emphases and are not mutually exclusive stages of development. First, children acquire phonemic awareness: They learn a host of complex rules about how our sound system works to create meaning. They come to understand that mental linguistic modifications of words can create rhyme and rhythm, which can produce melody, nonsense, or surprise. These are critical acquisitions that are essential for learning to read (Adams, 1990). Second, phonemic awareness lays the foundation for word recognition. To join the sound system with the printed form of words, children unconsciously induce a galaxy of rules. Fortunately, children do not need to understand all these rules any more than adults need to understand the rules of English syntax in order to converse with friends and colleagues. Third, once printed language can be decoded, comprehension of what is decoded develops.

Juel notes that there is stability in reading achievement across these three phases relative to peers. Students who are at the top of the class stay at the top; those on the bottom tend to stay at the bottom. For example, 88 percent of readers in the bottom quarter of their first-grade class will remain poor readers and be in the bottom quarter of their fourth-grade class. Eighty-seven percent of the average readers in the second grade will be average readers in the fourth grade. Although all children make gains in reading proficiency during the first four years of school, individual differences are persistent.

How might this be explained? Juel believes the critical factor might be amount of reading. In her study, first graders who were good readers read approximately 18,000 words during the year, whereas poor readers read about half that number. In fourth grade, these same good readers had read 178,000 words in school; whereas the poor readers had read about 80,000 words during their first four years of school. There is a terrible cycle here. Children who are low achievers are provided less opportunity to learn by reading. Because they do not read as frequently and widely, the lower achievers do not progress as rapidly as better achievers.

Juel reports that reading and writing are correlated approximately .38 to .60 in fourth grade. Extensive reading is a source of ideas, concepts, vocabulary, plot structure, and inspiration for writing. Juel's findings suggest that for both reading and writing, increasing the sheer amount of activity might improve competence. If we were to double the amount of reading and writing that the low group in a reading class performs, might this group be comparable to the top group by the time they reach fourth grade? This is a question for research and a challenge for innovation. In summary, Juel establishes that the acquisition of decoding is highly complex and builds upon itself. Providing ample opportunity for this complex, inductive, cognitive system to improve is essential to early reading.

Vocabulary Development

Michael Graves surveys some critical issues pertaining to vocabulary in reading. We learn *wordness,* that a word is different from an utterance or a speech. We learn origins, word constituents, strategies for learning new words, and to use word-building resources, such as dictionaries and context cues. Most critically, children learn to value words and to care about their use and their misuse.

Graves believes that most words are learned incidentally. By his estimates, as well as those of Nagy and others (1989), children learn 3,000 to 4,000 words per year in the intermediate grades. This estimate suggests that children learn 20 words per day, everyday in school. Even if more modest estimates of the number of words learned (i.e., D'Anna, Zechmeister, & Hall, 1991) are accepted, word learning must be incidental learning much of the time.

Graves makes the case that words are learned from verbal contexts such as sentences and paragraphs, which most frequently in turn, are understood as part of the texts in which they reside. The more such contexts the child experiences, the more vocabulary should be acquired—consistent with this expectation, vocabulary knowledge increases with the amount of time children spend reading in school. Time spent reading in language arts classes correlates with word knowledge at about .40 (Taylor et al., 1990). Of course, this relationship is likely to be bidirectional. Students with high vocabularies may choose to read more frequently and those who read more frequently acquire larger vocabularies. This bidirectionality is egalitarian however, with improved reading as a function of time spent reading both for low-achievers and high-achievers. Increases in the amount of reading increases vocabulary knowledge.

Although students learn words from context, they need strategies for learning efficiently. Graves reports that there is a 5 percent chance that a particular word will be learned from a single sentence context on the first encounter. He proposes, therefore, to teach students to use context cues to induce the meanings of words. His example of instruction is a program designed by a teacher around the theme of riddles. Riddles provide motivation for the cognitive effort of word learning. In this instruction the teacher used riddles as an analogy to word learning and taught the children to infer the unknown word, then read the context in which it was embedded, and think aloud about the possible meanings before arriving at a best meaning. Graves reports that an experimental group was superior to a control group in word learning with this method of instruction. Our guess is that the motivational benefits of the riddle theme and the cognitive benefits of the context-analysis strategies produced the gains in vocabulary development.

Comprehension Processes
There is a broad consensus in the reading field that the essence of reading is comprehension of text. If a child can decode the words in a passage but cannot comprehend the ideas in the passage, the child cannot be said to be a reader. Instruction in comprehension can be problematic for students, however. As Williams points out, directing student "to find the main idea or pick out the most important point" or "if you have picked out the most important sentence, you probably have found the main idea," will not suffice. These are merely restatements of the fact that the main idea is central.

Reading comprehension in the 1980s has been understood by researchers partially in terms of schema theory (Anderson & Pearson, 1984; Rumelhart, 1977). In this view, a student's comprehension of text depends greatly on her prior knowledge that pertains to the topic of the text. What you already know determines what you can understand from new passages. Williams explores schema theory as an avenue for explaining the comprehension deficits of students who are low achievers in reading.

Williams studied disabled readers using a sensitive experimental approach that illuminates the cognitive processing deficits of these readers. Williams first located reading disabled students who were approximately 13 years old, who had normal intelligence, and who read at least two years below their expected grade level. These students were considered to be "generally reading disabled" (GRD). She then designed two contrast groups, the first matched on age with the GRD students and the second matched on reading level with the GRD participants. The reading level group was younger, with a mean age of approximately 10 years but the same standardized reading level as the GRD. Of course,the general reading disabled reading group were expected to be lower than their age mates on most reading processes. Specifically, if the GRDs were lower than their reading level matched group on a particular process, that process would be a candidate explanation as a cause of the reading disability (see Guthrie, 1973).

Williams asked students to listen to a story, summarize each section of the story, and make a prediction about what would happen in the next section. The students described the theme and their bases for their selection of that theme. Although the GRD group performed at the same level as the reading level matched group with respect to summarizing, predicting, and identifying the theme, the GRD students were unique in one cognitive process. The GRD students imported a high number of irrelevant, implausible associations as they attempted to identify the themes of stories. They gave personal, idiosyncratic responses that were not related to the text. Williams concluded that these disabled readers were unable to evaluate which portions of their world knowledge (schemata) were relevant to the understanding of the story. They were unable to edit their own associations to identify the themes in the story. The GRD group seemed unable and/or unwilling to constrain their imports of prior knowledge to make them task relevant. In other words, increasing competence in comprehension requires increasing selectivity, evaluation, and judgement about which aspects of the learners' prior knowledge are relevant to comprehending a text. These findings are substantiated by research with highly skilled readers which illustrates that they evaluate and sift both the text and their own previous experience to optimize their learning (Bazerman, 1985; Guthrie & Kirsch, 1987).

Williams' work is extremely important because there are many comprehension interventions being deployed that are built upon the assumption that making personal associations to text content is a good thing. For some readers that may not be so. Alternatively, it may be that there are ways to keep even learning disabled readers on track, ways to encourage decidedly text-relevant associations. Because so much of reading comprehension instruction is targeted at learning disabled students and involves activation of prior knowledge, it seems essential to determine exactly how learning disabled students do respond to such instruction. Williams' work is an important first step, illuminating some potential hazards of prior knowledge activation strategies with weaker readers.

Reading Achievement

Rebecca Barr outlines her view of how the social structure of first grade classrooms is related to reading achievement. She observes that teachers make decisions about the structure of their classrooms in the context of district decisions, principal decisions, and student characteristics. Ability grouping reflects one widespread decision, although its frequency is decreasing with the adoption of whole language approaches. Barr reports from extensive observational studies the following conclusions: (a) the low group has a delayed start. The delayed group spends 2 to 4 times as much instructional time as the high group in the first preprimer in basal reading programs. (b) From that point forward, the high, medium, and low groups proceed at similar paces. The total amount of time spent in the first primer and the first reader is the same for the high group and the low group. By fourth grade in her longitudinal data, the amount of coverage through a basal system is the same for the high group and the low group. The high group starts at a higher level but the total amount of coverage is similar to that of the low group.

Although the high and low groups tend to proceed at the same pace through basal readers after the first portion of first grade, variations in this pace influence reading achievement dramatically. Reading acquisition is more rapid for all students in classrooms in which more time was allocated for reading instruction. Quantitatively, the amount of coverage measured in number of pages accounts for 83 percent of the variance in word learning and 49 percent of the variance in comprehension of primary age students. Consistent with other data reviewed earlier in this commentary, Barr concludes that increasing the amount of reading increases reading achievement.

Barr warns us that large amounts of content coverage in the absence of reading comprehension will not be profitable. There is no point in hurrying students through tasks they do not understand. She points out that, consistent with distinctions offered by Bloom (1976) and Berliner (1981), that engaged time and allocated time are different. Merely scheduling time for reading is insufficient. Students must be actively experiencing books and texts for which they have appropriate knowledge and prerequisite abilities. Engaged reading time is a function of the time provided in the schedule as well as the management expertise of the teacher. Choosing appropriate materials, getting a lesson started on time, sustaining motivation, and reinforcing achievement are all productive uses of class time. Barr's work reinforces the well-established conclusion that high achievement is associated with a large amount of time experiencing high quality instruction (e.g., Rosenshine & Stevens, 1986).

Barr notes that "teachers need to extend the time period to enable children to engage in more reading." For example, in literature-based programs, teachers can read the story aloud in unison with all children, have all students read with a partner, and request students to write personal responses to their reading. All of these procedures enhance the total engaged reading time within a given lesson. Barr's recommendation is timely in that a number of investigators are examining student-led discussion groups in middle and elementary school levels (Alvermann et al., 1990; O'Flahavan, 1990), sometimes as part of larger programs of comprehension instruction (Pressley et al., in press). Such groups are hypothesized to teach students how to take multiple perspectives on a story. A particularly important hypothesis, consistent with Vygotsky's (1978) theory is that participation in such groups for an extended period of time results in individual students internalizing the analytical give-and-take that occurs during discussion, resulting in improved thinking about and comprehension of text (see Pressley, et al., in press). This possibility makes obvious that there are important linkages between the cognitive bases of reading and the experiential bases of reading. Thus, just as we close this section on the cognitive bases of reading by considering the role of social interactions in the development of early literacy, we open the next section on experimental bases of reading with a discussion of social interactional effects on literacy.

Experiential Bases of Reading

There are many facets to the idea that reading is a social experience. Some view reading as a conversation between the reader and the author. For example, Jean-Paul Sartre (in Booth, 1988) made this claim:

> Reading is a pact of generosity between author and reader. Each one
> trusts the other; each one counts on the other; demands of the others

> as much as he demands of himself...there is then established a
> dialectical going-and-coming; when I read I make demands; if my
> demands are met, what I am then reading provokes me to demand
> more of the author, which means to demand of the author that he
> demand more of me. And visa versa, the author's demand is that I
> carry my demands to the highest pitch. (p. 200 in Booth)

Others focus more on meaning developed within an interpretive community. That is, the meaning of a narrative or of an historical text is an interpretation shared by a group of people (Fish, 1980). Consider a lesson in Fulgrum's *Everything I Know I Learned in Kindergarten*. One of his lessons was that, "When you go out into the world, watch the traffic, hold hands, stick together." The meaning of this counsel varies if said to a child, a professorial colleague, or a spouse. The appropriate summary for a story or a paragraph is relative to the social situation in which the story occurs. The child learns the social rules of meaning at home and she extends these social rules to the school if they fit the school situation (Heath, 1983). From this perspective, sharing the interpretation of a story is motivating because when a child understands a story, she joins the group of people who understand it as she does. She joins a community.

Reading Acquisition

Jana Mason proposes that a social, cognitive model is needed to explain reading acquisition, favoring Vygotsky's (1978) perspective in particular. Mason argues that home literacy influences language abilities. Home literacy refers to such factors as whether the family values reading and language play, whether the child has a library card, and whether there are many books in the home. Home literacy fosters language abilities such as classification of words, analogy, definition, sentence repetition, and listening comprehension. These language abilities are related to reading level at the end of first, second, and third grades. Mason concludes that language and social interaction undergird the acquisition of reading comprehension.

Our own view is that although the idea of the social mediation of language and literacy is appealing, there is not yet sufficient data to permit confidence in the conclusion that social factors determine early reading acquisition. A given social context such as a mother reading a story book to her child, or a family discussing a newspaper at a dinner table conversation, involves a large number of social, cognitive, and motivational variables. For young preschool children, for example, it is possible that a mother's emphasis on reading stories in a book runs parallel to her emphasis on language use and language play. The mother may enhance the child's literacy through her social interactions with the child or she may enhance the child's literacy through her language use and stimulation. Perhaps both the social interaction and the language stimulation are contributory. Alternatively, perhaps brighter, more responsive children elicit storybook reading from their parents. We need studies of how all these dimensions interrelate before coming to strong conclusions.

Narrative Comprehension

When children confront the world of print and its meaning, they have already acquired a narrative background schema because they have already experienced many stories with beginnings, problems to be solved, climaxes, and resolution. Grandmother's knee and the Disney channel afford such opportunities. In fact, as soon as children can form symbols they begin to make meanings through narrative. Bruner (1990) states that:

> One of the most ubiquitous and powerful discourse form in human communication is narrative. Narrative structure is even inherent in the practice of social interaction before it achieves linguistic expression. Narrative requires four constituents if it is to be effectively carried out. It requires a means for emphasizing human action or 'agentivity'-action directed towards goals controlled by agents. It requires that a sequential order be established and maintained—that events and states be 'linearlized' in a standard way. Narrative also requires a sensitivity to what is canonical and what violates canonicality in human interaction. Finally, narrative requires a narrator's perspective; it cannot be 'voiceless' (p. 77).

Even before speech, children grasp the basic ideal that human actions and their outcomes assume the structure of a narrative. Even so, when complex narratives are read, not all students understand the stories being read. Thus, Sharp, Bransford, Vye, Goldman, Kinzer, and Soraci propose that a system of "integrated media" (IM) might be powerful in promoting understanding of complex narratives. They propose that written stories and video representations of the narrative may be synergistically combined to enhance children's ability to make sense of stories.

Sharp and her colleagues place the integrated media in a theoretical framework that is drawn from research on mental models. They suggest that effective readers construct mental models (e.g., Holland et al., 1987) that contain information about the situation and scenes in a story. The mental models are like images, pictures, or movies, according to Sharp, et al. The reader can switch objects or persons around in the scenes and interpret the interactions of people in these "imaginary movies".

After the mental model for a story has been constructed from a literal interpretation of the meanings of the sentences in the text, the reader may develop higher-order meanings of the story. The power of integrated media, according to Sharp et al., is in assuring high quality mental models for both lower-and higher-skilled readers. Such representations increase the likelihood that higher-order messages can be induced from a story—that the manipulations required to derive higher-order under-standings are more certain given a multimodel presentation of the basic story compared to presentation using words alone.

Sharp et al., coined the term of "representational literacy" to describe the ability of young children to fluently "manipulate their own internal representations" of narrative. To explore the hypothesis that integrated media foster "representational literacy," Sharp, et al. presented kindergartners with a video of a story and read the story to them simultaneously. They asked the children to recall the story. Children who saw the video prior to hearing the story were able to remember the information in the story more fully than children who were shown an irrelevant video or children who were not shown any video. Unfortunately, these pilot data cannot form the basis of definitive conclusions. Perhaps the students in the integrated media condition merely re-membered video and never "understood" the sentences. A full study requires a comparison group in which subjects recall the video without hearing the sentences. Sharp et al.'s exploratory work, however, is highly provocative and promising. Multimedia that integrate video and text provide the opportunity for ingenious and powerful learning contexts that might support reading comprehension.

Textbook Construction

Isabel Beck reports ways that the community of writers and community of teachers can affect learning from text. She believes that: a) textbook authors assume students know far more than they do about history, geography, or politics; and b) the coherence of textbooks is remarkably remiss. The sequence of ideas in such texts often is not easy to follow. Connective ties are rarely included. Abstract ideas are not sufficient illustrated.

More positively, Beck and her colleagues at the University of Pittsburgh's Learning Research and Development Center argue that good teachers can compensate for these shortcomings of text. First, she reports that pre-reading instruction in the historical and conceptual prerequisites of an event, such as the Boston Tea Party, substantially improved the ability of students to comprehend text about historical events. These findings are consistent with schema theory. What we learn from a text depends on the amount, refinement, and structure of the knowledge that we bring to the new information.

Beck and her colleagues believe that relatively incoherent texts may be markedly improved through revision. She suggests that when texts are revised to include explanatory information, supplementary details, enriching elaborations, connective ties, and explicit statement of relationships, student comprehension of them is increased. Beck and her co-authors argue that texts that clarify, elaborate, explain, and motivate the students to attend to the most important information in a unit will be more comprehensible than texts lacking these qualities.

Beck believes that student background knowledge and text characteristics, both contribute equally to comprehension. Students who read revised texts comprehend them more fully, regardless of whether their background knowledge is high or low. In addition, students who learn extensive background knowledge comprehend texts more fully than students who do not have this knowledge regardless of whether texts are relatively coherent and easy to understand or incoherent to the reader.

To revise a text into understandable form usually requires extending its length. By adding connective ties, elaborations, and explicit statements of relationships, Beck attempts to afford to students more depth of understanding. Because effective texts must be longer, she suggests, the curriculum should concentrate on fewer concepts. Doubling the amount of reading in any one topic or concept requires that teachers either reduce the number of topics in a given curriculum area or double the length of time spent in classroom reading and homework activities. Judicious choices of concepts to be taught appears necessary. Beck suggests that depth may be provided through trade books and multiple resources in classrooms, including dictionaries, biographies, and treatments of cultural issues with multiple perspectives.

Assessment

Calfee develops the perspective that assessment of literacy might be better done if it is consistent with the types of literacy demands usually put on students—if it is authentic. Concerns about validity of standardized assessments have been raised throughout the 20th century, reiterated now because of the current emphases on standardized assessments by various levels of government, most prominently the concern about the uniformly poor marks earned on such tests by American students. Calfee makes the point that students may do poorly on standardized tests because the tests are not well connected to their experiences and understandings. Perhaps there is a better way.

In fact, the better way appears to be much like what teachers have done since schooling began. They evaluate the work that students perform for them. Such evaluations are now being cast as "informal assessments," including portfolios stuffed with student accomplishments, end-of-the-year projects, and lists of books the child has completed during independent reading. The problem is, "What to make of it?" This is an especially challenging proposition since many teachers "know" that such assessments tell them much more about their students than do Iowa Test scores, state-developed performance assessments, or the National Assessment of Educational Progress. District administrators typically have less confidence in the homemade measures, which vary from classroom to classroom. Administrators find comfort in the face validity of standardized comparisons between classrooms and schools, ones that can be made when all classrooms and schools are measured using the same stick (or in this case, test)! State and federal policy makers have almost no respect for the teacher-made assessments, persistently grounding their evaluations of student competence in numbers produced by standardized assessments.

For many traditionally-minded researchers, there is little doubt that the more defensible course with respect to assessment winds through the Educational Testing Service in Princeton and the Lindquist Center in Iowa City, so much so that the norms prepared at these centers are not only revered by political leadership but also inspirational to them. The inspiration is that such norms can be the start of national standards and goals. The idea is that once such standards are established, the pressure will build for states, school districts, principals, and teachers to go beyond teaching to the test—teaching the skills needed to tackle the test items, items presumed to be revealing about important competencies according to the standardized test makers and the policy chiefs. Many of those closest to the nation's children disagree, however, believing the face validity of informal, curriculum-based assessments is more than enough to justify the authentic approach over standardized assessments. Whether the assessments that seem valid in one teacher's classroom are valid in other classrooms is not a critical issue to many associated with the informal assessment movement. Instead, for many who identify with informal assessment, the important issue is whether assessments permit sound educational decisions for particular students in particular classrooms. The authentic assessment advocates believe their approach does so better than formal assessments, since informal assessments are sensitive to contextual features compared to standardized assessments.

The challenges for measurement researchers posed by informal assessments are formidable, beginning with issues of reliability and validity. It is critical to understand the impact of educational practices that are as widespread as informal assessment. If there are "better" and "worse" ways of doing such assessments, they need to be identified. Our own intuitions are that informal assessments can play a valuable role in educational planning. It has been known for a long time that teachers who know their pupils' strengths and weaknesses first hand are often capable of sizing up their pupils needs and responding to those needs. Determining how teachers, who are especially skillful at this informal assessment enterprise, make the decisions they make, seems to us to be an especially critical question that informal assessment research might answer. Calfee's chapter provides a sympathetic introduction to the importance of informal assessment and the daunting task confronting those who would study it.

Development of Reading as a Mediator of Learning

A pervasive theme throughout the chapters in this volume is that cognitive expertise in reading is the primary goal of reading instruction. Cognitive expertise develops as the student gains competence in decoding, vocabulary, strategies for comprehending narrative and informative text, and using prior knowledge to understand what she is reading. We concur that these cognitive objectives are essential to the student and consequently to the teacher of reading. However, we believe that there are additional qualities of the excellent reader that should be explored as goals of instruction. The qualities we emphasize are consistent with the view expressed by the authors in this volume that students should read broadly, frequently, and extensively to increase their cognitive expertise as readers.

We suggest that it is useful to recognize how fully students are oriented to enjoying new experiences and expanding their understanding of the world surrounding them. Students read to encounter novel people and places, to learn new concepts about intriguing topics, and to fulfill their personal needs. The motivational orientation of students is toward the topics and substance they read about rather than toward improving their cognitive expertise for reading in itself. In this light, there are three vital characteristics of mature readers that teachers may aspire to develop in students. First, mature readers are devoted to topics and contents of interest to them. Mature learners read about issues, subject matters, authors, and concepts that they either want to know about or need to know about (Guthrie & Greaney, 1991). The motivational orientation of these readers is to explore a literary world or enhance their knowledge about a subject that fascinates them. Gaining the cognitive skills of reading is rarely the primary motivation that leads a student to become an active, avid reader. The cognitive competencies are indispensable tools, however, that enable students to fulfill their aspirations.

The second trait of mature readers is that they are strategic (Pressley, Borkowski & Schneider, 1987). Mature readers use strategies such as imagery, self-questioning, and summarizing to pursue their interests and to accomplish their goals. In school and community contexts, mature readers choose books, articles and references on topics that are directly related to their conceptual knowledge, topical interests and personal goals (Bazerman, 1985; Guthrie & Kirsch, 1987). Across a broad range of cultural settings, mature readers select written material that is congruent with their beliefs, that addresses their personal needs and that aids in solving their problems (Reder & Green, 1983).

Third, mature readers are extensive in their choices of material. They read frequently, widely, and avidly to seek new ideas, information, and perspectives (Guthrie, Schafer & Hutchinson, 1991; Stanovich & Cunningham, in press). The amount of time a person devotes to reading, and the number of books and magazines a person reads are related to many aspects of mature reading. More active readers have more conceptual knowledge about topics of interest to them. More active readers are more likely to participate in social events in school or community situations. More active readers are more inclined to continue learning independently on the basis of their own choice when formal instruction has concluded.

When we view cognitive expertise as one of several traits of the fully mature reader, the objectives of reading instruction are extended beyond the cognitive goals to include substantive and motivational goals. When reading is a primary means for learning about history, literature, or human cultures, the substance takes a high priority as the goal of instruction, and the student's cognitive expertise forms an indispensable supporting role. We do not suggest that educators should decrease reading instruction or decrease cognitive strategy instruction. Rather, we propose that reading instruction should be embedded more fully in other learning activities. A student's understanding of a story may be enhanced by viewing the story on a video, hearing the story from a teacher, and reading the story herself. A student's learning of a science concept may be enhanced by performing experiments with the concept, explaining the concept, or reading about the concept in textbooks. Conceptual growth and reading growth are joint goals of instruction. In this view, acquisition of reading is optimized when the cognitive goals of reading are taught in the contexts of conceptually rich topics in literature, in science or history.

We offer five projections that flow from this viewpoint. These expectations may be explored qualitatively through observations of classroom instruction or quantitatively through experiments and correlational analyses:

1. Students comprehend texts more fully and remember them longer if they view the texts as a means for learning an idea or gaining an experience than if they view the texts as objects to be understood and recalled. This prediction is consistent with a number of theories, including American depth-of-processing perspectives (e.g., Craik & Lockhart, 1972) and Soviet activity theory (Wertsch, 1981).

2. Cognitive strategies are learned most rapidly when reading goals are immersed in substantive goals. Over time, students acquire comprehension strategies at higher levels if they read to accomplish intrinsically interesting literary, conceptual or social objectives than if they read for extrinsic purposes such as completing assignments or taking tests.

3. Students learn to search for ideas and locate information across a variety of texts, authors, and references most efficiently when the texts are provided as tools and resources among other tools and resources for learning curricular contents such as history, literature, science or geography. Tools that can be used to accomplish meaningful tasks take on more significance than tools that are used to accomplish nonmeaningful tasks.

4. The amount of independent, voluntary reading among students is higher when reading is substantively oriented rather than cognitively oriented. This is a motivational expectation consistent with the whole language view that experiences such as enjoying the story of an author, learning about children in other cultures, and reading to exchange ideas with peers, are the primary motivators of reading activity.

5. When reading is taught as one mediator of conceptual development, students acquire strategies for processing multiple representations of ideas. Students learn how to construct mental models from videos and texts and to integrate such models (e.g., as when the second author integrated his model of Peter Pan based on many readings of the childhood classic with the model of Peter Pan that developed as he watched the movie "Hook"). Students learn how to use multiple representations such as illustrations, flow charts, directions, videos, and texts when they are related to aconceptual theme in a curriculum.

Our understanding of reading will be deepened by designing inquiries that hold these five expectations up to the realities of classrooms. The chapters in this volume motivate and set the stage for such work.

References

Adams, M. J. (1990). *Beginning to read: Thinking and learning about print.* Cambridge, MA: The MIT Press.

Alvermann, D. E., O'Brien, D. G. & Dillon, D. R. (1990). What teachers do when they say they're having discussion of content area reading assignments: A qualitative analysis. *Reading Research Quarterly, 25(4),* 296-321.

Anderson, R. C., & Pearson, P. D. (1984). A schema-theoretic view of basic process in reading comprehension. In P. D. Pearson (Ed.), *Handbook of Reading Research* (pp. 255-293) New York: Longman.

Bazerman, C. (1985). Physicists reading physics: Schema-laden purposes and purpose-laden schema. *Written Communication, 2(1),* 3-23.

Berliner, D. C. (1981). Vocabulary knowledge. In J. T. Guthrie (Ed.), *Comprehension and Teaching: Research Reviews* (pp. 203-226), Newark, DE: International Reading Association.

Bloom, B. (1976). *Human characteristics and school learning.* New York: McGraw-Hill.

Booth, W. C. (1988). *The company we keep.* Berkeley, CA: University of California Press

Bruner, J. (1990). *Acts of meaning.* Cambridge, MA: Harvard University Press.

Craik, F. I. M., & Lockhart, R. S. (1972). Levels of processing: A framework for memory research. *Journal of Verbal Learning and Verbal Behavior, 11,* 671-684.

D'Anna, C. A., Zechmeister, E. B., & Hall, J. W. (1991). Toward a meaningful definition of vocabulary size. *Journal of Reading Behavior, 23,* 109-122.

Fish, S. (1980. *Is there a text in this class?* Cambridge, MA: Harvard University Press.

Guthrie, J. T. (1973). Reading comprehension and syntatic responses in good and poor readers. *Journal of Educational Psychology, 65(3),* 294-300.

Guthrie, J. T. & Greaney, V. (1991). Literacy acts. In R. Barr, M. L.

Kamil, P. Mosenthal & P. D. Pearson (Eds.) *Handbook of Reading Research,* vol. 2 (pp, 68-96). New York: Longman.

Guthrie, J., & Kirsch, I. (1987). Distinctions between reading comprehension and locating information in text. *Journal of Educational Psychology, 79,* 210-228.

Guthrie, J. T., Schafer, W. D. & Hutchinson, S. R. (1991). Relations of document literacy and prose literacy to occupational and societal characteristics of young black and while adults. *Reading Research Quarterly, 26*(1), 30-48.

Heath, S. B. (1983). *Ways with words: Language, life and work in communities and classrooms.* Cambridge: Cambridge University Press.

Holland, J. H., Holyoak, K. J., Nisbett, R. E., & Thagard, P. R. (1987). *Induction: Processes of inference, learning, and discovery.* Cambridge, MA: The MIT Press.

Kirsch, I. S., & Jungeblut, A. (1986). Literacy: Profile of America's young adults. *National Assessment of Educational Progress.* Princeton, NJ: Educational Testing Service.

Nagy, W., Anderson, R. C., Schommer, M., Scott, J. A. & Stallman, A. C. (1989). Morphological families and word recognition. *Reading Research Quarterly, 24*(3), 262-282.

O'Flahavan, J. F. (1990). Second-grader's social, intellectual, and affective development in varied group discussions about narrative texts: An exploration of participation structures. *U.S. Dissertation Abstracts International, 50*(11-A).

Pressley, M., Borkowski, J. G., & Schneider, W. (1987). Cognitive strategies: Good strategy users coordinate netacognition and knowledge. In R. Vasta & G. Whitehurst (Eds.), *Annals of child development, 5,* 89-129.

Pressley, M., El-Dinary, P. B., Gaskins, I., Schuder, T., Bergman, J. L., Almasi, J., & Brown, R. (in press). Beyond direct explanation: Transactional instruction of reading comprehension strategies. *Elementary School Journal.*

Ravitch, D., & Finn, Jr., C. E. (1987). *What do our 17-year-olds know?* New York: Harper & Row, Publishers. 1986 *State adult literacy initiatives: Report of a National Conference and a survey of state programs.* Alexandria, VA: National Association of State Boards of Education.

Reder, S. & Green, K. R. (1983). Contrasting patterns of literacy in an

Alaskan fishing village. *International Journal of the Sociology of Language, 42,* 9-39.

Rosenshine, B. & Stevens, R. (1986). In M. C. Wittrock (Ed.) *Handbook of Research on Teaching* (3rd ed.) (pp. 376-391). New York: Macmillan.

Rumelhart, D. E. (1977). *Introduction to human information processing.* New York: John Wiley & Sons.

Stanovich, K. & Cunningham, A. (1991) Studying the consequences of literacy within a literate society: the cognitive correlates of print exposure. *Memory & Cognition,*

Taylor, B. M., Frye, B. J. & Maruyama, G. (1990). Time spent reading and reading growth. *American Educational Research Journal, 27*(2), 351-362.

Vygotsky, L. S. (1978). *Mind in society.* (M. Cole, V. John-Steiner, S. Scribner, & E. Souberman, Trans.) Cambridge, MA: Harvard University Press.

Wertsch, J. V. (Ed. (1981). *The concept of activity in soviet psychology.* Armonk, NY: M. E. Shapre, Inc.

Winfield, L. F. & Lee, V. E. (1986, August). *Gender differences in reading proficiency: Are they constant across racial groups?* Paper presented at the annual meeting of the American Psychological Association, Washington, DC.

Contributors

Mariam Jean Dreher received her Ph.D. from the University of California, Riverside. She is an associate professor and Director of the Reading Center in the Department of Curriculum and Instruction at the University of Maryland. A former elementary school teacher and reading specialist, she is currently researching how students use texts and documents to search for specific information.

Wayne H. Slater is an associate professor in the Language Education Unit in the Department of Curriculum and Instruction at the University of Maryland. A former junior-and senior-high school teacher, he is currently investigating how causal relations affect students' reading comprehension and the affect of audience variables on students' writing.

Rebecca Barr is Director of Doctoral Programs and Chair of the Division of Instructional Theory and Practice at National-Louis University. She has authored several books on reading instruction and assessments, published extensively in major literacy, sociological, and psychological journals, and co-edited both volumes of the *Handbook of Reading Research.*

Isabel L. Beck received her Ph.D. from the University of Pittsburgh, where she is currently Senior Scientist and Professor in the Learning Research and Development Center. Her current research looks at acquisition of reading skills, learning from text, and instructional strategies. She is Editor-elect of *Cognition and Instruction.*

John D. Bransford, Centennial Professor of Psychology and co-director of the Learning Technology Center at Vanderbilt University, received his Ph.D. from the University of Minnesota. He has published extensively in the fields of psychology and education. His research focuses primarily on the nature of thinking and learning and their facilitation.

Robert C. Calfee received his Ph.D. from UCLA. He is presently a professor in the Committee on Language, Literacy, and Culture, and the Committee on Psychological Studies. A cognitive psychologist, his research interests include the effect of schooling on the intellectual potential of individuals and groups.

David D. Dunning received his Ph.D. from the University of Illinois. He has taught at the University of Delaware and is currently an assistant professor at Portland State University. He is currently investigating the efficacy of a reading group discussion strategy that highlights the connections between story events and characters' internal states.

Linda Gambrell is a professor in the Department of Curriculum and Instructional at the National Reading Research Center at the University of Maryland. She has published widely in journals such as *The Reading Teacher, The Journal of Reading, Reading Research Quarterly, Reading Research and Instruction,* and *Journal of Educational Research,* among others. Her research interests focus on classroom reading instruction, reading comprehension development, and in particular, participation structures during discussions of text.

Susan R. Goldman is co-director of the Learning Technology Center and Professor of Psychology at Vanderbilt University. A graduate of the University of Pittsburgh, her current research focuses on strategies for learning from text and integrated media, and on math problem solving skills.

Michael F. Graves, Professor of English Education and Reading at the University of Minnesota, received his Ph.D. from Stanford University. His research and development interest include writing readable instructional text, vocabulary development, comprehension development, and remedial instruction. He is author of numerous books, chapters, and articles.

John T. Guthrie received his Ph.D. from the University of Illinois. He is at present Professor of Human Development at the University of Maryland and Co-Director of the National Reading Research Center at the University of Maryland at College Park.

Connie Juel is Thomas Jewell Professor of Education and Director of Studies in Learning to Read in the McGuffey Reading Center at the University of Virginia. A graduate of Stanford University, she has published widely on literacy acquisition.

Charles K. Kinzer received his Ph.D. from the University of California at Berkeley. He is currently Associate Professor of Education and Research Scientist at the Learning Technology Center, Peabody College of Vanderbilt University. His research includes reading comprehension, vocabulary acquisition, teacher cognition, and the application of technology in education. He is also author or coauthor of numerous articles and several books.

Jana M. Mason is a professor of educational psychology at the University of Illinois at Urbana-Champaign. She has written extensively about young children's reading development. She is coauthor of *Reading Instruction for Today,* editor of *Reading and Writing Connections,* and coeditor of *Risk Makers, Risk Takers, Risk Breakers.*

Margaret G. McKeown is a Research Scientist with the Learning Research and Development Center at the University of Pittsburg, where she received her Ph.D. Her current work focuses on vocabulary acquisition and factors that influence learning from text.

Carol L. Peterman received her Ph.D. from the University of Illinois. She is an assistant professor at Portland State University where she teaches graduate courses in reading and language arts. Her research interests include language and literacy development in preschool and primary programs, teacher training in literacy, and methods of integrating literacy across the curriculum.

Michael Pressley is a professor of Human Development at the University of Maryland, College Park. He received his Ph.D. from the University of Minnesota. He has published numerous articles and book chapters.

Diane L. Miller Sharp is a research associate at the Learning Technology Center of Vanderbilt University. She received her Ph.D. from Vanderbilt University. Her research revolves around issues related to mental models and reading comprehension.

Salvatore A. Soraci is an Associate Professor and Director of the Cognitive Studies Program in the Department of Psychology at the University of Alabama. A Ph.D. graduate of Vanderbilt University, his research in cognitive psychology involves an examination of the relationship between cognitive and perceptual variables.

Janice Porterfield Stewart received her Ph.D. from the University of Illinois. She is currently an assistant professor at the Graduate School of Education, Rutgers University. Her research centers around children's early reading and writing awareness and behaviors, teaching the African-American child, and instructional models for teachers of young children.

Nancy J. Vye is assistant director of research at the Learning Technology Center of Vanderbilt University, where she received her Ph.D. Her recent work is concerned with the role of technology in creating effective contexts for problem solving and reasoning.

Joanna P. Williams received her Ph.D. from Yale University. She is currently Professor of Psychology and Education at Teachers College, Columbia University. Her recent research has focused on reading acquisition, comprehension, and learning disabilities. She is a former editor of Journal of *Educational Psychology.*

Index